ISLAMIC LAW OF BUSINESS ORGANIZATION: PARTNERSHIPS

Islamic Law and Jurisprudence—1
Series Editor: Zafar Ishaq Ansari

ISLAMIC LAW OF BUSINESS ORGANIZATION

Partnerships

Imran Ahsan Khan Nyazee

KITAB BHAVAN
New Delhi-110002

Kitab Bhavan
Publishers, Distributors, Exporters & Importers
1784, Kalan Mahal, Darya Ganj
New Delhi - 1100 02 (India)

Phone : (91-11) 23277392/93, 23274686, 30906494
website : www.kitabbhavan.com
Email : nasri@vsnl.com
Fax : (91-11) 23263383

Ist Published in Indian : 1999
Reprinted : 2006

ISBN : 81-7151-262-3

Published in India by :
Nusrat Ali Nasri for Kitab Bhavan
1784, Kalan Mahal, Darya Ganj
New Delhi - 1100 02 [India]

Printed in India at :
Lahooti Fine Art Press
1711, Sui Walan, Darya Ganj
New Delhi - 110002 (India)

Contents

FOREWORD

Islamic law, which is rooted in the Qur'ān and the *Sunnah* of the Prophet (peace be on him), has a chequered history of over fourteen centuries. During this long period the principles embodied in these two sources were elaborated and their legal implications were worked out by some of the finest and most pious minds. Muslim jurists carefully considered the different aspects of Islamic legal theory in great depth. Likewise, the detailed legal prescriptions were examined with great thoroughness. The laws so developed were applied in a variety of Muslim societies which, during all but a few past centuries, were among the most advanced in the world. Thus the legal heritage of Islam is characterized both by legal finese and diversity in addition to its having matured after being tried and tested over a long period of practical application.

During the nineteenth and twentieth centuries, however, leadership in most fields of life passed on from the world of Islam to the West. New sources of energy and power were tapped and exploited by Westerners with the result that they eventually acquired almost universal dominance and their institutions became models for all, including the Muslims. This is true of the institutions of business and finance as well. However, like other institutions in the West, these were also developed—consistent with the dominant secularist spirit and orientation of the times—in total disregard of heavenly guidance, a fact which poses some problems for Muslims. For they hold, as a matter of religious belief, that Islam is valid for all times and that it provides the most judicious guidance for different aspects of life. It would follow from these premises that the economic institutions inspired by Islamic principles (1) should be as viable in the present times as they were before, and (2) should be more conducive to human good than the institutions developed in disregard of the principles derived from heavenly guidance.

The recent decades have witnessed a strong assertion of Islamic identity. One of its manifestations is the insistence on the part of Muslims that all institutions of life—be they political, economic or whatever—should be brought in conformity with Islamic principles. This necessitates exploring Islamic principles relevant to the institutions concerned as well as developing clear ideas as to how those principles would be applied in the changed circumstances of the present age.

Imran Ahsan Nyazee has addressed himself to these very questions in the present work and has attempted to spell out the Islamic principles on which business enterprise should be based specially in the area of partnership. In this exercise Nyazee displays a strikingly acute awareness of Islamic laws on the subject. This, however, is matched by an equally striking awareness of the forms of business organization in vogue in the contemporary world. What is perhaps no less striking is the author's robust confidence in Islamic law and its distinct approach to the problems of life, including business and finance. Nyazee feels no need to apologize for the fact that Islamic legal prescriptions come into conflict with some of the business institutions and practices of the present times. In fact he feels unhappy with those Muslims who, instead of taking up the challenge to build institutions of business and finance in the light of Islamic principles, resort to the less strenuous task of uncritically appropriating Western institutions. Such persons tend to gloss over the fact that some of those institutions might be incongruous with Islamic principles, or explain away by adopting an easygoing attitude to Islamic law. Nyazee is convinced that the Islamic legal principles which are at variance with the contemporary laws and practices in business and finance are intrinsically sound and are preferable to their counterparts prevailing in the present times. The work primarily represents a serious scholarly effort to sort complicated questions such as those mentioned above, to enunciate Islamic principles relative to business enterprise, and to apply these principles in the changed context of present-day business.

We have had the privilege of publishing Nyazee's previous work—which was also his maiden work—*Theories of Islamic Law: The Methodology of Ijtihād* (Islamabad: 1994). That work was devoted to illuminating the theoretical bases of Islamic law. It was characterized by a boldness of approach emanating from the author's strong conviction in the intrinsic value of Islamic law apart from his redoubtable breadth of knowledge. We hope that the readers will find the present work equally characterized by those very attributes.

Islamabad
October 1997

Zafar Ishaq Ansari

Chapter 1

Introduction

1.1 The Importance of the Study

Islamic economics and Islamic banking have been in existence for more than two decades, and according to some reports the number of Islamic banks and financial institutions has now increased to two hundred. This activity is supported by the state in some countries,[1] while in others it is mostly in private hands. Some of the private institutions have witnessed partial success, but this should not be attributed to advances in forms of business organization, financial instruments and derivatives. The partial success of the banks is in reality due to the enthusiasm of the Muslim investors, who wish to invest their money in instruments and investment channels that are lawful according to Islam.[2] In the development of Islamic forms of business organization, financial instruments and derivatives, the role of Islamic banking is almost negligible. It is not clear whether those forms that have been implemented are Islamic in reality or only in name.[3] In fact, if one critically examines the literature on Islamic law and finance, one feels that many of the experts working in this

[1]Foremost among these states are Pakistan and Iran. The Malaysian government is also making commendable efforts in this direction.

[2]It is estimated that the funds that may be potentially available for investment could exceed \$60 billion. Roger Taylor, "Western Funds Scent Rich Rewards in Islam," FINANCIAL TIMES, Feb. 13, 1996, 17. "Western fund managers are eyeing a potentially huge area of business: up to \$60bn of assets which Islamic investors may be willing to place in equities." Among the Western funds named in this article are Wellington, Kleinwort Benson and Flemings.

[3]Of special interest here are the forms implemented in Pakistan; namely, modaraba (*muḍārabah*), musharaka (*mushārakah*), term participations certificates and so on. The modaraba contract, as applied in Pakistan, will be analyzed in a separate study.

area are up in a blind alley. They feel tied in by the apparently strict rules of the *sharī'ah* on one side and the sophisticated and speculative nature of the modern instruments on the other.[4] What could be the reasons for this lack of innovation and inertia? In response to this question, one could point out a number of reasons, but the foremost reason, in our view, is the defective approach to legal research in this field. This is illustrated, for example, by the views expressed in the highly acclaimed report of bankers and panel of experts issued in Pakistan more than a decade ago. The report observes:

> The modern financial institutions cannot conceivably function on the basis of unlimited liability. Cases of *mudarabat* are also few and far between. The traditional stipulations of Shirkaṭ and Mudarabat have therefore limited relevance in modern conditions.[5]

The importance of the issue of limited liability of modern institutions notwithstanding, the reply to this hasty view of the panel of experts and bankers is that this is not a question of historical statistics; it is a matter of following the general legal principles of Islamic law. The issue is not to be judged on the basis of how many instances of *sharikah* and *muḍārabah* can be listed,[6] but whether Muslims are sincere in, and ready for, observing the cherished legal principles of Islamic law—principles that seek to implement some of the basic norms of the *sharī'ah.* If the forms designed by the earlier jurists are not considered important, we cannot throw out the baby with the water; the legal principles that they sought to implement must be taken into account. Some of these vital legal principles governed the

[4]There has been a kind of explosion of derivative instruments in the Western financial markets in the last decade.

[5]*Report of the Panel of Bankers and Experts submitted to the Council of Islamic Ideology* (Islamabad, 1982). One can agree with this report that the contract of *muḍārabah* may have little relevance, but on grounds that are based on the nature of the contract. The explanation of these grounds can be found under the discussion of the contract in the third part of this book. The question here is: Why were modaraba companies floated when this was the view of the experts? What is the underlying contract of modaraba, if not the traditional *muḍārabah?* Is it *muḍārabah* in name alone?

[6]One wonders how these experts were able to determine the time lag between different instances of *muḍārabah*.

forms of business organization, and they should govern the modern forms too if these are to be deemed Islamic.[7]

As compared to these experts on banking, the father of modern management, Peter F. Drucker, writing about the concept of the corporation for a secular society, has the following to say: "We shall demand of it not only the performance of economic functions but the discharge of heavy social and political tasks."[8] He says again: "Does the institution strengthen the citizen's allegiance to his society by furthering the realization of society's ethical beliefs and promises."[9] These are questions that the Muslims occupied with the implementation of the Islamic forms of business organization should be asking today.[10] The beliefs and promises of the Islamic society can be realized in its forms of business organization only by understanding and implementing the important legal principles operating though the institutions. An outright rejection of the earlier forms of business organization as having "little relevance in modern conditions" has, to our mind, discouraged and actually prevented the comprehension of these principles. It is also our considered opinion that unless these broad principles are grasped and implemented, Islamic banking has little chance of succeeding in the long run.

This approach is not visible in Pakistan alone, it can be found, though to a lesser extent, in the Arab world as well where the Islamic banking movement is mostly in private hands. There appears to be a desire, an urgency, to gobble up, so to say, the concept of the corporation and other forms of institutions, and to absorb them within the Islamic fold.[11] This anxiety is understandable when banks having huge sums of money given by Muslim investors face the risk

[7]The principles referred to here are those that are either stated explicitly in the texts or are implied by the texts. These principles have been unanimously accepted by the jurists. They may be interpreted in different ways, but they cannot be done away with altogether.

[8]Peter F. Drucker, *The Concept of the Corporation* (New York: The New American Library, 1964) p. 16.

[9]Ibid. p. 24.

[10]And, of course, attempt to answer them too.

[11]This is witnessed in a blanket approval given by modern Muslim scholars to the concept of legal personality and consequently to the corporation. The Islamic Fiqh Academy (Organization of Islamic Conference (OIC)), following the opinions of these scholars, has done the same. Very few, if any, have stopped to reflect what the consequences of this acceptance are. Moreover, accepting legal personality does not mean the automatic acceptance of the modern business corporation within the fold of Islamic law. Further analysis is necessary. For a view permitting

of keeping this money idle due to a lack of valid financial instruments and avenues of investment. The need once again is to fully discuss and understand the basic issues and principles and to design the new forms of business organization as well as financial instruments around such principles.

During the period that Islamic banking has been in existence, much has been written on the Islamic forms of business enterprise. This work is commendable and is to be appreciated. At least an effort has been made. Most of this work has, however, been undertaken by economists for whom the economic issues have naturally been more important than the legal issues. The result is that some of the most important legal principles in this field have either been completely ignored or have not been given the attention they deserve.[12] In certain cases, where work has been undertaken by traditional scholars, the issues and principles of modern law have not been fully appreciated, especially those pertaining to the modern corporation. One important study has been undertaken in the West, which was exceptionally good, but it aimed at historical assessment rather than implementation in the modern world.[13]

The efforts being made by Muslim economists need to be appreciated, because they are doing their best to push the frontiers of the discipline. Doing something is much better than doing nothing, especially when they are trying to fill a gap left wide open by scholars of Islamic law. There is one problem, though, in this entire effort: constructing a building on a weak foundation is fraught with unpredictable consequences. If some of the basic legal issues in this field are not settled, how can we go ahead and implement the details? In addition to this, there may be some economists who have not devoted too much time to Islamic law, which in fact is not their field, and they may be misinterpreting the legal implications of some issues and principles, just as a student of law may misunderstand economic issues. For example, if we try to extrapolate some of the details of *muḍārabah* and *sharikah* and try to graft them on to the modern corporation without even analyzing the basic principles of

---

the corporation, see Aḥmad ʻAlī ʻAbd Allāh, *al-Shakhṣīyah al-Iʻtibārīyah fī al-Fiqh al-Islāmī* (Khartoum, n.d.).

[12]The fault does not lie with the economists, but with scholars of Islamic law, who have not made the necessary effort.

[13]See Abraham L. Udovitch, *Partnership and Profit in Medieval Islam* (Princeton, 1979).

the corporation, or of *muḍārabah* for that matter, the result may be nothing short of total confusion.

What needs to be done, therefore, is to clearly understand the basic legal principles operating within the Islamic forms of business organization developed by the earlier jurists. Once these principles have been identified and their operation fully understood, an effort should be made to apply the principles to the modern forms of partnerships and corporations. If the modern business institutions do not conform with the Islamic principles, it would be necessary to examine the changes that may legalize these forms and enable them to function smoothly in the modern world. Finally, it will be imperative to examine ways in which these institutions may be able to lawfully invest their money in projects and instruments as well as to raise money for such investments. This applies to ordinary corporations as well as financial institutions. The final point is important not only for the design and implementation of the Islamic commercial enterprise, but it also furnishes the groundwork on which primary markets as well as the secondary markets including those in derivatives are to be structured. All this analysis can, therefore, provide the basic material for banking activity as well.

This book intends to deal with all these issues, but all this cannot be achieved in a single volume. The study has, therefore, been split into two volumes. Both volumes have been designed in a way that they can serve as textbooks for use in law courses, or even in courses on Islamic economics and business studies. The first volume is called the *Islamic Law of Business Organization: Partnerships,* while the second *Islamic Law of Business Organization: Corporations*. The second volume contains material that should be studied after the first volume has been read. To make the second volume somewhat independent, however, there is some spill over from the first volume into the second. This is expected to help the readers who might not have been able to read the first volume.

The present volume deals with the Islamic law of business organization with a focus on partnerships. It attempts to provide a thorough grounding in the Islamic law of *sharikāt* and its underlying principles. It also attempts to identify the farthest reaches of this law, that is, the extent to which the earlier jurists were able to develop it. From these limits, this study moves forward to propose new forms of business organization that would accommodate some of the existing modern forms and also advance in other more interesting directions.[14] To achieve this last objective, a comparison between the important principles of Islamic law and those of modern law becomes necessary. All these tasks are intended to reach the overall objective of updating, so to say, of the principles of Islamic law, that is, explain them in a manner that makes them applicable in the modern age. Whether this purpose is ultimately achieved is left to the reader to decide. One thing is certain, though, that this is a dynamic area and developments in this law will continue as business activity increases under the Islamic forms of organization.

1.2 The Goals of the Study

The goals of the study may be listed in specific terms as follows:

1. To identify the basic principles of the Islamic law of partnership along with the underlying contracts and relations that exist between the partners, and to draw out these rules for further analysis and comparison.

2. To indicate how far these rules are similar to and different from the rules of Western law and what distinctions are fatal for preserving the integrity of Islamic law when it is applied to modern forms.

3. To attempt an identification of the path that Islamic law of business organization will take in the future in the light of modern needs and also in the light of developments in other legal systems.

4. To prepare the ground for the future development of Islamic corporations and Islamic corporate finance (including Islamic financial engineering) as an independent subject.

---

[14]The methodology employed for extending the law in this area should not be interpreted as *ijtihād* of some kind. The method used is called *takhrīj* in the Ḥanafī system. It seeks to extend the existing broad and general principles derived by the jurists from evidences in the Qur'ān and the *Sunnah*. *Ijtihād* employs such evidences directly whereas *takhrīj* uses the derived principles. The former is mainly the domain of the legislator, while the latter is mostly the method of the jurist and the judge. This book, in some ways, may also be considered a text in the system of *takhrīj* or reasoning from principles.

1.3 Some Difficulties on the Way

There are some difficulties involved in the study and understanding of the Islamic law of business organization. These are not insurmountable, but the reader needs to be cautioned as some of these problems may lead to considerable confusion. Stated simply, the problems are:

1. New forms of funds and instruments have been introduced under the name of *mushārakah* and *muḍārabah*.[15] The rules of these forms may or may not have any resemblance with the rules available under the same names in Islamic law. The reader should consider each set of rules separately and then bring them together for analysis.

2. The use of the term *sharikah,* borrowed from Islamic law or from the Arabic language, by the Arab law to mean partnerships as well as corporations is likely to create a communication gap between Arab scholars and those accustomed to considering partnerships and corporations as two distinct categories.[16] The distinction is somewhat blurred in Arab law where qualifying adjective is used with the term *sharikah*, like *musāhamah* for instance, for maintaining a distinction. The precedent for this, however, is found in Islamic law itself where the term *sharikah* is qualified to denote different forms. Those accustomed to a clear distinction between partnerships and companies should note this difference.

3. One possible outcome of the use of the term *sharikah* in Arab law as described above may be that someone not fully acquainted with the distinctions may think that some of the rules cut across all forms of *sharikah.* This would not be correct, and the analogy should not be brought into the discussion of Islamic law of *sharikāt.* Thus, the rules of *sharikah* and *muḍārabah* cannot be picked up at random and applied to modern corporations, because these are two different systems and relations

---

[15] The terms used in the Pakistani law are *modaraba* and *musharika*.

[16] When the words Arab law are used in the context of *sharikāt,* it is primarily the Egyptian law that is intended. The Saudi law now prefers the term *niẓām* (institution) for corporations. See, e.g., Ṣāliḥ ibn Zābin al-Marzūqī al-Buqamī, *al-Sharikāt al-Musāhamah fī al-Niẓām al-Sa'ūdī* (Mecca: Umm al-Qurā University, 1987).

found in one may have nothing to do with those in the other.[17] Further, while Muslim scholars will readily accept the modern corporation as Islamic, because of the dire need to use it, it needs to be analyzed more deeply before a final acceptance is possible. The current research on the subject lacks depth and a superficial acceptance of the concept can play havoc with the rules.

4. An analysis and comparison of the rules of Islamic law with those of Western law in the field will become more complex as Western law moves toward the acceptance of the entity concept for partnerships as well. In other words, in American law, for example, all forms of business organization including partnerships may soon have legal personality (*shakhṣīyah i'tibārīyah*).[18] This further enhances the need to study the concept of the corporation more deeply if the rules of Islamic law are to be given effect in modern forms of business.

1.4 Structure of the Study

This volume has been divided into five parts. The first part deals with the meaning of *sharikah* in Islamic law as well as some basic concepts. The understanding of the basic concepts is, perhaps, the most important part of the study as far as the work of the *fuqahā'* is concerned. It attempts to bring out the basic rules and the underlying contracts and relationships between the partners or between the *muḍārib* and the *rabb al-māl.* These concepts are compared with their counterparts in modern law at each stage. The second part of the study is devoted to the first category of *sharikāt* in Islamic law as developed by the Ḥanafī school; namely *'inān* and *mufāwaḍah.*[19] The methodology adopted for this part, as well as the one following it, is to give separate treatment to the views of the four Sunnī schools. This helps in bringing out the true distinctions between the views

[17]This is irrespective of what has been attempted in Arab law, especially the Egyptian law.

[18]The Uniform Partnership Act has upheld the entity concept, and most states are expected to adopt it. What this means is that in the USA, partnerships too will have legal personality.

[19]Forms like *sharikat al-amwāl* and *sharikat al-a'māl* are included within these two terms as will be shown later.

of different schools.[20] Thus, for example, the reader will be able to identify that the term *mufāwaḍah* means different things in different schools and we may have several forms that we are talking about when we use the term *mufāwaḍah*. Likewise, the *'inān* partnership. The third part deals with the first category of partnerships according to the majority of the Sunnī schools. The fourth part deals briefly with the second category of partnerships that are not considered true *sharikāt*. These are *muḍārabah, muzāra'ah* and *musāqāh*. There may not be much interest in the last two of these, but they have been included so as to make the study complete.[21] The fifth and final part in the main analyzes the modern law of partnership in the light of the principles of Islamic law identified in the first four parts. It also proposes new forms of partnership based on the principles of Islamic law. These new forms are actually being practiced in the Western world, but they have been amended in the light of the principles of the *sharī'ah*.

---

[20] For a quick view of the distinctions, refer to the table at page 238 of this study.

[21] An opinion has been expressed about the problems of the "agricultural tax" in Pakistan, which may be of interest to some.

Part I

The Nature of Partnership in *Fiqh* and Law

Chapter 2

Definition of Partnership in *Fiqh* and Law

The word for partnership in Islamic law is *sharikah*. Some jurists prefer to use the word *shirkah*,[1] because of which the word in Urdu is *shirkat*. There is, however, no difference in the meaning of the different applications of the word. In Muslim countries where the English common law is applied, a distinction is made between partnership and companies or corporations with respect to terminology so as to identify the difference in the legal forms. In Arab countries, on the other hand, the word *sharikah* is applied to mean partnerships as well as corporations. To distinguish between the legal forms, additional terms are used. Thus, a company or a corporation is called *sharikah musāhamah*. This method of naming different legal forms of the business enterprise does not affect terminology alone; it has some conceptual implications as well. It may have caused or is likely to cause some confusion for researchers.

The purpose of this chapter is to identify the meaning of partnership in both law and Islamic law and to point out that some care has to be exercised in the use of the term *sharikah* in the present times. A brief comparison between a partnership and a corporation will, therefore, be necessary.[2]

---

[1] See Aḥmad ibn Muḥammad ʻAlī al-Muqrī al-Fayyūnī, *al-Miṣbāḥ al-Munīr*, 2 vols. (al-Qumm: Dār al-Hijrah, 1414), art. "shariktuhu" vol. 1, p 311; Kamāl al-Dīn Muḥammad ibn al-Humām al-Siwāsī al-Iskanadarī, *Fatḥ al-Qadīr ʻalā al-Hidāyah Sharḥ Bidāyat al-Mubtadī*, vol. 5 (Cairo: Muṣtafā al-Bābī al-Ḥalabī, 1389/1970) p. 6 (hereinafter referred to as Ibn al-Humām, *Fatḥ al-Qadīr*).

[2] These distinctions have been drawn from the perspective of Islamic law.

2.1 Definition in *Fiqh*

We shall first examine the literal meaning of the word *sharikah* and then turn to the various technical meanings reflected in the definitions provided by the jurists.

2.1.1 The literal meaning of *sharikah*

The word for partnership, as stated earlier, is *shirkah* or *sharikah* and some linguists prefer the former. In the literal sense, the word *sharikah* is used in two meanings:

1. **Mixing or *ikhṭilāṭ*.** Here it means the mixing of the shares, that is, the capital contributed.[3] Ibn al-Humām describes *ikhtilāṭ* as the attribute of the property that is found in a mixed or mingled state, which is "mixing of the shares so that one of them cannot be distinguished from another."[4] He distinguishes this meaning from *ishtirāk*, which is an act of the partners and the object of this act is wealth. This means participation. Thus, when two partners participate, they bring about the mingling of wealth (*khalṭ*) and the wealth is held jointly by them.[5]

2. **The contract of partnership.** Ibn al-Humām describes the second meaning of *sharikah* as the contract of partnership itself, because it is the cause of *khalṭ*. Thus, when the phrase *sharikat al-'aqd* is used, it serves as an elaboration.[6] Insofar as a contract is the union of two statements and the legal effects that flow from it, the emphasis in this meaning is upon the "relationship that exists between two (or more) partners."[7]

2.1.2 The technical meaning of *sharikah*

We have seen that there are two literal meanings of the term *sharikah*. The meaning assigned to the word by the jurists does not go beyond

---

[3]See Ibn Manẓūr, *Lisān al-'Arab*. In *Tāj al-'Urūs* it is the participation of the partners.

[4]Ibn al-Humām, *Fatḥ al-Qadīr*, vol. 5, p. 6.

[5]Loc. cit.

[6]Loc. cit.

[7]This is the basis of a partnership in modern law, and has been emphasized by the Ḥanafī jurists. The emphasis on this relationship between the partners is inadequate with the majority schools.

these meanings, because partnership arises either through a contract or through the mixing of wealth. It is for this reason that the jurists have divided the types of partnership into: *sharikat al-ibāḥah* (or common sharing of things); *sharikat al-milk* (co-ownership); and *sharikat al-'aqd* (partnership through contract).

After a thorough search in *fiqh* literature, we were not able to find a definition of partnership that covers all three types. 'Abd al-'Azīz al-Khayyāṭ feels that the reason for this is the difference between the rules and conditions for the various types of partnerships.[8] To overcome this difficulty, al-Khayyāṭ tries to give a general definition by building upon a definition given by the Ḥanafī jurists and another one formulated by the Ḥanbalīs. The Ḥanafī definition he chooses defines *sharikah* as "the exclusive right of two or more persons to a single subject-matter."[9] We would like to disagree with al-Khayyāṭ here about the propriety of this definition as a general definition. The definition has been given in the *Majallat al-Aḥkām al-'Adlīyah*[10] as a definition for *sharikat al-milk* (co-ownership) and it is not a definition of *sharikah* in the sense of the partnership contract or even a general definition. The Ḥanabalī definition he chooses is taken from *al-Mughnī*: "Joint right of ownership or transaction."[11] Now, this definition is general, but it is too wide and includes the contract of agency as well, because agency is "participation in a transaction by the principal and the agent."[12]

A similar difficulty is found in finding a general definition for *sharikat al-'aqd* or partnership through a contract. We have not been able to discover a general definition that covers all types of *sharikat*

[8] 'Abd al-'Azīz al-Khayyāṭ, *al-Sharikāt*, 2 vols. (Amman: Wizārat al-Awqāf, 1971) vol. 1, p. 33 (hereinafter referred to as al-Khayyāṭ, *al-Sharikāt*). 'Īsā 'Abduh, *al-'Uqūd al-Shar'īyah al-Ḥākimah* (Cairo: Dār al-I'tiṣām, 1977) p. 48, has also expressed a similar opinion. He says that the technical meaning varies with the type of partnership.

[9] Al-Khayyāṭ, *al-Sharikāt*, vol. 1, p. 33.

[10] Commission of Ottoman Jurists (1867–77), *Majallat al-Aḥkām al-'Adlīyah* (Constantinople, 1305 AH). See §§1045 and 1060.

[11] Al-Khayyāt, *al-Sharikāt*, vol. 1, p. 3.

[12] Muwaffaq al-Dīn Abū Muḥammad 'Abd Allāh ibn Aḥmad ibn Muḥammad Ibn Qudāmah, *al-Mughnī fī Fiqh Imām al-Sunnah Aḥmad ibn Ḥanbal al-Shaybānī* (Cairo: al-Maṭba'ah al-Salafīyah wa-Maktūbātuhā, 1962) vol. 5, p. 3 (hereinafter referred to as Ibn Qudāmah, *al-Mughnī*). The word used is *taṣarruf*, which actually means the right to transact, but may apply to the right of disposal as well.

al-'aqd. It becomes necessary, therefore, to examine each type of partnership separately to understand the meaning of *sharikah* in Islamic law. Once these separate meanings are understood, we will attempt to derive a general definition of *sharikat al-'aqd*, whatever its worth.

Sharikat al-ibāḥah (common right to acquire ownership)

Sharikat al-ibāḥah is defined as the "common right of the people in ownership by acquisition or gathering of things that are *mubāh* (permissible for such acquisition) and are not originally owned by anyone."[13] This type of partnership, then, is the participation of the people in the common right to own things that are not owned by anyone. In other words, all things not owned by any individual or group of individuals exist in a kind of partnership of the people generally and this partnership grants this right to all the members of the community so as to be able to convert a thing to personal ownership. These things can pass into the ownership of individuals through two ways: actual gathering or acquisition, like gathering firewood or the revival of barren lands, and by bringing about the cause of acquisition, like placing a pan for gathering rain water or throwing a net in the water for fish.[14]

It is obvious that today such a partnership would be difficult to form. All things not owned by the citizens are owned by the state, except for things that are free like air or rain water. Today, forests, land, lakes and all other things are owned by the state, which is an individual in the eyes of the law—a corporation. Thus, an individual may not be permitted to throw his net into water for fish if the state has chosen to grant licenses for such an economic activity.

The concept of *sharikat al-ibāḥah* highlights the nature of the Islamic state, that is, it raises the question whether the concept of juristic person is compatible with Islamic law as designed by the jurists. In this case, the concept of the state as a juristic person clashes with the concept of *sharikat al-ibāḥah*, but the problem may be found in Islamic law generally, and will come up again and again in this book. To those who may have the permission of the sultan in mind, as an argument, in the grant of lands after revival (*iḥyā*

[13] *Majallah*, §1045.

[14] The acquisition of ownership here pertains to the ownership of the *res nullius*.

al-mawāt), it is suggested that such permission does not imply the existence of the state as a legal person.[15]

Sharikat al-milk (co-ownership)

Co-ownership or *sharikat al-milk* is defined by the *Majallah* as "the existence of a thing in the exclusive joint-ownership of two or more persons due to one of the bases of ownership, or it is the joint claim of two or more persons for a debt that is due from (is the liability of) another individual arising from a single cause."[16] Ibn 'Ābidīn defines it as "the joint ownership of a number of persons in an *'ayn* (ascertained thing) or in a *dayn* (debt)."[17] There is no difference in these definitions, except that the second definition does not elaborate that the debt arises from a single cause.[18]

The concept of *sharikat al-milk* and its rules are very important for understanding the Islamic law of business organization. The reason is that whenever a *sharikat al-'aqd* collapses, that is, becomes *fāsid* or *bāṭil,* the rules for the sharing of earned profits and the division of property revert to those of *sharikat al-milk.*

Sharikat al-'aqd (partnership)

The definition of this partnership is the real goal of our search. *Sharikat al-'aqd* or partnership through contract is the same thing as "partnership" in law. It is to be noted, however, that there are different types of partnership in Islamic law. Islamic law attempts to assign separate rules for each type, therefore, a common definition that covers all types is difficult to identify. We will examine the various definitions given by the schools and then explore the possibility of a common definition that covers all types.

Ḥanafī School. The Ḥanafīs define *sharikat al-'aqd* as "an agreement between two or more persons for common participation in

---

[15]That is, it cannot be assumed that the Islamic state was a corporation just because ownership in revived lands had to be confirmed by the state.

[16]Ibid. §§1061, 1091.

[17]Muḥammad Amīn ibn 'Uthmān ibn 'Abd al-'Azīz ibn 'Ābidīn, *Radd al-Muḥtār 'alā al-Durr al-Mukhtār Sharḥ Tanwīr al-Abṣār* (Cairo: Muṣṭafā al-Bābī al-Ḥalabī, 1966) vol. 4, p. 301 (hereinafter referred to as Ibn 'Ābidīn, *Ḥāshiyah*).

[18]The debt should have arisen from a single transaction in favor of two or more persons, who would then become co-owners. If the debts originated from separate transactions, a co-ownership cannot be established.

capital and profits."[19] This definition has been designed for one type of partnership called *sharikat al-amwāl* or contract partnership through participation with wealth. There are other types of partnerships that cannot be included in this definition. These are: *muḍārabah, sharikat al-a'māl,* and *sharikat al-wujūh.* In these three types there is no participation in capital, and the definition given requires this. In most Ḥanafī books the definition provided is that of partnerships that require participation in wealth or capital.

Mālikī School. It is defined by the Mālikīs as "a permission from each of the participants to the others for transactions in his wealth and on their own behalf, while retaining the right to transact personally (in such wealth)."[20] This definition, like the definition formulated by the Ḥanafīs, is applicable to partnerships with capital. This is evident from the words "his wealth." Thus, partnership through labour is excluded as is *muḍārabah*, because the former does not involve capital and in the latter the wealth belongs to the *rabb al-māl* and not to the the *muḍārib. Muḍārabah* is also excluded through the use of the word "permission," because permission is granted from one side, that is, by the *rabb al-māl* alone to the *muḍārib*, and the *rabb al-māl* does not retain the right to transact personally in the wealth.

There is another definition given by al-Dasūqī: "Partnership is the permission by each partner to his companion for transacting for the partner and for himself in wealth."[21] As far as the Mālikī school is concerned, this is quite a comprehensive definition. By the use of the word "wealth" in place of "his wealth," as in the previous definition, partnership in labour is included. *Sharikat al-wujūh,* as we shall see later, is void according to the Mālikīs. The definition, however, does not include *muḍārabah* or *qirāḍ* (the term preferred by the Mālikīs). The reason is the same, as in the previous definition, and pertains to "permission by each partner" when permission in *muḍārabah* is from one side alone.

---

[19] *Majallah,* §1329.

[20] The definition is from *al-Mukhtaṣar* by Khalīl as quoted in al-Khayyāṭ, *Sharikāt,* vol. 1, p. 42. A similar definition is found in al-Khirashī, *Sharḥ al-Mukhtaṣar,* vol 6, p. 35.

[21] Muḥammad ibn Aḥmad ibn 'Arafah al-Dasūqī, *Ḥāshiyat 'alā al-Sharḥ al-Kabīr li-Abī al-Barakāt Sīdī Aḥmad al-Dardīr 'alā Mukhtaṣar al-Khalīl* (Cairo: 'Īsā al-Bābī al-Ḥalabī wa-Shurakāh, 1931–34) vol. 2, p. 348 (hereinafter referred to as al-Dasūqī *Ḥāshiyah*).

Al-Khayyāṭ has quoted a definition from al-Dardīr, which is better than the two definitions provided above. In this definition partnership is "a contract between two or more owners of wealth for joint trade or it is a contract for shared labour and shared profits."[22] This definition is better as it highlights the purpose of the partnership, which is the sharing of profits by the partners. It is, however, limited to partnerships permitted by the Mālikī school.

Shāfi'ī School. Al-Ramlī says in the *Nihāyat al-Muḥtāj* that *sharikah* "in its literal meaning is mixing and technically it is an established undivided right in a single thing or it is a contract implying this."[23] This definition does not indicate participation by the partners in transactions nor does it indicate the purpose of the partnership, which is the acquisition of profits and participation in them. Further, this definition is restricted to co-ownership and partnership in wealth, because the other forms of partnership are not valid according to the Shāfi'īs. *Muḍārabah* is not included in this definition either. We shall see later that the Shāfi'ī law of partnership is very narrow and highly restricted. We shall also attempt to understand the reason for this restricted version of partnership law. All that the Shāfi'ī law permits by way of business organization is included in this definition, namely, *sharikat al-milk* and a restricted form of *'inān* based on *māl*.[24]

Ḥanbalī School. Ibn Qudāmah has defined partnership in *al-Mughnī* as "participation of two or more persons in transactions."[25] This is the first definition among the several we have considered so far in which its author has tried to cover *muḍārabah* alongwith the other types of partnership. We shall see, however, that delivery of the capital of *muḍārabah* to the *muḍārib* and the non-participation of the owner of capital in transactions is an essential condition of *muḍārabah*. The definition, therefore, cannot apply to *muḍārabah*. In addition to this, the definition includes both the principal and his

---

[22]See al-Khayyāṭ, *al-Sharikāt*, vol. 1, p. 43.

[23]Shams al-Dīn Muḥammad ibn Abū al-'Abbās Shihāb al-Dīn Aḥmad ibn Aḥmad ibn Ḥamzah al-Ramlī, *Nihāyat al-Muḥtāj li-Sharḥ al-Minhāj* (Cairo, 1967) vol. 5, p. 3 (hereinafter referred to as al-Ramlī, *Nihāyat al-Muḥtāj*).

[24]The reader may refer to a comparative table provided at the end of part 3 for a quick review.

[25]Ibn Qudāmah, *al-Mughnī*, vol. 5, p. 3.

agent in a contract of agency, because there is joint participation in transactions by these two. Moreover, this definition does not indicate the purpose of the contract, which is the earning and sharing of profits. It is, therefore, not a very useful definition.

A wider definition of *sharikat al-'aqd*

It is for this reason that 'Alī al-Khafīf attempted a definition of contractual *sharikah* that would cover more forms. He says, "It is a contract between two or more people for participation in capital and its profits, or for participation in profits without participation in capital."[26] He explains that in the first case it is called *sharikat al-amwāl* and in the second case it is called *muḍārabah*. He does not mention anything about partnership in labour or partnership in credit-worthiness.[27]

This definition can be expanded to include the remaining two types. Thus, we may rephrase it as:

> It is a contract between two or more people for participation in capital and its profits, or participation in transactions in someone else's capital and its profits, or participation in profit without participation in capital or transactions.[28]

The real utility of a comprehensive definition may be doubted, however, the aim here is to indicate the main purpose of a partnership and in how many ways this is possible or is permitted. This expanded definition is not true for all the four schools. It applies to the views of the Ḥanafī school alone, and with slight modification to the Ḥanbalī school as well.

---

[26]The Arabic text of the definition provided by 'Alī al-Khafīf is as follows:

هي عقد بين اثنين أو أكثر على الاشتراك في المال والربح ، أو على الاشتراك في الربح دون الاشتراك في رأس المال.

[27]See 'Alī al-Khafīf, *al-Sharikāt fī al-Fiqh al-Islāmī* (Cairo, n.d.) p. 18.

[28]The Arabic text for the new definition could be as follows:

هي عقد بين اثنين أو أكثر على الاشتراك في المال والربح ، أو على الاشتراك في التصرف في مال الغير وربحه ، أو الاشتراك في الربح دون الاشتراك في رأس المال أو التصرف.

It can be seen from this definition and those that have preceded that Islamic law tries to pin down the actual form of partnership, that is, the way participation is taking place. We will see from the discussion that follows that the Western law leaves the matter open to the wishes of the partners and focuses on the relationship that subsists between partners, that is, whether this relationship was for sharing profits irrespective of the form of participation.

2.2 Definition of Partnership in Law

In the field of Islamic law, we have scholars from different legal systems contributing to scholarship in the field of Islamic business organization. Even economists are participating in the ongoing discourse. It is, therefore, important to clarify what we mean by law. For the present discussion, law means legal systems based upon the English common law. In most Arab countries, the law is based in the main on the French legal system. This may not cause problems in communication, but the terminology employed in Arabic may not have its equivalents for the systems following the English common law. The use of the term *sharikah* in modern Arab law is one term that is likely to cause some confusion. We should, therefore, make an effort to clarify the terms at the outset.

The word *sharikah* is applied in Arab law to mean all kinds of business organizations, whether these are partnerships or corporations with their own fictitious personality. The precedent for employing the term in this manner is found in *fiqh* itself: the use of the term *sharikah* and then its qualification with terms like *ibāḥah, milk, ʿaqd, aʿmāl* and *wujūh*. The situation is further complicated when one examines Scottish law, which assigns a legal personality even to partnerships.[29] The new American Uniform Partnership Act attempts to do the same, that is, it assigns legal personality to partnerships. In American law, there has been a long debate about the entity and aggregate concepts, that is, whether a legal personality can be assigned to a partnership. It appears that the entity concept is now going to prevail because of the pressures of business and the ease of the going concern.

[29]Earnest H. Schamell, *Lindley on the Law of Partnership* 12th ed. (London: Sweet and Maxwell, 1962) p. 121 (hereinafter referred to as Lindley, *The Law of Partnership*).

We shall first examine the definition of partnership in systems that follow the English common law. The meaning of *sharikah* as used in modern Arab law will then be looked at briefly to indicate that there must be some precision in the use of the terms.

The word partnership is generally used, in English common law systems, to identify the form of business organization that is based on the aggregate concept. In such a form, individuals pool their resources for sharing the common profits arising out of their venture. The property of such an organization is owned by the partners as a co-ownership. As distinguished from this, the form of business organization called the company or the corporation is a legal entity in its own right. The property of such an organization is owned by the entity itself, and the claims of the shareholders are represented by share certificates.[30] In Arab law, the word *sharikah* is used for both kinds of organizations, that is, whether they are organized around the aggregate concept or around the entity concept. Additional qualifying names are then used for making distinctions. Let us look for the meaning of partnership first.

Partnership is a contract; the emphasis, however, is always on the **relationship** that arises from this contract, whether the contract has been concluded expressly or is implied by the relationship.[31] The word relationship means the rights and duties that exist among the partners and are owed to each other as well as to the third parties dealing with their joint partnership. Over time, there have been many definitions for partnership. Thus, the English Partnership Act of 1890, in §1 defined it as:

> Partnership is a relationship that subsists between persons carrying on a business in common with a view to profit.[32]

The Civil Code of New York defined it as:

> Partnership is the association of two or more persons for the purpose of carrying on business together and dividing its profits between them.[33]

---

[30]In fact, the share certificate is property in its own right and the owner has the full right of disposal over it.

[31]It should be obvious that a legal relationship has to be viewed in terms of some basic contract or contracts. These are contracts like agency and surety.

[32]As quoted in Lindley, *Law of Partnership,* p. 14.

[33]Loc. cit.

Lindley has quoted other definitions too. For example, the definition given by Parsons is:

> Partnership is the combination by two or more persons of capital, or labor, or skill, for the purpose of business for their common benefit.[34]

This definition is similar to the definition that we have arrived at for Islamic law above. The definition given by Pollock, also quoted by Lindley, is:

> Partnership is the relation which subsists between persons who have agreed to share the profits of a business carried on by all or any of them on behalf of all of them.[35]

This is an expanded form of the definition given in the English Partnership Act of of 1890. The (Pakistan) Partnership Act 1932 defines partnership in §4 as:

> Partnership is the relationship between persons who have agreed to share the profits of a business carried on by all or any of them acting for all.

Most of these definitions are similar, so let us attempt to analyze the last definition and list its major characteristics:

1. Partnership is the relation subsisting between two or more people and is not merely an agreement or a contract between them, even though this relation may have been established on the basis of an agreement or contract.
2. The purpose of the formation of a partnership must be trade and, therefore, clubs and associations cannot be considered partnerships.
3. There has to be an agreement or a contract between the partners, and the relationship known as "partnership" cannot arise prior to such agreement or contract. This excludes co-ownership.

[34]Ibid. p. 15.

[35]Loc. cit.

4. The contract must indicate as its main purpose participation in profits, whether this indication is express or implied. It is not necessary to indicate participation in loss, because the creditor in certain cases may be considered a partner in profits.[36]

5. It is not necessary that all the partners contribute by way of labour or skill.[37]

6. Similarity of the subject-matter of the partnership is not necessary. Thus, one of the partners may participate with his labour when the other is participating with his property.

7. Actual mixing of capitals is not required when the participation is by way of property or wealth.[38]

2.3 Comparison and Implications

From a superficial examination of these characteristics, one can say that Islamic law will not accept the creditor as a partner[39] because this will invoke the rules of prohibition of *ribā*. Accordingly, sharing of loss is an essential characteristic of a partnership, because it excludes loan giving creditors as partners. While the characteristic at number 6 is possible in *muḍārabah,* the rules of liability may be quite different in Islamic law for this contract. The details will be explained on the proper occasion.

We shall also see later that the underlying contracts in a partnership have different conditions attached to them and Islamic law may have some additional underlying contracts that are not found in modern law. Thus, for example, both are based upon the contract of agency to enable partners to carry on business through "all or any of them acting for all." The rules of agency itself are different in the two systems.[40] Due to this difference, Islamic law introduces the contract of *kafālah* (surety) into partnerships, but modern law does not. We shall examine these details in the study of the basic concepts.

---

[36]To understand this, an examination of §6 of the Partnership Act, 1932 is necessary.

[37]In other words, some partners may even be sleeping partners.

[38]While Islamic law treats mingling of capitals as essential for determining the issues of liability, modern law treats it as an accounting problem.

[39]Neither does modern law.

[40]For an explanation see §6.1.2, pp. 59–61 in this book.

Chapter 3

The Formation of a *Sharikah*

The art of conveyancing was fairly developed in Islamic law. The title of this discipline was *shurūṭ*. Al-Ṭaḥāwī, the Ḥanafī jurist, wrote two voluminous books on the topic called *al-Shurūṭ al-Ṣaghīr* and *al-Shurūṭ al-Kabīr*.[1] Al-Sarkhsī also discussed the discipline in his book *al-Mabsūṭ*.[2]

Those who study Islamic law from the original sources will notice that the jurists focus on a technical term and then associate a host of conditions with this term. One reason for doing this is that when a contract is concluded, the mere use of the term discussed implies all the conditions that the jurists have associated with it. The use of the term is, therefore, enough, and there is no need to restate all the associated conditions.[3] Some readers may get the impression from this that a number of other possible conditions have either been excluded by the jurists or have not been taken into account. This is usually not the case. The use of the term in the offer and acceptance by the parties will automatically invoke the basic stipulations associated with the term,[4] but it does not prevent the parties from stipulating additional conditions, even if this radically alters the basic contract. The

[1] Abū Ja'far Aḥmad ibn Muḥammad ibn Salāmah al-Ḥajrī al-Ṭaḥāwī, *Kitāb al-Shurūṭ al-Kabīr* (Baghdad, 1966). Jeanette Wakin has written a book on the topic called *Function of Documents in Islam* (Albany, 1972).

[2] Shams al-A'immah Abū Bakr Muḥammad ibn Abī Sahl Aḥmad al-Sarakhsī, *Kitāb al-Mabsūṭ*, 30 vols. (Cairo Maṭba'at al-Sa'ādah, 1324–31/1906–13) (hereinafter referred to as al-Sarakhsī, *al-Mabsūṭ*).

[3] In law this is usually referred to as the "implied contract."

[4] For example, for the implications and conditions of the contract of *'inān*, the earlier jurists would refer to it as *muqtaḍā 'aqd al-'inān* or the "implied contract of *'inān*."

law of partnership is a clear example of this method. Let us illustrate this.

The *'inān* partnership in Islamic law can be of several types, as we shall study in the following chapters. There is a special *'inān* and a general *'inān.* This distinction is achieved either through the contract of *wakālah* by invoking a general or special agency and in another form by forming the partnership for one type of trade or for all types of trades.[5] Further, the basic type of *'inān* does not include the contract of *kafālah,* but this contract can be stipulated as an additional condition to widen the scope of activities and consequential liabilities. Doing so yields an entirely new partnership. The details of how these contracts are actually invoked will be explained later.[6] The question here is that if one person says to another, "I have concluded an *'inān* partnership with you," which of the foregoing types is intended? According to the jurists, by the use of the absolute term *'inān,* it is the general *'inān* without the contract of *kafālah* that is intended.[7] In discussing *'inān,* therefore, the jurists are discussing this general *'inān* in their books. The rest of the conditions desired by the parties will have to be stated explicitly by them in addition to the absolute term. Likewise, if a special *'inān* is intended, the absolute term *'inān* will have to be restricted expressly to the *'inān khāṣṣ* or *'inān* for a single trade. This method is true for *fiqh* in the entire law of contract.

One has to be careful, however, when assuming what is intended. The concept of contract may differ from one school to the other. The absolute term, therefore, has to be linked to the views of the school. In the above case of *'inān,* for example, what we have said is true of the Ḥanafī school. In the Shāfi'ī school, the concept of partnership is very narrow. In this school, when the absolute term is used, it is not the general *'inān* that is implied, but the special *'inān* based on special agency. Thus, the *'inān* partner in the Shāfi'ī school may not have the right to enter into credit transactions, unless he takes special permission from his partner. In the Ḥanafī school, a partner

---

[5]The *fuqahā'* usually employ it in the latter sense. The Modaraba (Floatation and Control) Ordinance, 1982 (Pakistan), for example, uses the terms "single modaraba" and "multiple modaraba" to convey a similar meaning.

[6]The explanation is spread out in part 3 of this book under different forms of partnership.

[7]The term "general" here would mean general for all types of trade. For the details of the implied contract of *'inān* see al-Sarakhsī, *al-Mabsūt,* vol. 11, p. 156.

has implied permission for credit transactions by virtue of the *'inān* contract itself, because what was concluded was the general *'inān*.

Today, these problems are avoided when the contracts are reduced to writing and the detailed conditions are spelled out, but the writings of the jurists are based on this method. Perhaps, many of these problems were avoided in the time of the earlier jurists when such contracts were reduced to writing, but most of the works of the contracts in *fiqh* are structured for oral agreements. This discussion also indicates that mingling opinions from different schools is a business fraught with hazard. One has to be very careful when doing so. This is also the basic reason why the discussion of the principles of partnership have been kept separate for each school in this study.[8] We may now look at some of the ways in which partnership is formed in Islamic law.

3.1 The Oral Agreement

According to the Ḥanafī school, there is a single *rukn* (element) of the contract of *sharikah,* and this is the form (*ṣīghah*) or offer and acceptance (*ījāb* and *qabūl*).[9] This is true for all contracts according to this school. The majority of the schools maintain that there are five elements of the contract of *sharikah.* These are the two parties to the contract, the subject-matter (capital); work with capital, and the *ṣīghah.*[10] Except for the form (*ṣīghah*), the rest of these elements are conditions according to the Ḥanafīs. The distinction lies in the fact that, according to the Ḥanafīs, if there is something wrong with the *ṣīghah,* the contract is void (*bāṭil*), but if there is something wrong with the conditions, the contract is not void, but vitiated (*fāsid*). A *fāsid* contract is unenforceable, unless the offending conditions are removed. Once removed, the contract can become valid. A void contract, on the other hand, cannot be set right or reformed. A new contract will have to be concluded where possible. The *fāsid* category may, in some cases, save a lot of unnecessary expense. As the majority schools do not have a category called *fāsid,* they cannot make the

[8]In fact, this separation of analysis has been maintained for the first category of partnerships. The second category of partnerships—*muḍārabah, muzāra'ah* and *musāqāh*—have been discussed in the usual manner adopted for analysis.

[9]Al-Sarakhsī, *al-Mabsūṭ,* vol. 11, p. 168.

[10]Abū al-Walīd Muḥammad ibn Aḥmad ibn Muḥammad ibn Rushd (Averröes), *Bidāyat al-Mujtahid wa-Nihāyat al-Muqataṣid,* vol. 2 (Beirut, n.d.) p. 189 (hereinafter referred to as Ibn Rushd, *Bidāyat al-Mujtahid*).

distinction made by the Ḥanafīs and are bound to consider all the essential conditions as elements.[11]

In addition to the use of the absolute term as the *ṣīghah* for a type of contract, it is important to note that Islamic law follows the objective theory of contracts and not the subjective theory. In Western systems following the English common law, the objective theory is given importance, while in the French system and those following it, the subjective theory is given priority. Following the objective theory means that words used in a contract are assigned their ordinary meanings and the law will not try to dig into the inner intentions of the parties, unless the words used are contrary to the very objective of the contract. Parties will, therefore, be bound by the terms used. This highlights the use of absolute terms for contracts by Muslim jurists, because the use of such terms favours the objective theory.

There are, in *fiqh* books, detailed discussions about what type of words are suitable for concluding the contract of partnership. A good source for these is the *Fatāwā 'Ālamgīrī*.[12] All these words are intended to convey the meaning of *sharikah* in their ordinary meanings or when used in a specific context. There is no dispute among jurists, however, that *sharikah* is concluded by words used for the past tense. Some even permit its conclusion through words used for the present and future tenses, though the Ḥanafīs are somewhat strict about the use of the future tense. The interrogative form is not considered suitable for concluding a contract of partnership.

The Ḥanafīs stipulate that the term *mufāwaḍah* must be used for concluding that contract so that its extreme conditions are fully implied. Al-Sarakhsī says:

> Al-Ḥasan has related from Abū Ḥanīfah that the *mufāwaḍah* is not concluded except by the use of the term *mufāwaḍah,* so much so that if it is not used, the partnership concluded is a general *'inān. 'Inān* is sometimes general and sometimes special. This is interpreted to mean that most of the people do not understand all the *aḥkām* of *mufāwaḍah,* therefore, consent cannot be implied, unless these *aḥkām* are fully understood. The express employment of the term *mufāwaḍah* is considered a

[11] A violation of a condition will naturally render the contract void.

[12] Commission of Sulṭān Muḥīy al-Dīn Awrangzeb 'Ālamgīr (1659–1707) *al-Fatāwā al-'Ālamgīrīyah*, 6 vols. (Būlāq, 1310 A.H.).

> substitute for such knowledge. If, however, the two parties clearly understand the rules of *mufāwaḍah,* the contract is valid if the general conditions of *mufāwaḍah* are expressly mentioned, even if the word is not used, because it is the conditions that are important not the words.[13]

In this passage, al-Sarakhsī explains the importance of using the word *mufāwaḍah* in the contract and elaborates the conditions under which it may be given up. If these are not met, the partnership constituted will not be *mufāwaḍah,* but a general *'inān.* The texts of the jurists also make it quite clear that if the word *sharikah* is used by itself, it implies a general *'inān.* As for the special *'inān,* it needs elaboration of the type of trade for which it is intended. Another special form of *'inān* is based upon the grant of a special agency instead of a general agency for the partnership. Likewise, the fixing of the duration of the partnership (*tawqīt*) needs and express stipulation.[14]

3.2 Writing Down the Contract

The jurists considered the writing down of contracts or conveyancing as an independent discipline called *al-shurūṭ.* The leading jurist in this field, whose books have reached us, was al-Ṭaḥāwī. He says in his book *al-Shurūṭ al-Ṣaghīr:*

> Allah, the Mighty, the Glorious, has said in His Book about debts that are delayed by some for others, "O ye who believe, when you deal in debts delayed for a stated period, write them down."[15] He, therefore, ordained for the believers the writing down of such debts, so that it may be a protection for the wealth of the creditors and the rights of the debtors. He then said about immediate debts, "Unless it be spot trade that you transact among yourselves; there is no blame on you if you do not record them in writing."[16] He, thus, granted flexibility in the relinquishment of writing, but without rejecting the right to

[13] Al-Sarakhsī, *al-Mabsūṭ,* vol. 11, p. 154.

[14] Zayn al-'Ābidīn ibn Ibrāhīm ibn Nujaym, *al-Baḥr al-Rā'iq Sharḥ Kanz al-Daqā'iq* (Cairo, 1893) vol. 5, p. 168 (hereinafter referred to as Ibn Nujaym, *al-Baḥr al-Rā'iq*).

[15] Qur'ān 2 : 282.

[16] Qur'ān 2 : 282.

> record them, because the removal of blame is the granting of an option and freedom without a prohibition.... He, then, said, "Witness [your contracts],"[17] that is, for them to become a proof of what they have written, because a document in itself is not a proof; it becomes (admissible as) evidence when it is proved (by the testimony of witnesses).... He further said, "He (the scribe) should not avoid the recording of it as he has been directed by Allah." This indicates that He intended by a document the best way that they can record it....[18]

About the number of copies of a document, he says:

> If each one of them demands... that he be in possession of a document recording what has been transacted among them, in accordance with what we have mentioned, he (the scribe) should make two identical documents (copies) without there being the discrepancy of a single word, and without loss of meaning.[19]

Al-Sarakhsī too records in the section on *shurūṭ* in *al-Mabsūṭ*, the benefits of written documents, especially with respect to trade.

> Know that *'ilm al-shurūṭ* (conveyancing) is one of the most important disciplines and one of the most technical... and it has many benefits.
>
> 1. The preservation of wealth: We have been commanded to preserve wealth and not to waste it.
> 2. The avoidance of disputes: A document becomes a decisive ruling between the contracting parties and they have recourse to it at the time of dispute, and it becomes a means of suppressing distress (*fitnah*).
> 3. The avoidance of *fāsid* contracts.
> 4. The elimination of ambiguity: As time passes, the contracting parties are likely to be unsure about the

[17]Qur'ān 2 : 282

[18]Al-Ṭaḥāwī, *al-Shurūṭ al-Kabīr* along with *al-Shurūṭ al-Ṣaghīr* in the margin, vol. 1, p. 3.

[19]Ibid. p. 382.

> exact amount of a counter-value (*badal*), or about the extent of the period (*ajal*). When each one of them has recourse to the document there is no cause left for doubt. Likewise, their deaths are likely to cause doubts for their heirs, going by the normal behavior of human beings, who would not abide by their trusts. On recourse to the document, there is no cause for disagreement among them.

> It is, therefore, necessary for each person to make an effort to learn the *shurūṭ*, because of their immense benefit.[20]

Are we, in this modern age, in a position to say more than what al-Sarakhsī has said about the importance of conveyancing? He explains further in the chapter on *sharikah:* "The purpose, then, of a document is reliance and precaution. It is, therefore, necessary that he (the scribe) write in the most reliable manner avoiding all chances of allegations (of a lapse)."[21] He says again: "He begins the description of *sharikāt al-'inān* and about how the two parties should record the deed of this partnership between them. Partnership is a contract that extends (into the future). Recording of a deed is, thus, recommended in such a contract so that it becomes a decisive proof between them in case of dispute."[22]

In early Ḥanafī books we find specimens of the contract of partnership. We record here a contract mentioned by Muḥammad ibn al-Ḥasan al-Shaybānī and transmitted by al-Sarakhsī and other Ḥanafī jurists. The contract is one of *sharikat al-'inān* that is general.

> This is what is agreed upon by so and so. They have participated in this partnership with the fear of Allah in fulfilling their trusts. The *kātib* then explicitly states the amount of capital contributed by each one of them, and says that this is now in their joint possession (ownership), and with which they can both buy jointly as well as severally. Each one of them will operate in accordance with his considered opinion and will sell on cash as well as on credit.... [He then writes] whatever the profit arising from it will be shared by them in proportion to the

---

[20] Al-Sarakhsī, *al-Mabsūṭ,* vol. 30, p. 168.

[21] Ibid., vol. 11, p. 155.

[22] Loc. cit.

> contributed capitals, so also the loss and whatever is consequential to it.... They have agreed to enter into this partnership in such and such month and such and such year [he then records the date].[23]

We also find specimens of such contracts in *al-Shurūṭ al-Ṣaghīr*.[24]

From the foregoing statements we conclude that the contracts of partnership and their recording was not too different from what it is today; in fact, the stipulations about writing are almost identical. There is one important point that needs to be elaborated and this pertains to the deed as admissible evidence in itself without any further supporting evidence in the shape of testimony of witnesses who attested the document. This point has been mentioned by al-Ṭaḥāwī. The position is almost similar in the law for partnerships. For example, in Pakistani law, the rights of partners, and duties owed to each other, do not come into operation by the mere recording of the partnership deed. The law requires that the partnership with its deed be registered with the registration authority for these rights to be secured.[25] Further, such registration enables the partnership to transact business in its own name and also seek the recovery of its claims in its own name. Most other documents require to be notarized in order to be admissible. All these conditions can be added to the partnership deed of an Islamic partnership, because they seek to help the judicial system and cut down lengthy judicial procedures.

3.3 Partnership by Act of the Parties

Contracts are concluded in Islamic law by the gestures of parties. Modern writers discuss such acts within the *ṣīghah* as if it is useful only for dumb people or in simple situations. It is, however, an important rule. If accepted in a wider form, it will grant the courts the right to determine whether a contract or a quasi contract existed between the parties. This is done for partnerships too in the law where the court may determine whether the relationship existed between the parties as evidenced by their acts, even if a formal contract had not been concluded. The jurists, however, are reluctant to accept the conclusion of partnerships through the acts of the parties.

[23]Ibid. pp. 155–56; see also Ibn Nujaym, *al-Baḥr al-Rā'iq,* vol. 8, p. 168.

[24]See al-Ṭaḥāwī, *al-Shurūṭ al-Kabīr,* vol. 2, pp. 726, 736.

[25]The Partnership Act, 1932, §§56–71.

It is futile here to discuss and analyze the lengthy procedures that lead to the incorporation of companies and the issuance of the certificate of incorporation. The reason why this discussion will serve no useful purpose at this stage is that the nature and form of an Islamic corporation are not settled. It is only when this new form is accepted will such a discussion be fruitful. That discussion is, therefore, moved to the volume on the Islamic corporation.

Chapter 4

Types of Partnership

Modern writers, following the *Majallat al-Aḥkām al-'Adlīyah,* mention three broad forms of partnership in Islamic law: *sharikat al-ibāḥah, sharikat al-milk* and *sharikat al-'aqd.*[1] As compared to this, the earlier jurists focus on the last two. The reason is that *sharikat al-ibāḥah* is merely a common right to acquire property that is free; it is participation in a common right. In fact, the first transaction in property acquired this way, or the mere act of acquisition, terminates this common participation, as the property passes into private ownership. This is not true of *sharikat al-milk* or *sharikat al-'aqd,* which begin with an initial mixing of shares.

The purpose here is not to study the first two types of the three forms, but we shall consider *sharikat al-milk* (co-ownership) briefly and compare it with *sharikat al-'aqd,* because many rights revert to the former when a partnership is terminated or becomes unenforceable (*fāsid*).

4.1 Co-ownership (*Sharikat al-Milk*)

Ibn 'Ābidīn defines it as follows: "*Sharikat al-milk* is ownership by a number of persons of an *'ayn* (ascertained property) or *dayn* (debt not ascertained by weight or measure or other means) arising through inheritance or through exchange (*bay'*) or through other means."[2] The *Majallah* elaborates upon the terms *'ayn* and *dayn* separately. Co-ownership in an *'ayn* is "the joint and exclusive ownership of two or more persons resulting from one of the causes of ownership,

---

[1] *Majallah,* §1060 This is the first use of the term *sharikah* in a broad sense. The term is then qualified with other terms like *ibāḥah, milk* and *'aqd.*

[2] Ibn 'Ābidīn, *Ḥāshiyah,* vol. 4, p. 301.

like purchase, gift, acceptance of a bequest, inheritance, or by the mixing (*khalṭ*) of their property in a manner that does not accept distinction or separation."[3] Co-ownership of a *dayn* occurs "when two or more persons are owed a debt attached to the *dhimmah* (liability) of another person, a debt that has arisen from a single cause. This is a common debt and is held in co-ownership between them. If the cause is not common, the debt is not in co-ownership."[4]

This shows that co-ownership or *sharikat al-milk* is of two types: co-ownership in *'ayn* and co-ownership in *dayn*. There is no disagreement about *sharikat al-milk* in an *'ayn*, but the jurists disagree about a *dayn*. The majority of the Ḥanafīs permit it on the ground that a gift is permitted in it. Those who oppose them say that this partnership is metaphorical, just as gift in it is metaphorical, because it (a gift) is in reality the relinquishment (*isqāṭ*) of the rights to a claim. Most prefer the Ḥanafī view.[5]

The single element (*rukn*) of this type of *sharikah* is *khalṭ* or the mixing of two *'ayns* or two *dayns*. This may occur due to the act of the owners or by the act of others, and they have no option to revoke it in the second case. This leads to a mandatory co-ownership and co-ownership by choice. These are called *sharikat al-jabr* and *sharikat al-ikhtiyār*. Some jurists derive further distinctions on the basis of the mode of occurrence of ownership, but these details do not serve any purpose for our discussion.

4.1.1 The conditions of co-ownership

1. The co-owner is like a stranger *ajnabī* with respect to the share of the other co-owner. Thus, he cannot use or dispose of the share of the co-owner. The only exception is a house, which may be used by both.

---

[3] *Majallah,* §1060.

[4] Ibid. §1068.

[5] Ibn 'Ābidīn, *Ḥāshiyah,* vol. 4, p. 299. Would this mean that a *dayn* may be sold or mortgaged? The first thing to notice here is that when we use the term *dayn,* we do not mean one arising out of a money loan. What we mean is a debt created through a credit transaction, like selling of goods on credit. In any case, if a debt can be sold, then, this would be useful for financing the accounts receivables of a partnership or a corporation. Whether this would be hit by the principle of prohibition of a *dayn bi al-dayn* needs to be investigated.

2. A co-owner cannot sell his joint share without the permission of the other co-owner.[6] The ownership is undivided in every particle (*mushā'*), therefore, giving possession of such property is also impossible without permission.[7]

3. The share of one co-owner in the possession of another co-owner is governed by the rules of *wadī'ah* (deposit). If.one co-owner deposits such property further with a third party without the permission of his co-owner, he is liable for compensation (*ḍamān*) if the property is destroyed.

4. Joint receipt of revenue amounts to *sharikat al-milk* in such revenue. The rule is extended to govern *sharikat al-'aqd* as well.

5. **Transactions in jointly owned debts.** This is a detailed topic and it cannot be discussed here. Briefly, however, the right to demand the recovery of a debt belongs to each co-owner jointly and severally. Any debt possessed by one partner is governed by the rules of *sharikat al-milk* applicable to an *'ayn*. Further, postponement in the period of a debt cannot be given by one co-owner without the permission of the other.[8]

[6] *Majallah,* §1088. This assertion of the *Majallah* is somewhat confusing as some schools claim *ijmā'* (consensus) on the permissibility of the sale of such a share. In law, one co-owner can, without the consent of the others, transfer his interest—in the case of land, his equitable interest—to a stranger so as to put him in the same position as regards the other owners as the transferor was himself before the tranfer. Perhaps, what the *Majallah* implies is that there is no restriction on the transfer of the share, but this must be done with the permission of the other owners. The Islamic law of pre-emption (*shuf'ah*) would also affirm such a conclusion at least for the property affected by this law.

[7] A co-owner can sell his share without the permission of the other co-owners according to some schools. It is for this reason that the Islamic Fiqh Academy (OIC) attempts to validate the sale of the shares held in a corporation. The reasoning, however, is defective, because they treat a corporation like a *sharikat al-'aqd* and a partner cannot sell his share in a partnership to an outsider without the specific permission of the other partners. This is true in *fiqh* as well as in law.

[8] For the details of the above conditions see *Majallah,* §§1091–1112; al-Kāsānī, *Badā'i' al-Ṣanā'i',* vol. 7, pp. 3552–56.

4.2 Distinction Between *Sharikat al-Milk* and *Sharikat al-'Aqd*

In law, *sharikat al-milk* is not referred to as a partnership, but as a co-ownership. Nor does co-ownership form the basis of partnership in law. We do find in law books on the topic a distinction drawn between co-ownership and partnership. We shall attempt something similar here, but from the point of view of Islamic law. The following distinctions may be drawn:

1. The *rukn* (element) of *sharikat al-milk* is the mixing of shares (*khalṭ*), whether this is mandatory or by choice. The *rukn* of *sharikat al-'aqd* is offer and acceptance, called the *ṣīghah* (form), which is the cause of its existence and not the mixing of shares.

2. Sharing of profits is not necessary in *sharikat al-milk* in ascertained property. In joint claims of debt, it is not permitted, because it will amount to *ribā.* The very purpose of *sharikat al-'aqd,* on the other hand, is the seeking and sharing of profits.

3. The division of the usufruct or revenues of *sharikat al-milk* always follows the ratio of shares. Al-Kāṣānī says that there is consensus (*ijmā'*) on this.[9] In a contract of partnership, this ratio may be altered, at least according to the Ḥanafīs and the Ḥanbalīs.

4. The relationship between co-owners is that of strangers (*ajānib*), but if authority to transact is granted the rules of agency take over, which does not lead to a sharing of profits, but may lead to entitlement to wages. The contract of partnership not only establishes the relationship of agency, but also becomes a cause for the sharing of profits. Likewise, in the law, a co-owner may sell his interest to a stranger, but a partner may not sell his share in the partnership property.[10] He may sell his interest in the partnership as a member, and this too with the permission of other partners and in accordance with §29.

5. When the shares in a co-ownership are partitioned or apportioned, sale by a co-owner becomes possible without the

[9] Al-Kāsānī, *Badā'i' al-Ṣanā'i',* vol. 7, p. 3547.

[10] The Pakistan Partnership Act, 1932, §§15 & 19.

permission of the other co-owner(s). This is not possible in a contract of partnership where permission is always required. In other words, co-ownership is terminated as soon as *khalṭ* is destroyed, but such separation cannot terminate a partnership, which requires a formal termination.

The distinctions drawn in law between partnership and co-ownership are more or less similar, except in some of the details. These have been elaborated by Lindley.[11]

4.3 Types of Partnership (*Sharikat al-'Aqd*) in *Fiqh*

In this section, we will discuss the different types of *sharikat al-'aqd* found in *fiqh*. The section following this will deal with partnerships in law. The present section is extremely important for the purpose of this study, especially the comparison between schools.

There is considerable difference among the schools about the way the different types of partnerships are classified. The reasons for this will become visible when we make some progress. The lack of uniformity about the types of contract partnership (*sharikat al-'aqd*), however, makes it difficult to understand which partnership is legal according to whom, and which school is using what term for a particular type of partnership. To solve this riddle, we will first describe the types listed by each school and then propose a general structure for understanding the various types. This derived structure will then serve as a criterion for judging the legality or otherwise of a partnership according to the different schools and will also provide a framework for the analysis of their views.[12] We will begin with the classification of the types according to the majority schools.

4.3.1 Types of contract partnership according to the majority

The contract partnership, according to the majority, is divided into five types:

---

[11]Lindley, *The Law of Partnership*, p 75.

[12]It is difficult to comprehend why most scholars keep on repeating the usual classification into *sharikat al-amwāl*, *sharikat al-a'māl* and *sharikat al-wujūh* without taking the trouble to examine how these forms are related to *'inān* and *mufāwaḍah*. This popular classification will be questioned here and then rejected in favour of a more useful classification.

1. *sharikat al-'inān;*
2. *sharikat al-mufāwaḍah;*
3. *sharikat al-abdān* (or *a'māl*);
4. *sharikat al-wujūh;* and
5. *muḍārabah.*

This classification is available with the Ḥanbalī school, and is expressly mentioned by the author of *al-Mughnī.* Thus, Ibn Qudāmah says: "*Sharikah* is of two types: *Sharikat al-amlāk* (co-ownership) and *sharikat al-'uqūd.* This section is for *sharikat al-'uqūd,* which is of five types: *sharikat al-'inān, abdān, wujūh, muḍārabah* and *mufāwaḍah.*"[13] As for the Mālikīs and Shāfi'īs, the contract partnership is of four types and they consider *qirāḍ* or *muḍārabah* as an independent contract. Al-Ramlī says in *Nihāyat al-Muḥtāj:* "And it (*sharikah*) is of four types. First is *sharikat al-abdān*... *sharikat al-mufāwaḍah*... and the third is *sharikat al-wujūh,* and these are illegal (*bāṭilah*). The fourth is *sharikat al-'inān.*"[14] The same meaning is found in al-Shāfi'ī's text,[15] in al-Muzanī's text,[16] as well as in that of most jurists of the Shāfi'ī school; and likewise, in the texts of the Mālikīs.

We do not find an express statement in the Mālikī texts that *qirāḍ* or *muḍārabah* is a type of contract partnership, except what is stated in *Ḥāshiyat al-Dasūqī,* which is a later Mālikī text: "This type is an addition to partnerships, because there is in it a type of participation prior to the division of profits."[17] This means that there is a kind of participation in the profits prior to their division. In the Shāfi'ī view, *muḍārabah* is permitted on the analogy of *musāqāh.* Thus, al-Ramlī says: "And it (*qirāḍ*) is an analogy on *musāqāh* on the common ground of work as a basis with some capital from him (the *rabb al-māl*) in each one of them, along with some *jahālah* (uncertainty) of compensation (*'iwaḍ*). It, therefore, takes most of the

[13]Ibn Qudāmah, *al-Mughnī,* vol. 5, p. 3.

[14]Al-Ramlī, *Nihāyat al-Muḥtāj,* vol. 5, p. 3.

[15]Muḥammad ibn Idrīs al-Shāfi'ī, *al-Umm* (Cairo: Maktabat al-Kullīyāt al-Azharīyah, 1961) vol. 3, p. 206 (hereinafter referred to as al-Shāfi'ī, *al-Umm*).

[16]Al-Muzanī, *Mukhtaṣar,* p. 109 (in al-Shāfi'ī, *al-Umm* vol. 7) (hereinafter referred to as al-Muzanī, *Mukhtaṣar*).

[17]Al-Dusūqī, *Ḥāshiyah,* vol. 2, p. 517.

other's *aḥkām*."[18] *Musāqāh* in the Shāfi'ī view is a type of *ijārah* (hire). Is it then valid to say that *qirāḍ* is a type of partnership according to the Shāfi'īs? The discussion of this issue will come up later along with that of the position taken by the Mālikīs. We may, however, turn to the views of the Ḥanbalī school about *muzāra'ah* and *musāqāh*. Ibn Qudāmah says:

> The accepted view of the school is that *muzāra'ah* is valid, if the seed is being given by the *rabb al-arḍ* (landowner) and the work is being done by the worker. Aḥmad has stated this explicitly as reported by a group and it is the opinion of the jurists generally, and is also the opinion of Ibn Sīrīn, al-Shāfi'ī and Isḥāq, because it is a contract in which the *rabb al-māl* and the worker participate in growth. Thus, it is necessary that the entire *ra's al-māl* (capital) come from him, like *musāqah* and *muḍārabah*.[19]

As the Ḥanabalīs consider *muḍārabah* to be a contract and they associate *muzāra'ah* and *musāqāh* with it, it is clear that all three are partnerships in their view. According to the Mālikīs and Shāfi'īs, on the other hand, all three are identical, but they are types of *ijārah* rather than partnership.

The contract of partnership, therefore, has two main categories according to the majority. The first category has four types: *'inān, mufāwaḍah, wujūh* and *abdān*. The second category has three types: *muḍārabah* or *qirāḍ, musāqāh* and *muzāra'ah*. This is a category that is disputed as to whether it is partnership or hire.

4.3.2 Types of contract partnership according to the Ḥanafīs

Al-Qudūrī says: "The second category is *sharikat al-'aqd*, and this is of four types: *mufāwaḍah, 'inān, sharikat al-ṣanā'i'* (of artisans); and *sharikat al-wujūh*."[20] He, then, states in the chapter on *muḍārabah*: "*Muḍārabah* is a contract for participation (*sharikah*) in profits with wealth from one of the partners and work by the other."[21] There is

[18] Al-Ramlī, *Nihāyat al-Muḥtāj*, vol. 5, p. 3.

[19] Ibn Qudāmah, *al-Mughnī*, vol. 5, p. 417.

[20] Abū al-Ḥusayn Aḥmad ibn Muḥammad al-Qudūrī al-Baghdādī, *Kitāb al-Mukhtaṣar* (Cairo, n.d.) chapter on *sharikah* and *muḍārabah* (hereinafter referred to as al-Qudūrī, *Mukhtaṣar*).

[21] Ibid.

no difference between this statement and that of the majority, except that it is explicit insofar as *muḍārabah* is considered a type of partnership, just as we found in the statement of Ibn Qudāmah. A similar statement is made by al-Marghinānī in *al-Hidāyah* as part of the *matn* (original text): "The second category is that of *sharikat al-'uqūd*... and these are of four types: *mufāwaḍah, 'inān, sharikat al-ṣanā'i'* and *sharikat al-wujūh.*"[22] This statement too is more or less similar to that of the majority, but from this place onward the similarity ends. We are now dealing with a maturer and more developed legal system whose legal structures and analyses are complex. It gives us the types and also the legal basis for the types. This is not a bias in favour of the Ḥanafī legal system, but the plain truth. The statements that follow, therefore, need to be examined with a great deal of care and attention.

The author of *al-Hidāyah*, while discussing *sharikat al-wujūh*, says: "*Sharikat al-wujūh*... is concluded by way of *mufāwaḍah*, because *kafālah* and *wakālah* can be inserted with respect to the transactions, but if it is concluded in absolute terms, it is formed into an *'inān.*"[23] This is a completely different approach. It means that *sharikat al-wujūh* is not an independent type; it has to be concluded as a *mufāwaḍah* or as an *'inān*. It also shows that the classification of the basic types have something to do with the contracts of *wakālah* and *kafālah*.

Is this approach followed by al-Marghinānī alone or does it run throughout the Ḥanafī school? Let us examine the views of some of al-Marghinānī's predecessors. The author of *al-Mabsūṭ*, al-Sarakhsī says: "As for *sharikat al-'aqd,* it has four types that are valid: *mufāwaḍah, 'inān, sharikat al-wujūh,* and *sharikat al-taqabbul* also called *sharikat al-abdān* and *sharikat al-ṣanā'i'*."[24] Again, there is not much difference between this statement and that of the majority, but while talking about *sharikat al-a'māl* he says: "This type of partnership is sometimes concluded as *'inān* and sometimes as a *mufāwaḍah*, when the conditions of *mufāwaḍah* are found.[25] He further adds: "And we elaborated earlier that *sharikat al-wujūh* is *mufāwaḍah* at

[22]'Alī ibn Abū Bakr ibn 'Abd al-Jalīl al-Farghānī al-Marghinānī al-Rushdānī Burhān al-Dīn, *Kitāb al-Hidāyah Sharḥ Bidāyat al-Mubtadī* (Cairo, 1368/1948) vol. 3, p. 3 (hereinafter referred to as al-Marghinānī, *al-Hidāyah*).

[23]Ibid., vol. 3, p 11.

[24]Al-Sarkhsī, *al-Mabsūṭ*, vol. 11, p. 151.

[25]Ibid., vol 11, p. 155.

times, and *'inān* at others."[26] Al-Kāsānī, in his usual manner, is more systematic: "*Sharikat al-'uqūd* is of three types: *sharikah* with wealth, *sharikat* with labour—called *sharikat al-abdān* or *sharikat al-ṣanā'i'* or *sharikat al-taqabbul*—and *sharikah* with credit-worthiness."[27] After elaborating the mode of participation, that is, wealth, labour or skill, and credit-worthiness, he describes their legal formats: "About the elaboration of the permissibility of each of these three types, our jurists have said that they are permitted whether these are concluded as *'inān* or as *mufāwaḍah*."[28]

After establishing that there are two bases for classification, the type of capital contributed and the type of the legal format, let us look at what the later systematizers have to say. Ibn al-Humām in *Fatḥ al-Qadīr,* commenting on the views of al-Marghinānī, says: "It is stated to confirm (analytical) consistency... that it is implied that *sharikat al-ṣanā'i'* and *sharikat al-wujūh* are not constituted as *mufāwaḍah* nor as *'inān,* but it is not like this as we will mention in what follows. The basis for the division is what was stated by the two Shaykhs, Abū Ja'far al-Ṭaḥāwī and Abū al-Ḥasan al-Karkhī, when they said that *sharikah* is of three types, *sharikah* with wealth, *sharikah* with work and *sharikah* with credit-worthiness, and each one of these is formed as *mufāwaḍah* or as *'inān.*"[29] In conclusion, we may repeat what was said by Ibn 'Ābidīn: "It was incumbent upon him to say that there are six types."[30] What Ibn 'Ābidīn means by this statement that there are the following six types:

1. *Sharikat al-amwāl* by way of *mufāwaḍah.*
2. *Sharikat al-amwāl* by way of *'inān.*
3. *Sharikat al-a'māl* by way of *mufāwaḍah.*
4. *Sharikat al-a'māl* by way of *'inān.*
5. *Sharikat al-wujūh* by way of *mufāwaḍah.*
6. *Sharikat al-wujūh* by way of *'inān.*

---

[26]Ibid.

[27]Abū Bakr ibn Mas'ūd al-Kāsānī, *Kitāb Badā'i' al-Ṣanā'i' fī Tartīb al-Sharā'i'* (Cairo: Sharikat al-Matbū'āt al-'Ilmīyah, 1909–10) vol. 7, p. 3531 (hereinafter referred to as al-Kāsānī, *Badā'i' al-Ṣanā'i'*).

[28]Ibid., vol. 7, p. 3534.

[29]Ibn al-Humām, *Fatḥ al-Qadīr,* vol. 5, p. 5.

[30]Ibn 'Ābidīn, *Ḥāshiyah,* vol.4, p. 303.

With respect to *muḍārabah,* there is no disagreement among the Ḥanafīs that it is a type of partnership. This was stated clearly by al-Qudūrī as recorded above. Likewise, *muzāra'ah,* when declared legal by the Ḥanafīs, is considered a type of *sharikah.* The author of *al-Hidāyah* says: "Both (Abū Yūsuf and Muḥammad)[31] said it is valid, because of what is related from the Prophet (peace be upon him) about his transaction with the people of Khaybar upon half of the produce of crops, and further because it is a contract of *sharikah* between wealth and labour. It is, therefore, permissible on the analogy of *muḍārabah.*"[32] About *musāqāh* he says: "The discussion about it is similar to the discussion of *muḍārabah.*"[33]

We, therefore, conclude that the contract of partnership is classified by the Ḥanafīs into two categories and then further classified into nine types:

I. The First Category:

(a) *Sharikat al-amwāl* by way of *mufāwaḍah.*

(b) *Sharikat al-amwāl* by way of *'inān.*

(c) *Sharikat al-a'māl* by way of *mufāwaḍah.*

(d) *Sharikat al-a'māl* by way of *'inān.*

(e) *Sharikat al-wujūh* by way of *mufāwaḍah.*

(f) *Sharikat al-wujūh* by way of *'inān.*

II. The Second Category:

7. *Muḍārabah.*
8. *Muzāra'ah.*
9. *Musāqāh.*

When we compare these views of the Ḥanafīs with those of the majority, we find that *sharikat al-wujūh,* according to the majority, is an independent contract and it is not to be qualified as *'inān* or *mufāwaḍah.* In fact, it is the *sharikat al-māl* alone that is called *'inān* or *mufāwaḍah* by these schools.[34]

---

[31] We will see later, under the discussion of *muzāra'ah,* that Abū Ḥanīfah does not consider *muzāra'ah* to be legally permissible.

[32] Al-Marghinānī, *al-Hidāyah,* vol. 4, p. 53.

[33] Ibid. p. 59.

[34] And even in this case the statements of the majority schools are not very clear.

4.3.3 Classification preferred for this study

The classification of partnership that we would like to prefer for this study is the one outlined by the Ḥanafī school. There are several reasons for this. The first and foremost reason is that it provides a structure for legal analysis that is not available in the classification adopted by the majority schools. Second, it provides a detailed structure of a developed system of law against which we can measure the views of the majority schools about the legality and illegality of certain forms. Finally, this classification enables comparison with modern forms of partnership, as we shall see during the course of this study. We will, however, attempt to alter the way it has been presented above for the sake of systematic analysis. There are two grounds for dcing so:

1. The focus in this study is on the relationships that exist between the partners in the different types.[35] Thus, when we examine the meaning of *sharikah* as a contract, we find this contract to be either *'inān* or *mufāwaḍah.* The relationships, then, flow from these two types of contracts as well as the other types of contracts they incorporate within them.

2. The second ground is also the reason for dividing the Islamic forms of partnership into two main categories. We do not find such a division stated explicitly in the works of the jurists, but when we pay attention to the distinction between the types of *sharikāt,* we find labour or skill being contributed from both sides or from one. It is on this basis, then, that we may divide them into two broad categories or classifications. In the first category work is present or possible by both or all the parties, while in the second category work or management is permitted by one party alone.

On the foregoing grounds, we may say that the contract of partnership is divided into two broad types according to the Ḥanafīs insofar as there is work from both sides or from one side alone. The first category, in which there is work from both sides, is divided on the basis of the nature of the governing contracts into two types: *'inān* or *mufāwaḍah.* Insofar as the *'inān* contract may incorporate

[35] Such a focus is to be found in modern law.

the contract of agency alone or agency plus surety,[36] we divide the *'inān* into two further types. Further divisions of *'inān* are possible on the basis whether the agency is general or special and whether the partnership is for all types of trade or for a specialized trade, but too much detail is likely to prove more cumbersome than helpful. These details will naturally come up within the broad categories.

The second category, in which there is work from one side alone, has three types: *muḍārabah, muzāra'ah* and *musāqāh.*

In all, we have the following classification for *sharikat al-'aqd* (henceforth to be referred to as **contract partnership**) in Islamic law:

A. **The First Category of Partnerships**

(a) *'Inān* Ordinary

a. With wealth as its subject-matter

b. With work as its subject-matter

c. With credit-worthiness as its subject-matter

(b) *'Inān* with the contract of *kafālah*

a. With wealth as its subject-matter

b. With work as its subject-matter

c. With credit-worthiness as its subject-matter

(c) *Mufāwaḍah*

a. With wealth as its subject-matter

b. With work as its subject-matter

c. With credit-worthiness as its subject-matter

B. **The Second Category of Partnerships**

(a) *Muḍārabah*

(b) *Muzāra'ah*

(c) *Musāqāh*

The second type of *'inān* mentioned above, that is, *'inān* with *kafālah* will be explained later. This study has been structured upon the above classification. In what follows, we will analyze each of these

---

[36]It will be explained in detail, under the discussion of *'inān*, that the Ḥanafīs permit the inclusion of the contract of surety (*kafālah*) even in the *'inān*. This leads to a new form of partnership that is never discussed in modern books on the subject.

types and see which of these are permitted by each school. We will also try to understand whether the terms used by the schools convey the same forms of partnership or some other form.[37] The purpose is to analyze how far each school is willing to go in the field of Islamic business organization. This classification can also serve in the analysis of the views of the other schools, besides the four Sunni schools, as well as the views of independent jurists. This extended study has been avoided here as it would make the book voluminous and the task cumbersome.

4.3.4 Types of partnership in law

In this section, we will list briefly the types of partnership found in English common law, especially in Pakistani law. The various types of companies will also be listed, even though they are not partnerships. Finally, we will list some of the partnerships or companies that all go under the broad title of *sharikāt* in Egyptian law, which is representative of the Arab law.

Types of Partnerships and Companies in English and Egyptian Law

Business organizations are basically of two types: partnerships and companies. The distinction between them is based upon the concept of legal personality. Partnerships are based upon the aggregate concept, while companies rest on the entity concept. In other words, partnerships do not have legal personality, but companies do.

Partnerships are divided into two broad types: ordinary partnerships and limited liability partnerships. The Pakistani law does not have limited liability partnerships, however, a new section 6-A introduced into the existing law attempts to create limited liability for banks participating in partnerships.[38] The ordinary partnership is divided further into two types depending upon whether the agency

[37]For example, the term *mufāwaḍah* used by the three schools that permit it—that is, the Ḥanafīs, the Mālikīs and the Ḥanbalīs—means three different forms of partnership. The classification of partnerships adopted in this study will make it very easy to understand such distinctions.

[38]See §6A of the Pakistan Partnership Act, 1932. A substitute for this provision has been suggested in the last part in the chapter dealing with limited partnerships and partnerships with legal personality. The Companies Ordinance, 1984, in sections 110 and 111, also provides for something similar, but it is a company nevertheless.

incorporated in it is general or special. The limited liability partnership, on the other hand, has general partners, who have unlimited liability, and limited partners, whose liability is limited to the extent of their shares, and who do not interfere in the management of the firm. This type of partnership was introduced into the English law in 1908. The idea was borrowed from the French law. The American law too has this form.

Companies are first divided into those that are working for profit and those that are called non-profit companies. They are further divided into those with limited liability and those with unlimited liability. The liability of the shareholders, in those with limited liability, may be limited by shares or by guarantee to the extent of the guarantee. The companies working for profit are divided into public and private companies depending upon whether the general public has been asked to subscribe to the shares. Companies having the liability of their members limited to the extent of their shares are called corporations in the United States of America. We will not go into the detailed distinctions between these companies, because this information can be grasped better from any book on company law; the purpose here is mere identification.

In Egyptian law, the word *sharikah* is applied to mean companies as well as partnerships. The *sharikāt* are first divided into civil and commercial (*madanīyah* and *tijārīyah*). This division is linked to the division of the courts under the same name.[39] The *sharikāt* are then divided with respect to their formation into *sharikāt al-ashkhāṣ* and *sharikāt al-amwāl*. We will focus here on the commercial *sharikāt*.

Commercial *sharikāt* that are formed as *sharikāt al-ashkhāṣ* are of several types. First is the *sharikat al-taḍāmun*. This is a company having corporate personality in which the liability of the members is unlimited. It is, therefore, similar to a company with unlimited liability in Pakistani law. Next comes the *sharikat al-tawṣiyah al-basīṭah*. This is a limited liability partnership, but this type has another variation in which the capital is divided into shares with a face value, which moves it into the next classification of commercial *sharikāt* under the name of *sharikat al-tawṣiyah bi al-ashum*. The latter type is merely an administrative arrangement under the limited liability partnership. We then have the *sharikat al-muḥāṣṣah*. This is what has been called by Lindley an "undisclosed partnership."[40]

---

[39]For the details of such classification see al-Khayyāṭ, *al-Sharikāt*, vol. 1, 32.

[40]Lindley, *Law of Partnership*, p. 25.

The second type of commercial partnerships are called *sharikāt al-amwāl.* The first type in this category is called the *sharikat al-musāhamah.* This is what is called a public limited company in Pakistani law and a public corporation in American law. We then have the *sharikat al-tawṣiyah bi al-ashum.* It is a variation of the limited liability partnership, as mentioned earlier. Finally, we have what is called *al-sharikah dhāt al-mas'ūlīyah al-maḥdūdah.* This is what we call a private limited company in Pakistan and in the USA it would be a corporation that has not gone public.

After identifying some basic facts about the types of partnerships and companies in the different legal systems with which we are concerned in this study, let us turn to the fundamental concepts identified for this study. A study of these concepts will enable us to draw out certain basic principles that will be applied to different forms of business organizations throughout the rest of the study.

Chapter 5

Fundamental Concepts I: The Firm and its Different Notions

5.1 The Economist and the Firm

The concept of the firm visualizes an organization that replaces a large number of market transactions that would otherwise have to be undertaken by individuals. By gathering these functions within it, the firm reduces and sometimes eliminates costs required for negotiating the numerous transactions. It is a team use of inputs giving a centralized position to some party in the contractual arrangements.[1] Ronald Case, an economist at the Chicago Law School, once said: "Within the firm, the market transactions are eliminated and in place of the complicated market structure with exchange transactions is substituted the entrepreneur-co-ordinator who directs production."[2] The result is economies in transaction costs.[3]

The widest term used to convey the idea of business activity is business enterprise. Business enterprise connotes a unit of ownership in pursuit of profits.[4] Economists, on the other hand, prefer to use the term "firm." In a modern economy, the economists say, production is carried out by firms and not individuals. As compared to this,

---

[1]Posner, *Economic Analysis of Law* (Boston: Little, Brown and Company, 1972) §14.2, 290.

[2]R. A. Posner and K. E. Scott, *Economics of Corporation Law and Securities Regulation* (1980) p. 2, as quoted in J. H. Farrar, *Company Law* (London: Butterworths & Co., 1985) p. 4.

[3]J.H. Farrar, *Company Law,* p 4.

[4]N. S. Buchanan, *The Economics of Corporate Enterprise* (1940) 15, as quoted in J. H. Farrar, *Company Law* (London: Butterworths & Co., 1985) p. 4.

in a simple economy, production is possible by individuals who specialize in producing goods and services. As societies and technology grow more complex, however, the problem of coordination by the price system becomes increasingly difficult and costly. This pushes the firm to the forefront as an organizing principle. In place of a variety of market transactions, which require time and cost for their negotiation, the firm purchases some agents of production and hires others. The economists construct their analysis around this idea of the firm.

5.2 The Accounting Notion of the Firm

The concept of the firm, perhaps, precedes the time of the economists. It appears to have been born out of the needs of the merchants. There was a commercial necessity to look at a group or association of persons as a single person. This idea facilitated, primarily, the keeping of accounts of associations of person. It is, therefore, referred to as "the mercantile notion of the firm."[5] In the early days, when modern corporations had not been born, accountants used to view partnerships or other forms of collective business activity as a single person or individual. These partnerships were not based upon the entity concept, that is, they were not assigned a personality by the law, but merchants and their accountants used to assign them a personality in their books. Thus, anything that a partner may contribute became the capital of the firm. In terms of Islamic law, we would say that the accountant assigned a *dhimmah* (personality) to the firm,[6] even though it was not a legal reality. The firm could continue to maintain this status in the books even if one of the partners left the firm or died.

5.3 The Lawyer's Notion of the Firm

It is for this reason that the modern law of partnerships appears to acknowledge this concept. Section 4 of the partnership law applied in undivided India and later in Pakistan, for example, acknowledges this concept.[7] Likewise, after the registration of the partnership, this law

[5] Lindley, *Law of Partnership,* pp. 29–30.

[6] The assignment of personality in the law and *dhimmah* in Islamic law leads to the creation of legal capacity or *ahliyah.*

[7] See The Partnership Act, 1932. The section states:

grants the partnership the right to sue in the name of the partnership and also the right to be sued in its own name.[8] The details of this concept have been described by Lindley in his well known book on the subject.[9] This acknowledgment of the concept of the firm by the law does not mean that the law assigns a personality to the partnership. This brings us to the way lawyers view firms.

For lawyers the idea of the firm exists, but to analyze the underlying legal relationships between the partners or the shareholders, it is the exact species that is given importance. A firm for the lawyer is either an association of persons, a partnership, a limited partnership or a corporation, as well as the several variations attached with each type. A partnership and a corporation have been two distinct concepts for lawyers although the distinction is rapidly fading. A corporation is assigned legal personality by the law, but a partnership is not. In certain jurisdictions, in different countries, even partnerships have been assigned legal personality.[10] In the United States there has been a protracted debate as to whether the partnership should be viewed through the aggregate concept or the entity concept. Recently, the new Uniform Partnership Act has preferred the entity concept and assigned legal personality even to partnerships. The actual adoption of the law, of course, depends upon individual states. Once this is done, there will be very little distinction between the accounting notion of a partnership as a firm and its legal notion.

5.4 The Mercantile Notion of the Firm and Islamic Law

Does Islamic law acknowledge the mercantile notion of a firm? The answer is yes, but it does so for partnerships that incorporate the

4. *Definition of "partnership", "partner", "firm", and "firm name"*.—"Partnership" is the relation between persons who have agreed to share the profits of a business carried on by all or any of them acting for all.

Persons who have entered into partnership with one another are called individually "partners" and collectively "a firm", and the name under which their business is carried on is called the "firm name".

[8] Ibid. §69(1).

[9] Lindley, *Law of Partnership*, pp. 29–30.

[10] Scotland is one example. Ibid. Some forms that are partnerships without personality in English law have been assigned personality in French law and hence in the Egyptian law.

contract of *kafālah* (surety) within them. Thus, the notion is associated with the *mufāwaḍah* partnership, but not with the ordinary *'inān*. Al-Sarkhsī says:

> (If two partners in *'inān* have a claim for a debt on an individual, and one of them agrees to postpone it, the other partner is not bound by this,)[11] as against two partners in a *mufāwaḍah*. Because, the participants to a *mufāwaḍah*, insofar as this is a practice of traders, are like a single individual. Postponement of claims is also a practice of the traders. Thus, the act of one is like the act of the other. In the *'inān* partnership, on the other hand, they have not become like a single individual. Further, in the *mufāwaḍah* partnership each partner has a right to claim what is due to the other."[12]

This is a very precise statement about the mercantile notion of the firm. Al-Kāsānī clarifies the concept further by distinguishing it from the concept upheld by lawyers. He says: "The act of one of them in this partnership (*mufāwaḍah*) is like the act of both, and the statement of one of them is like their joint statement. They are in fact (legally) two persons, but in the *aḥkām* rules of trade they are one individual."[13]

The precision of the Ḥanafī jurists in analyzing this concept is at its height here. Even the modern law does not achieve this type of precision in this case, which brings us to the question: On what legal basis does modern law recognize the concept of the firm? Is it based upon the contract of surety as in *fiqh*? The answer is no. It is implicitly based upon a wider meaning assigned to the contract of agency. This will be obvious in the following chapters dealing with the basic concepts.

5.5 The Mercantile Notion of the Firm and Corporate Personality

At this point it would be appropriate to suggest minor corrections to two views presented in modern times about this issue. The first

---

[11]The text in parenthesis is from Ḥākim al-Shahīd's *al-Kāfī*, which means that these are al-Shaybānī's views, if not his words.

[12]Al-Sarakhsī, *al-Mabsūt,* vol. 11, pp. 174, 190, 121.

[13]Al-Kāsānī, *Badā'i' al-Ṣanā'i'*, vol. 7, p. 3570.

view is that of Abraham L. Udovitch presented in his excellent book *Partnership and Profit in Medieval Islam.* This book, with its penetrating research, has been of immense benefit for this study. Referring to the view of al-Sarakhsī on *mufāwaḍah* being treated as a single individual, he says:

> The Ḥanafī *mufāwaḍah* partnership constitutes the single exception to the approach outlined in the preceding paragraphs. This institution is the closest approximation found in Islamic law to corporate entity.... If in this statement, we were to substitute the word law for the word commerce, it would constitute a fairly accurate and acceptable definition of a corporation.[14]

We would like to disagree here. Al-Sarakhsī was referring not to the concept of the juristic person here, but was elaborating with great precision the mercantile notion of the firm. This was further elaborated by al-Kāsānī. Islamic law, as expounded by the *fuqahā'* does not acknowledge the concept of the juristic person, but it does not mean that the *fuqahā'* were not aware of the concept. The details on this issue are very important and have been discussed separately in the study on *Corporations and Islamic Law.* S.M. Hasanuzzaman, apparently following Udovitch and referring to the statement of al-Sarakhsī says: "Another institution in addition to these two institutions which, at least, according to the famous jurist al-Sarakhsī enjoys the status of a legal person is *shirkah mufāwaḍah.*"[15] The response to this is the same.

The Financial Accounting Standards Board of the Financial Accounting Organization for Islamic Banks and Financial Institution states:

> Recent Fiqh thinking has extended the concept [of fictitious personality] to companies and other similar entities, including an Islamic bank. This recent thinking means that an Islamic bank is considered an accounting unit

---

[14]Abraham L. Udovitch, *Partnership and Profit in Medieval Islam* (Princeton: Princeton University Press, 1979) pp. 99–100. Footnotes omitted.

[15]S.M.Hasanuzzaman, "Limited Liability of Shareholders: An Islamic Perspective," *Islamic Studies,* 28:4 (1989) pp. 353, 355.

> separate from its owners or others which have provided the bank with funds.[16]

It is surprising that the Financial Accounting Standards Board is unaware of the accounting notion of the firm. In any case, the response to this assertion is that accommodating the concept of legal personality is not such an easy matter. Drafting a section in a code of law, or in a book of rules, or acknowledging this concept is not going to solve the problem. In fact, it is exactly at that time that the problem will start. The concept of a juristic person as manifested in the corporations clashes with certain basic rules of Islamic law.[17] There is a need to harmonize this concept with traditional Islamic law before a final ruling is possible. Nevertheless, as far as accounting standards are concerned they can proceed on the accounting notion of the firm. The issue whether or not Islamic law acknowledges the concept of a juristic person does not stand in their way.

The conclusion to be drawn from the above discussion is that a clear distinction must be made between the accounting notion of the firm and the concept of the corporation. The earlier Muslim jurists made this distinction, the modern partnership law maintains it, and so should modern scholars dealing with the issue; confusing the two concepts could prove devastating for legal analysis. An indication of the mercantile or accounting notion of the firm by Muslim jurists in books of *fiqh* in no way means that the corporation is acknowledged by Islamic law.

---

[16] Financial Accounting Standards Board, *Objectives and Concepts of Financial Accounting, Presentation and General Disclosure Standard and Information about the Organization* (Jeddah, 1994) p. 50.

[17] This has been shown in the study on *Corporations and Islamic law* mentioned above.

Chapter 6

Fundamental Concepts II: Contracts Underlying Partnerships

The contract of partnership is called a contract, but in reality it is structured upon a cluster of basic contracts.[1] This is true for Islamic law as well as modern law. Once the main contract is available, it does have its own effects too, but the basic rules that govern the relationship between partners, their various rights and liabilities, and even the rights owed to third parties are governed by the underlying contracts. To facilitate our understanding of the operation of the underlying contracts, we will approach the issue in three ways: 1) The operation of underlying contracts in a single contract of partnership; 2) The effects of the contract of *sharikah* in conjunction with the underlying contracts; 3) The operation of the underlying contracts when two contracts of partnership are combined, and this takes place in the contract of *muḍārabah* as well as the ordinary *ʿinān.*

6.1 The Effects of Underlying Contracts in a Single Contract of Partnership

There are four basic contracts that can operate on a partnership. All four, however, do not exist together. These contracts are: the contract of *amānah* (trust); the contract of *wakālah* (agency); the contract of *kafālah* (surety); and the contract of *ijārah* (hire).

The contract of *kafālah* does not operate in the second category of partnerships described earlier, that is, it does not operate in *muḍārabah, muzāraʿah* and *musāqāh.* The contract of *ijārah* (hire),

[1] As will be obvious in the following pages, the method of analyzing partnerships in terms of basic contracts is to be found in the Ḥanafī school. The other schools are somewhat vague on the issue.

on the other hand, does not have any role to play in the first category of partnerships, that is, *'inān* and *mufāwaḍah.*

The first form of partnership in the first category is the *'inān.* The contracts that underlie *'inān* are the contract of *wakālah* and *amānah.* The second type of partnership in the first category is the *mufāwaḍah* contract. This partnership includes within it the contracts of *wakālah, kafālah* and *amānah.*[2] As for *musāqāh* and *muzāra'ah,* which fall in the second category, include the contracts of *amānah* and *ijārah.* The details of all these types will be considered later, but for the present we need to examine the effects of each of the underlying contracts when they are included in different partnerships.

6.1.1 The contract of *amānah* (trust)

This contract is present in every type of partnership, either as part of the contract of agency, as in *'inān, mufāwaḍah* and *muḍārabah,* or as independent of the contract of *wakālah,* as in the contracts of *muzāra'ah* and *musāqāh.*

By virtue of this contract, the capital or property of the partnership is held in trust by one partner on behalf of the other partners.[3] Thus, if the property of the partnership is lost or destroyed without negligence and without a delict, the liability for bearing such loss is on the owner of the property in proportion to his share. That is, each partner will be liable for his own share and the partner managing the property will not be liable for it.[4] All the rules revert to this contract irrespective of the contract of *sharikah* being valid or void or vitiated. In other words, the effects of the contract of *amānah* are not eliminated through the elimination of the governing contract of *sharikah.*

Amānah (trust) is a relationship that pervades the entire Islamic law of contract. Wherever one person holds property on behalf of

[2] We have seen in the types of partnership discussed earlier that, according to the Ḥanafīs, this contract may be included in *'inān* as well, but by stipulation. This point will be discussed further within the *'inān* partnership. The resulting partnership is what the Ḥanbalīs later called *mufāwaḍah.*

[3] Al-Marghinānī, *al-Hidāyah,* vol. 3, p. 10.

[4] The rules applied here are those of the contract of *wadī'ah,* which would be something similar to the trust fund theory in the law insofar as fiduciary duties are imposed.

another, the rules of this contract are automatically invoked. Examples are agency, bailment, *biḍā'ah, waqf* and all the partnerships. All fiduciary relationships are determined in the light of this contract.

6.1.2 The contract of *wakālah* (agency)

By virtue of the contract of *sharikah*, each partner becomes the agent of the other partner or partners. Each act undertaken by a partner on behalf of the partnership, whether right or wrong, is governed by the contract of *wakālah*. In order to understand the operation of this contract within a partnership, a distinction made by the Ḥanafī school needs careful examination. The Ḥanafīs make a distinction, with respect to the acts of the agent, between the *ḥukm* (effects) of the contract and the *ḥuqūq* (rights of performance) of the contract.[5] The *ḥukm* of the contract means the main objective or purpose of the contract, or the primary effects that follow from a transaction. The *ḥuqūq* of a contract are considered to be the means adopted to complete the main objective or the primary effects. In a transaction of sale, for example, the *ḥukm* is the transfer of ownership or the passage of title to the buyer in the goods bought and to the seller in the price of such goods. When the sale has been made by an agent, the title in the goods bought passes at once to the principal. The *ḥuqūq*, however, stay with the agent. The *ḥuqūq* in a sale involve the delivery of the price to the seller, the right to demand delivery of the goods and to take possession of the goods. In addition to these, the agent also has the right to stipulate options, to reject the goods on the basis of defects and to terminate various types of options.[6] In other words, the performance of the contract belongs to the agent. As compared to this, the title in the goods will always pass to the principal and not the agent; the *dhimmah* of the agent is not affected. The *ḥuqūq* always belong to the agent and the principal, according to the Ḥanafīs, cannot be sued for performance.

This distinction drawn by the Ḥanafīs affects what we call joint and several liability of the partners in a partnership. For instance, if

[5]Udovitch compares this with the transactions of the *socius* for a partnership in Roman Law. Abraham L. Udovitch, *Partnership and Profit in Medieval Islam*, p. 98. The problem is that Roman law did not have a developed theory of agency, whereas the Ḥanafī school did have a developed theory of agency. It appears that the Ḥanafīs accommodated the idea of separation between the *ḥukm* and the *ḥuqūq* of a contract for its obvious utility for the Ḥanafī theory of agency.

[6]Al-Sarakhsī, *al-Mabsūṭ*, vol. 11, p. 156.

the partner as agent buys something for the partnership, his other partners are his principals to the extent of their shares in the partnership. The title to the goods purchased will pass to the other partners in proportion to their shares in the partnership. The parties dealing with the partnership can only demand payment for the goods from the partner who made the transaction. It is this partner who is liable for making the payment. This partner, of course, has the right to collect the payment in proportion to the shares from each partner. The seller of the goods, therefore, cannot sue the other partners for the price, nor can the other partners sue the seller for the delivery of the goods; this right belongs to the partner-agent who made the transaction. To put it differently, the title in the goods has passed to all the partners, but the rights and obligations pertaining to performance stay with the partner making the transaction.

These rules affect the contract of *sharikah* that is based upon the contract of *wakālah* alone and is not supported by other contracts like *kafālah*. Al-Sarkhsī, while discussing the contract of *'inān*, says:

> If one of them (the partners) acknowledges a debt against their joint trade, but the other partner denies this, then, the partner acknowledging the debt is liable for the entire amount if he was the one who transacted it, because the *ḥuqūq* of the contract revert to the party to the contract, whether he is an agent or is transacting for himself. If he acknowledges that both of them transacted the debt, he becomes liable for half, because for one-half he is acknowledging on his own account and for the other half for his partner.[7]

He then elaborates this by saying:

> If one of them buys something for their joint trade and finds a defect in the property, the other partner does not have the right to return the property on account of such defects; because return due to defects is one of the *ḥuqūq* of the contract, and these belong to the party concluding the contract. The other partner is a stranger with respect to half the purchase and is a principal with respect to the other half. The principal does not possess the right

[7]Ibid. p. 174.

> to sue the buyer on account of defects for what his agent has purchased.[8]

It is important to note here that the other schools of Islamic law do not have this complication, which is introduced only by the Ḥanafī school.[9] The first impulse of modern writers, who mix opinions from different schools without proper reflection, would be to reject the Ḥanafī distinction and follow another school. Unfortunately, this would not be possible in the law of partnership. This will be obvious after a major part of this book has been read. Nevertheless, there is no harm in indicating here that in the law of *sharikah,* the Shāfi'ī law is higly restricted, because of the narrow contract of *wakālah* preferred by this school. Accordingly, Shāfi'ī law barely goes beyond the co-ownership. The Mālikī law too is limited. It is only the Ḥanbalī law that may be comparable to Ḥanafī law in this area. In our opinion, however, the Ḥanbalī opinions in this field appear to be the adoption of the Ḥanafī opinions, and sometimes those of the other two schools, without fully exploring the principles operating behind those principles. This may appear to be a harsh view to some, but this conclusion has been forced upon us by a thorough study of this field.[10]

Even when such factors are ignored, it is suggested that the distinction drawn by the Ḥanafīs between the *ḥukm* of a contract and its *ḥuqūq* is highly useful, especially in the area of the Islamic law of business organization. This will become obvious after the distinction is employed in this study at the proper occasion for making new proposals. Further, the Ḥanafīs can very easily do away with this distinction, if the need arises, as we shall see in the next topic.

6.1.3 The contract of *kafālah* (surety)

In the previous section, we said that the *ḥukm* of the contract belongs to the principal, while the *ḥuqūq* belong to the agent or the person concluding a contract. The principal, therefore, cannot be sued for

---

[8]Loc. cit.

[9]The work of some modern writers implies that they too make this distinction. See generally 'Abd al-Razzāq Sanhūrī, *Maṣādir al-Ḥaqq fī al-Fiqh al-Islāmī* (Beirut: Dār Iḥyā' al-Turāth al-'Arabī, n.d.). This, however, is not an accurate view.

[10]Some of the problems arising out of this will be obvious to the reader when we discuss, in chapter 15, the first category of partnerships found in the Ḥanbalī school.

the price when the agent-partner has purchased something for the partnership. Likewise, the principal cannot be sued for the delivery of the subject-matter if the agent-partner has sold something belonging to the partnership. This is true when the partnership is based upon the contract of *wakālah* alone and the contract of *kafālah* is not included in it.[11] If the partners were to stipulate that the partnership will also include the contract of *kafālah,* which is built into the *mufāwaḍah* anyway, then, each partner becomes a surety for each of the other partners.[12] In such a case, each partner can be sued for the performance of the contracts concluded by one partner. Thus, each partner will become liable for the amount of the price. This has two constituents. First, he stands surety for the price in proportion to his own share and secondly, he stands surety for the share of his partner. This enables the creditor to sue each one of them severally or all of them together. This gives rise to joint and several liability of the partners that we find in the modern law of partnership.

The distinction drawn by the Ḥanafīs between the *ḥukm* and the *ḥuqūq* of a contract vanishes with the introduction of the contract of *kafālah* into a partnership.[13] The only part that remains is that the other partners are still not in a position to sue the debtors of the partnership. This right still belongs to the partner dealing with the debtors or third parties. This problem can be overcome in other ways, but it does not concern us at the moment.

6.1.4 The contract of *ijārah* (hire)

The operation of the contract of *ijārah* in the Islamic law of partnership is viewed in two ways: its operation in a valid partnership and its operation in a vitiated or *fāsid* partnership.

The operation of *ijārah* in a valid partnership

The contract of *ijārah* operates in some forms of partnerships, which are usually not considered partnerships, and these are *muzāra'ah* and

[11]Al-Marghinānī, *al-Hidāyah,* vol. 3, p. 10.

[12]Ibn al-Humām, *Fatḥ al-Qadīr,* vol. 5, p. 20.

[13]It appears that Udovitch, without considering the operation of the contract of *kafālah,* confuses its operation in the *mufāwaḍah* partnership with corporate entity of some kind. See Udovitch, *Partnership and Profit in Medieval Islam,* p. 99.

musāqāh.[14] In these contracts, the hire contract requires that there be fixed duration for the partnership, because *ijārah* is not permitted without the fixation of a period. This does not mean, however, that all the rules of *muzāra'ah* and *musāqāh* are determined by the rules of *ijārah.* Thus, *ijārah* is not permitted with undetermined wages, but these two forms of partnership permit this. It is in this form of undetermined wages that the rules of *sharikah* are applied and lead to the sharing of profits.

The operation of *ijārah* in a vitiated partnership

When the contracts of *muḍārabah, muzāra'ah* and *musāqāh* are declared vitiated (*fāsid*), their rules revert to those of a *fāsid ijārah.* The worker in such a case is entitled to reasonable wages (*ajr al-mithl*), whether or not the vitiated partnership produced some profit. On the other hand, if the worker did not undertake any work, he would not be entitled to anything even if some profits have been generated on their own.

6.2 The Effects of *Sharikah* in Conjunction with the Underlying Contracts

The primary purpose of the contract of *sharikah* is the sharing of profits.[15] This is exactly what this contract does and nothing more. While all the rules are controlled by the underlying contracts, these contracts do not and cannot provide for the sharing of profits. This can be seen by examining the contract of *wakālah,* which is the basic underlying contract in a partnership. The mere agent, who is not a partner, is not entitled to a share in the profits through the contract of agency alone. He can only share the profits with the principal when their relationship is further strengthened by the contract of *sharikah.*[16]

---

[14]The Shāfi'īs and even the Mālikīs do not consider these two forms as partnerships. In their view, they are types of *ijārah* on the analogy of *musāqāh,* which is proved through a text itself. For the permissibility of these forms see chapter 18 below.

[15]The primary objective of agency is the acquisition of ownership, while that of partnership is the sharing of profits. Al-Kāsānī, *Badā'i' al-Ṣanā'i',* vol. 7, p. 3532.

[16]Loc. cit. Likewise, a creditor cannot share the profits of a partnership. The law permits such sharing of profits, but does not call such creditor a partner. See §6 of the Partnership Act, 1932.

This operation of the contract of *sharikah* is brought out when profit has been earned, but the *sharikah* is declared *fāsid* for some reason. How will the profit earned be distributed among the partners in this case? As the rule of *sharikah* about sharing profits is eliminated, the rules of co-ownership or *sharikat al-milk* take over. Thus, if A and B contributed equal capitals to their partnership, but agreed to share profits in the ratio of 30% and 70% respectively, this ratio will not be maintained if the partnership is vitiated. The rules of co-ownership will apply and the profits will be shared in the ratio of 50 : 50, which is the same as the capital contribution.

6.3 Two Partnerships in One and the Rules of *Istidānah*

The underlying contracts operating in a single partnership impose certain restrictions on the powers of the partners to act on behalf of the partnership. To break out of these restrictions, the Ḥanafīs permit the formation of two partnerships in one. The most important issue in this respect is the power to buy on credit. For example, in the *sharikat al-'inān* that is constituted through the contribution of capital and is based on general agency (*wakālah 'āmmah*), each partner has the right to buy and sell on credit (*nasī'atan*). There is a restriction imposed by the underlying contract of *wakālah* that the partner cannot purchase on credit beyond the amount of the contributed capital. In other words, the total accounts payable at any moment cannot exceed or be in excess of the combined capital of the partnership (ignoring the profit earned at that moment). What if the firm needs to buy more, that is, on credit so that the accounts payable may exceed the contributed capital?

This is permitted by the Ḥanafīs through the authority of *istidānah*. The partners authorize *istidānah* and all the excess profits earned this way are considered to arise not from the original *'inān* partnership based on *māl,* but a second *'inān* partnership that is based on credit-worthiness or *'inān* that is *sharikat al-wujūh*. The same holds true in the contract of *muḍārabah*. Thus, al-Kāsānī says: "Likewise, the *istidānah*. In fact, after the authorization it is *sharikat al-wujūh*. It is another contract beyond the *muḍārabah*."[17]

[17] Al-Kāsānī, *Badā'i' al-Ṣanā'i'*, vol. 8, p. 3618. The contract of *muḍārabah* has other features too that severely restrict its utility for modern applications. See chapter 17 below.

We may raise the question here as to what is the need for such a device? Why does authority of *istidānah* require another contract, which amounts to *sharikat al-wujūh*? We shall study later that it is permissible in *sharikat al-'inān* to stipulate excess profits for one of the partners if he performs more work as compared to the other partners. We will also study that in a *sharikat al-wujūh* excess work is of no consequence, because the profit is being earned on the basis of credit-worthiness and not on the basis of the capital contributed or on the basis of work. This is the basic principle of *sharikat al-wujūh* according to the Ḥanafīs. Combining the two into a single partnership would lead to a clash of the two basic principles underlying these two forms of partnerships, or as the jurists would say, it would lead to combining two conflicting conditions in one contract. It is for this reason that the Ḥanafīs maintain that the authority of *istidānah* requires *sharikat al-wujūh* between the two partners and it is a contract beyond the first partnership, whether this partnership is *'inān* or *muḍārabah*.

Now this problem does not exist in the other Sunnī schools. As for the Mālikīs and Shāfi'īs, the problem does not exist because *sharikat al-wujūh* is not legal anyway, in their view.[18] The question of *istidānah,* therefore, does not arise in their systems. As for the Ḥanbalīs, they permit *sharikat al-wujūh,* and with it permit the stipulation of varying profits. In addition, they include the contract of *kafālah* into the *sharikat al-wujūh.* They can, therefore, combine the two partnerships into one, but their legal analysis on the issue needs careful examination, and we shall return to it at the proper occasion.[19] *Istidānah* in *muḍārabah,* however, is not permitted by any of the other schools. It is only the Ḥanafī school that permits it. The reason for the Mālikīs and Shāfi'īs is obvious, while in the Ḥanbalī school, as in the others, the contract of *muḍārabah* does not include *kafālah.* This point may have far-reaching consequences for the modern applications of *muḍārabah.*[20]

The above discussion brings us to the relationship between *istidānah* and *kafālah* that is built into a partnership. The authority

---

[18]See chapters 12 & 13 for the types of partnerships permittted by these two schools.

[19]See the discussion of partnerships in chapter 15, especially sections 15.1 and 15.2.

[20]In fact, there are several problems with the contract of *muḍārabah,* especially its varying nature, because of the introduction of new arrangements as profit is earned.

of *istidānah* is implied by the contract of *kafālah* when it is included in a partnership. Thus, the types of partnership that include this contract do not need the *wilāyat al-istidānah.* It is only the Ḥanafīs and Ḥanbalīs who uphold such partnerships. We shall study the details later, but if the reader wishes to have an overview, he may refer to the analysis in chapter 16. The contract of *kafālah,* however, cannot be inserted into the contract of *muḍārabah,* and another partnership based on credit-worthiness is needed on top of the *muḍārabah* contract. What, then, is the difference between *istidānah* based on *kafālah* and *istidānah* existing independently? The difference lies in the liability of a partner authorizing the *istidānah* alone and the same partner acting as a *kafīl.* With simple *istidānah,* the authorizing partner is liable for the price of the goods purchased on credit to the extent of his own *ḍamān* alone. In *istidānah* rising up from *kafālah,* he is liable not only for his own share, but also for the share of his partner. In other words, in the first case the partner does not become liable for the entire debt, but in the second case he does; liability becomes several as well as joint.[21]

6.4 Contracts Underlying Partnerships and Corporations in Modern Law

We have seen above how the four contracts of *amānah, wakālah, kafālah* and *ijārah* regulate, along with the rules of co-ownership, the entire law of partnership in Islam. In the modern law of partnership, we find that the partners can buy and sell on credit, they have joint as well as several liability, and they enjoy all kinds of rights and liabilities that are available through the Islamic contract of *kafālah.* Do the modern partnerships, then, incorporate the contracts of agency as well as surety? In modern law, the only contract underlying the partnership is that of agency. The distinction is that the contract of agency in law is based upon the principle: *qui facit per alium facit per se* (he who does a thing through another does it himself). The agent in law is a mere servant of the principal and all his acts are attributed to the principal. Thus, if an agent buys on credit for the principal, it is as if the principal made the purchase himself. Anson says: "When the principal gives to an agent express authority to contract on his behalf, he is bound as regards third parties by all acts of

[21] This distinction is very important for understanding the nature of liability in the Islamic law of business organization.

the agent, which are done within the limit of that authority."[22] This implies that the authority of the agent/partner is not unlimited and it depends on how much authority is delegated by the partners to each other. Such an arrangement makes the situation uncertain for third parties dealing with the partnership. In Islamic law, one may say that the creditors will be able to identify their rights by the name and type of the partnership they are dealing with.

What about the corporation? Do these relationships exist among the shareholders or between the shareholders and the corporation? The answer is no. This shareholders have no such relationship among themselves and no contract like *wakālah* or *kafālah* exists between them. There is no such contract between the shareholder and the corporation either. The corporation does have a contract with the directors and other employees—they are its agents and employees, but that is a totally different arrangement and has nothing to do with the present discussion. The nature of the contract between the shareholder and the corporation has been discussed at some length in the chapter on the meaning of the corporation in a study on *Islamic Law of Business Organization: Corporations* by the author.

---

[22] Anson, *English Law of Contract*, p. 532.

Chapter 7

Fundamental Concepts III: The Bases for Entitlement to Profit

Partnerships and all other forms of business organization are set up primarily for a single objective: the sharing of profits through joint participation. We have stated earlier that sharing of profits in Islamic law arises from the contract of partnership. Nevertheless, the question remains: what is the basis of sharing these profits, that is, what are the factors that *fiqh* recognizes as valid bases for entitlement to profit? This may be stated in a different way: in how many legal ways may individuals cooperate with each other in order to share profits jointly earned? One common way is to contribute money or capital to the joint venture, but is it possible to share profits on the basis of labour, for example? These are questions that we will attempt to answer in this chapter. After examining the valid bases in *fiqh,* we will also briefly indicate the valid bases in modern law. The views of the Ḥanafīs and Ḥanbalīs are quite similar on the issue. We shall, therefore, examine their views together and then look at the opinions of the Mālikīs and the Shāfiʿīs.

7.1 Entitlement to Profit (*Istiḥqāq al-Ribḥ*) according to the Ḥanafīs and Ḥanbalīs

Al-Kāsānī, the Ḥanafī jurist, states:

> The rule, in our view, is that entitlement to profit is either due to wealth (*māl*) or work (*ʿamal*) or by bearing a liability for loss (*ḍamān*). As for entitlement due to wealth, it is obvious, because profit is a growth in wealth and belongs to its owner. It is for this reason that the *rabb al-māl*

> in a contract of *muḍārabah* is entitled to profit and likewise the partner (*sharīk*). In the case of *ḍamān* (liability for bearing loss), if the *muḍārib* were made to bear the liability for loss, he would be entitled to the **entire profit** (of the *muḍārabah*). This is due to his *ḍamān,* and it is the revenue (*kharāj*) of the *ḍamān.* The Prophet (peace be upon him) said: "Revenue is based upon the corresponding liability for bearing loss." Thus, if the liability for bearing the loss falls on him, the *kharāj* belongs to him too.[1]

Al-Kaāsānī, then, provides a rational argument quoting the example of an artisan. The artisan makes an article for someone and charges more for it than he would be paid had he been a mere employee of another person. The reason for charging more, when he is self-employed, is that he bears the liability of loss of materials used. The loss would be borne by his employer if this artisan were a mere employee. The reason for charging more is, therefore, due to the underlying *ḍamān* that he provides.[2]

The views of the Ḥanbalīs are almost similar. Thus, Ibn Qudāmah, the author of *al-Mughnī,* says:

> In our view, *ḍamān* is a basis for entitlement to profit on the argument of *sharikat al-abdān* (work partnership). The acceptance of work involves *ḍamān* for the person accepting work (as an independent contractor) and provides a basis for entitlement to profit. It is, therefore, similar to the acceptance of wealth in *muḍārabah.* The worker through his work is entitled to profit; it is thus like a *muḍārabah.*[3]

Here too the concept of *ḍamān* is acknowledged as a basis for entitlement to profit, even though the reasoning employed is somewhat different from that employed by the Ḥanafīs. We shall see later that the actual application of the concept of *ḍamān* by the Ḥanbalīs is somewhat inadequate and has not been carried to its full legal potential.

---

[1] Al-Kāsānī, *Badā'i' al-Ṣanā'i',* vol. 7, p. 3545.

[2] Loc. cit.

[3] Ibn Qudāmah, *al-Mughnī,* vol. 5, p. 7.

The above statements make it clear that there are at least three reasons for entitlement to profit: wealth, work and the liability for bearing loss. These three bases enable the Ḥanafīs and Ḥanbalīs to permit *sharikat al-māl* (wealth), *sharikat al-abdān* (work) and *sharikat al-wujūh* (pure *ḍamān* according to the Ḥanafīs). These bases also enable them to permit excess profits for excess work, though the Ḥanafīs tend to ignore it in the case of *sharikat al-wujūh.*

All this is important, but it is not the end of the matter. The statements of these jurists conceal a vital principle, which is revealed to us if we pursue their reasoning to its logical limits. It is a principle that is little understood and is leading to considerable confusion in modern times, especially when attempts are made to extrapolate the rules of the *sharikah* to apply them to corporations and to issues of liability. Let us try to understand and elaborate this rule and see whether it is consistent with the rest of the law.

In a passage quoted above, al-Kāsānī says that if the worker (*muḍārib*) in a contract of *muḍārabah* were asked to bear the liability for loss, he would be entitled to the **entire profits** of the *muḍārabah.* This implies that in such a case there would be nothing for the *rabb al-māl.* But the *rabb al-māl* has paid wealth, and we have said that wealth is a basis for entitlement to profit. This amounts to an apparent contradiction: wealth is a basis for profit, yet we are denying profit to the *rabb al-māl.* Why?

The answer to this riddle is that wealth is a basis for entitlement to profit, but not alone. It needs additional support and this comes from *ḍamān.* In other words, in a contract of *muḍārabah,* the *rabb al-māl* is entitled to profit, because he has contributed wealth and has also undertaken to bear the liability for loss. This shows that *ḍamān* is always associated with wealth; it is built into it. The principle, therefore, is: **Wealth is a basis for entitlement to profit along with a corresponding liability for bearing loss.** This is the meaning of the tradition: *al-kharāju bi al-ḍamān.* A little reflection shows that this is not the entire meaning of this tradition.

The principle is applied not only in partnership law, but in the entire Islamic law of contract. It still needs another qualification, and this is ownership (*milkīyah*). In order for the owner of wealth to be entitled to profit on the basis of wealth, three conditions must be met: he must contribute wealth; he must bear the liability for loss; and he must continue to retain ownership in the wealth contributed (or in the things it is exchanged for after transactions). This principle is valid in the general law of contract as well. It determines the entitlement to usufruct or mesne profits when the passing of the title in the goods (*milkīyah*) is in question. The issue pertains to the theory of contract and is beyond the scope of this book. However, the question of retaining *milkīyah* in the wealth of the partnership will be taken up in the next concept on entitlement to profit.

When we combine these sub-rules, we have what the Ḥanafīs would call *ḍamān al-māl.*

7.2 Entitlement to Profit and the Mālikī View

According to the Mālikīs, a partner is entitled to profit on the basis of wealth contributed to the partnership. Where a partner contributes work along with wealth to a partnership, his work is considered subservient to wealth. This means, apparently, that work in itself is not a valid, or at least independent, basis for entitlement to profit. Ibn Rushd says: "The third element is work (*'amal*) and it is subservient according to Mālik, as we said, to wealth and is not treated as an independent basis. According to Abū Ḥanīfah, it is treated as an independent basis with wealth."[4]

If this is the position, how do the Mālikīs uphold the validity of *sharikat al-abdān* as well as *muḍārabah*? It is stated in *al-Mudawwanah al-Kubrā:* "What do you think, if two persons participate with labour, and they are butchers, who do not need capital.... (He said:) There is no harm in this, like partnership in *dirhams,* because when they participate with manual labour, such labour is considered a substitute for *dirhams.* Thus, whatever is valid for *dirhams* is valid for manual labour."[5]

Accordingly, we can conclude that work, when it is not dependent on wealth, is to be considered a valid basis for entitlement to profit. If wealth accompanies labour, labour becomes subservient to wealth. In *muḍārabah,* for instance, the labour contributed by the *muḍārib* is not accompanied by wealth. The same is the case with *sharikat al-abdān,* which is not dependent upon capital.

This brings us to the question of stipulating a higher ratio of profits for a partner who devotes more of his time to the partnership, or a working partner as against a sleeping partner. Mālik does

---

[4]Ibn Rushd, *Bidāyat al-Mujtahid,* vol. 2, pp. 253–54.

[5]'Abd al-Salām ibn Sa'īd ibn Ḥabīb al-Tanūkhī Saḥnūn, *al-Mudawwanah al-Kubrā,* vol. 5, pp. 42–43 (hereinafter referred to as Saḥnūn, *al-Mudawwanah al-Kubrā*).

not permit the stipulation of a higher ratio of profits for excess work; the ratio of profit must always be proportional to the capital contributed. In place of excess profits, the working partner is entitled to reasonable wages (*ajr al-mithl*) for his additional work. It is stated in *al-Mudawwanah al-Kubrā*:

> This, in my view, is like Mālik's statement about two persons participating in a partnership with one of them contributing 100 *dirhams* and the other 50 *dirhams,* on the condition that the profit will be shared equally. Mālik said that this is not valid, and they should divide the profit in proportion to their capitals. The owner of the extra 50 *dirhams* contributes his labour towards 25 of these, because both are working for the additional 50. Thus, the owner of the additional 50 works for 25 of these and his partner too works for the extra 25 out of 50. His partner is, therefore, entitled to reasonable wages for this work. If they do not make a profit and make a loss, the loss is shared by them in proportion to their capitals, but the owner of the 50 *dirhams* is still entitled to reasonable wages for the work he has done.[6]

We see that in this way Mālik permitted a salary for the additional work done by a partner, if his work is proportionately more than the ratio of his capital.

The Mālikīs do not permit *sharikat al-wujūh,* because *ḍamān* is not an independent basis in their view. This appears somewhat surprising when there is a tradition from the Prophet (peace be upon him) that emphasizes a principle that is generally accepted in Islamic law: *al-kharāju bi al-ḍamān.*

7.3 Entitlement to Profit and the Shāfi'ī View

The Shāfi'īs permit a single basis for partnership and this is wealth (*māl*). They, therefore, do not permit *sharikat al-wujūh,* which is based upon *ḍamān* nor do they permit *sharikat al-abdān,* which is based upon labour. As for *muḍārabah,* which is based upon work

[6] Ibid., vol. 5, p. 45.

from one side, they permit it as a type of *ijārah* and not as a partnership. They permit it on the analogy of *musāqāh* for which there is a supporting text (*naṣṣ*).[7]

7.4 Is Land a Basis for Entitlement to Profit?

There is considerable controversy within the majority of the Sunnī schools about the contract of *muzāra'ah,* and many of the jurists do not permit this contract. The contract is permitted by Abū Yūsuf and al-Shaybānī in the Ḥanafī school and the Ḥanbalī school appears to follow their opinion. The details of this dispute have been discussed in the section on *muzāra'ah* in the third part of this book.[8]

It appears that the real distinction between the two views within the Ḥanafī school, with Abū Ḥanīfah denying validity to the contract, is linked to the principle that entitlement to profit is based on a corresponding liability to bear loss. Further, the bases for entitlement to profit are capital (*māl*), labour (*'amal*), and *ḍamān* or the surety that you will pay for the loss when you are not contributing anything. The two principles when combined tell us that **in business you are allowed to gain on what you can lose.** When you give money, you also accept the accompanying risk of loss. It should be noted here that we are not talking about potential loss or the loss due to the capital staying idle. We are talking about loss in the original principal sum. The same goes for labour, as the entire labour can be lost. *Ḍamān* amounts to the same thing as capital, with the difference that nothing is being paid in advance. We now raise the question: Is land a basis for entitlement to profit? The reply would be that if a loss can occur in land, it should also be entitled to profit. Abū Ḥanīfah appears to be saying that no loss can occur in land and it cannot be a basis for entitlement to profit. As *muzāra'ah* is the sharing of profit, the owner of land cannot be allowed the profit or yield because land is not subject to loss. Abū Yūsuf and al-Shaybānī, on the other hand, appear to be saying that the seed contributed by the landowner should be considered his capital and his land should be assigned the status of real estate, because of which additional profits have been permitted in regular partnerships based upon labour

---

[7]See, e.g., al-Ramlī, *Nihāyat al-Muḥtāj,* vol. 5, pp. 245–46.

[8]See chapter 18 below. Even the Shāfi'īs and Mālikīs do not permit *muzāra'ah,* except that the Shāfi'īs do so when it is subservient to *musāqāh,* which in itself is based upon a text.

(*sharikat al-'amal*), whether *'inān* or *mufāwaḍah*. According to Abū Ḥanīfah, then, *muzāra'ah* is not valid, because land is not a basis for entitlement to profit. The details will be discussed later.

7.5 Bases for Entitlement to Profit in Modern Law

The English law of partnership of 1860 considered wealth, skill and labour as valid bases for entitlement to profit to the exclusion of all other things. The law of 1932, applied in India, and subsequently in Pakistan, and which is still working, did not have such restrictions. It is, therefore, possible for a person to be a partner without contributing any property, skill or labour. Lindley says:

> AGREEMENTS to enter into partnership, like all other agreements, require to be founded on some consideration in order to be binding. Any contribution in the shape of capital or labour, or any act which may result in liability to third parties, is a sufficient consideration to support such an agreement.[9]

The Law, in fact, leaves these issues to be settled by the partners among themselves.

It is also possible for a person, in modern law, to participate in the profits of a partnership and still not be a partner. Section 6 of the Pakistani law of partnership states that sharing of profits is not conclusive proof that the beneficiary is a partner, especially in the case of a creditor who has given a loan to the partnership and in certain cases shares the profits with the partners.[10] Likewise, an employee who takes part of the profits as compensation for work done[11] as well as the heirs of a deceased partner or even an ex-partner.

The true test of a person being a partner, as stated in the definition earlier, is the existence of a relationship of partnership between them. The bases for entitlement to profit in law, we may conclude,

---

[9]Lindley, *Law of Partnership*, p. 101.

[10]This is covered by §6 of the Partnership Act, 1932, and may be said to be the prototype of the relationship between the shareholder and the corporation. For a discussion see Imran Ahsan Nyazee, *Corporations and Islamic Law* (to be published).

[11]§6(b) of the Partnership Act, 1932 provides for a relationship that may be considered similar to *muḍārabah*, but the servant or agent is not a partner.

are all those factors that are found in Islamic law as well as many others. The ability to determine what these factors will be in a particular partnership is left to the partners. The main thing we notice here is that in the case of persons contributing money to a partnership, they become entitled to profits when ownership in their money has passed on to the partnership, as in the case of a creditor sharing profits, or even when such ownership is retained by the person giving the money, as in the case of a regular partner.

For the first category of partnerships in Islamic law, on the other hand, retaining ownership in the capital contributed is the true test of being a partner. In the second category of partnerships, especially *muḍārabah,* this test is applied when profits have emerged. If we apply this test to modern law, that is, the test of retaining co-ownership, we find that it will hold true in most cases. The exception will be the creditor sharing profits. This brings us to the next concept of ownership of the capital of the firm.

The above discussion tells us that there are three bases in Islamic law for entitlement to profit. These are based upon capital, labour and credit-worthiness. Land is not considered a basis for such entitlement by the majority of the jurists. The three bases have been assigned legal names by the Ḥanafī jurists as follows:

1. *Ḍamān al-māl* or the willingness to bear loss on capital, while retaining ownership of the capital.

2. *Ḍamān al-'amal* or the willingness to perform the contract, that is, complete the work assigned irrespective of who has accepted the work.

3. *Ḍamān al-thaman* or the willingness to pay the purchase price of the commodity bought on credit.

The loss to be borne by each party is always in proportion to the *ḍamān* provided.

Chapter 8

Fundamental Concepts IV: Ownership of the Capital of the Firm

In the previous chapter, we have shown that contributing capital alone does not entitle one to profit in the Islamic law of partnership, unless two further conditions are met. The conditions are the built-in liability for bearing loss and the co-ownership of the capital of the firm. In this chapter, we shall briefly examine the concept of joint ownership (*milk mushtarak*) in a partnership. This concept is important not only for partnership, but also for determining the legal validity of subscribing to the capital of the corporation as well as determining the existence of *ribā* in business transactions.[1] These two concepts cannot be elaborated here as they are somewhat complex. They have been explained in the study on corporations by the author referred to earlier.

As far as partnerships are concerned, the concept of co-ownership in the capital of the partnership is explored from two perspectives. The first is the case of a valid partnership, while the second is the case of a *fāsid* partnership.

It has been stated earlier that a partnership does not have legal personality, and is based on what is called the aggregate concept as against the entity concept. The capital of a partnership is, therefore, held in joint ownership by the partners. As compared to this, in a corporation, which is based upon the entity concept, the capital and assets belong to the corporation itself. The capital of a partnership in *fiqh*, and in law, is considered the wealth of the partners and so are the profits in a *muḍārabah*.

---

[1] An essential rule for the existence of *ribā* is the transfer of ownership in the exchanged counter-values from one party to the other.

The implications of this, in case of a valid partnership, can be seen in the rights and duties associated with the ownership. A single example will suffice, and this example illustrates the concept of co-ownership in *muḍārabah.* Thus, in a valid *muḍārabah,* if the *rabb al-māl* is selling a house, which has another house adjacent to it belonging to the *muḍārabah,* then the *muḍārib* has the right to buy this house through preemption, but for himself, not for the *rabb al-māl.* This is possible if profits have emerged in the *muḍārabah* (or in the house of the *muḍārabah*). If there are no profits, the *muḍārib* does not have this right. If, on the other hand, the house adjacent to the house of the *muḍārabah* is being sold by a stranger and no profits have emerged in the *muḍārabah,* it is only the *rabb al-māl* who has the right to buy the adjacent house through preemption. If profits have emerged, then, both the *rabb al-māl* and the *muḍārib* have a joint right of preemption.[2]

It is possible for us to apply the rules underlying this example to other forms of partnerships based upon capital, labour or credit-worthiness. Will these rules hold true for the corporation? The answer is no. One way we can visualize this situation is when two adjacent houses are owned by single corporation. If the corporation wants to sell one house, can a shareholder claim a right to buy the house on the assumption that he is part owner of the adjacent house. Another way, which is better, is if one of the houses is owned by a corporation and the next one by a shareholder. If the shareholder is selling his house, can another shareholder exercise the right of preemption on the ground that he is part owner of the house owned by the corporation. The answer is no. The second shareholder has nothing to do with the house owned by the corporation.

In the case of a *fāsid* partnership, the rules of co-ownership take over. In a partnership based upon capital, all its assets will be divided up among the partners in proportion to their capital contribution. If an excess ratio of profits was stipulated for a partner, according to those who permit it, he will not be entitled to this and will be paid reasonable wages for additional work. The case of the *muḍārabah* is similar. The *muḍārib* will not be given anything out of the profits, but he will be entitled to reasonable wages. The rules in this case will revert to a *fāsid ijārah.*

The rules for partnership are almost similar in the law with some variations. What is interesting is that even in a corporation, when

---

[2] Al-Kāsānī, *Badā'i' al-Ṣanā'i'*, vol. 8, p. 3637.

it is wound up, the rules of co-ownership will take over after all the creditors have been satisfied. Why? The reason is that the personality of the corporation now stands erased and what is left is joint claims on property. Before it died, the corporation gave back what it had to those who contributed to its wealth, whether these were creditors or shareholders. During its life, however, it was the sole owner of all its assets.

8.1 Ownership, *muḍārib* and borrower

To understand the implication of ownership for purposes of *ribā,* we may compare the case of a *muḍārib* and a borrower. A *muḍārib* takes money from the *rabb al-māl* on the understanding that he will share the profits with him. In this case the *rabb al-māl* retains ownership of the capital he has contributed. As compared to this, if this *muḍārib* were a mere borrower and he borrowed money from an investor on the understanding that he will share the profits with the creditor, the transaction would entail problems. First, ownership in the amount borrowed would be transferred to the borrower and he will be under an obligation to repay the entire amount after the stipulated period. This will invoke the rules of *ribā.* Any amount paid by the borrower out of the profits will be interest, whether such amount is a fixed part of the profits or is a percentage of such profits. This is not permitted. It may be noted that the Partnership Act, 1932 in §6 permits this arrangement with a creditor without designating him as a partner. Islamic law cannot permit this due to the prohibition of *ribā.*

Another difficulty that will arise in the transaction of the borrower is that the arrangement will clash with the principle of liability: *al-kharāju bi al-ḍamān.* As the creditor does not own, anymore, the amount he lent to the borrower, he is in no way liable for any loss that may arise out of the business transaction. The entire liability for loss in the borrowed amount has shifted to the borrower. This entitles him to the entire profit. As the creditor has no liability for losss, he is not entitled to any profit; Islamic law will not permit this. The arrangement with the creditor contemplated under §6 is, therefore, un-Islamic.

The reason for describing this situation is to invite the reader to think about the similarities between this situation and the position of the ordinary shareholder. Was the former the prototype for the latter?

Chapter 9

Fundamental Concepts V: Liability of Partners for Debts

We shall first examine the liability of partners for the debts of a partnership in *fiqh* and thereafter, briefly, look at the liability of partners in law. We shall be referring to the Ḥanafī version of *fiqh* on partnerships throughout this chapter, unless otherwise indicated, for the obvious reason that concepts pertaining to business are more fully developed in this school.

9.1 Liability of Partners in *Fiqh*

The liability of a partner for the debts of a partnership is unlimited, and Islamic law does not legitimate the concept of limited liability as we know it in modern law for corporations and the limited partnership.[1] Limited liability is the satisfaction of the debts of the partnership from the entire assets of the partnership including profits or from whatever is left after a loss has been made. This means that the creditors do not have access to the personal wealth of the partners, wealth that has not been contributed towards the capital of the partnership.[2]

---

[1]This is explained in this chapter as well as with each type of partnership discussed in later chapters. In doing so we have examined this concept according to the different schools.

[2]Basically, limited liability arises from the concept of a juristic person, but the law appears to assign this liability more or less arbitrarily and also takes it away in the same manner. An example of such arbitrary assignment is in the case of limited partners in a limited liability partnership. For one explanation of the issue see Dias, *Jurisprudence,* pp. 251–65.

The liability of a partner arises mainly due to two things: loans (*qarḍ*) and purchases on credit. In Islamic law, all expenses related to the credit purchase, like transportation costs, are included in the value of the credit purchase. In modern times, the meaning of the credit purchase may be expanded to mean all accounts payable.

The issue of liability has two sub-issues: 1) the limit of the liability of a single partner, and 2) the identification of the person from whom the satisfaction of these debts is demanded or the person towards whom the *muṭālabah* is directed, that is, who is to be sued? We shall attempt to examine both sub-issues keeping in view the separate requirements of the different types of partnership.

9.1.1 Liability of partners and requirements of *muṭālabah* in *sharikat al-'inān* and *muḍārabah*?

In the *'inān* partnership, a partner has the same rights and powers that a *muḍārib* has in a *muḍārabah*? Thus, he has the right to sell and purchase on credit by virtue of the contract of partnership alone. The right to purchase on credit, in both forms, cannot go beyond the amount of capital employed in the partnership. If the firm has $1000 as its capital, the credit purchase cannot extend beyond this limit of $1000. The right to raise money for purchase beyond this amount or buying on credit beyond the amount of capital does not belong to a partner by virtue of the contract of partnership, that is, it is not implied by the term *sharikah* as used in the contract. The partner, intending to exceed this limit, has to take special permission for the other partner for doing so. Al-Sarakhsī has the following to say:

> If he authorizes him to raise money against the capital of the firm (*istidānah*) or to raise it against the (credit-worthiness of the) *rabb al-māl*, and he purchases a slave girl for the *muḍārabah* and thereafter the *muḍārib* raises 1000 against the (assets of the) *muḍārabah* and purchases a(nother) slave girl with this, he is buying for himself exclusively. The loan is also within his personal liability. There are those who say that *istidānah* is merely a purchase on credit and *istiqrāḍ* differs from it, and does not enter into the implied authority of *istidānah*. **The correct view, however, is to say that authorization for raising of a loan (*istiqrāḍ*) is *bāṭil*.**[3]

[3]Al-Sarkhsī, *al-Mabsūṭ*, vol. 22, p. 180.

This statement of al-Sarakhsī is extremely important, not only for the law of partnership, but for the entire field of Islamic finance. The first thing we understand from this statement is that a partner or a *muḍārib* cannot make the other partner or the *rabb al-māl* liable for any loans that he may raise for the firm through *istiqrāḍ* (debt financing), whether or not the partner has authorized *istidānah*. The details of the whole statement will be discussed in the chapter on *muḍārabah*, but for the present purposes we conclude that the partner in *muḍārabah* (that is the worker) and in *'inān* does not possess the authority to raise loans. The second point and this is more important is that any authority granted for raising loans is in itself a nullity (*bāṭil*). Why does al-Sarakhsī say this? Are business loans not allowed in Islamic law? The answer is yes, they are not allowed, but this statement has to be qualified. Raising of loans with a fixed period of repayment are not permitted in Islamic law even when there is no interest (*ribā*) involved. We have explained this issue elsewhere in great detail and the reader may have recourse to that source.[4] The only loan acknowledged by Islamic law is called a *qarḍ ḥasan,* which is a loan that resembles a gift or charity. The reason is that the use of the amount of money is gifted to the beneficiary for an undetermined period. It is not permitted to fix the period or repayment in such a loan, and it is preferred that the lender wait till the beneficiary enjoys a period of financial ease. The lender, however, has the legal right to recall the loan any time he likes. A business cannot be run on such loans. Further, even if a partner raises such a loan, it will be a personal loan, because the nature of the loan is such. It is obvious that a person cannot run a partnership on charity.

Now that loans are out of the picture, and so is the liability for their repayment, we can focus of the credit purchase (*shirā' bi al-nasī'ah*). The credit purchase offers us two situations for analysis:

1. Prior to *istidānah*, and

2. After *istidānah.*

Liability before *istidānah*

The partner concluding a credit purchase possesses this right with some restrictions. The first restriction is that his purchase should not

[4]Imran Nyazee, *The Concept of Ribā and Islamic Banking* (Islamabad: Niazi Publishing House, 1995) pp. 42–50, 61, 145.

exceed the capital of the firm. In other words, at any moment the entire accounts payable should not exceed the capital of the firm. It is obvious that to work out the capital, the accounts receivable will have to be taken into account. The second condition, which applies to credit purchase through barter, is that the counter-value in which payment is promised should be present in the firm. The reason is that if payment is made ultimately with a substitute, it may lead to disputes of valuation. Further, setting off one commodity as payment against another may amount to the exchange of a debt for a debt (*dayn bi al-dayn*), and this is not permitted. Today, this condition should not apply when all payments are worked out in terms of fiat money. Accordingly, al-Sarakhsī says:

> By virtue of an absolute agency, the agent (partner) possesses the right to buy on cash and on credit as against the principal (the other partner). Likewise, by an absolute contract of *sharikah.* When one of the partners buys on credit, however, with (delayed) payment in cash, a measurable or weighed commodity (fungible), if he has in his possession the capital of the firm of the same genus, his purchase is valid on account of the firm. If he does not possess such a genus, his purchase will be for his personal account, because permitting such a purchase would amount to involving the principal in (purely) debt dealings. The partner is *sharikat al-'inān* and the *muḍārib* do not possess the authority of *istidānah* by virtue of the absolute contract alone.... If their authority of *istidānah* is presumed, the credit will exceed the capital of the partnership or of *muḍārabah.* The partners have not given their consent to their other partners for entering into (credit) transactions, except to the extent of what is deemed to be the capital of the firm. In this case, therefore, such a purchase would be for his personal account.[5]

We may conclude from the above that the *rabb al-māl,* or the partner in *sharikat al-'inān,* has no liability for the excess purchases made on credit without authorization. The reason is that if the partner concluding the transaction was to act in accordance with the restrictions imposed, the accounts payable will not exceed the capital of the firm. As stated above, because Islamic law does not permit

[5]Al-Sarakhsī, *al-Mabsūṭ,* vol. 11, pp. 173–74.

loans, and loans cannot be raised, this statement can be changed to say that the liabilities of the firm will never exceed the assets under normal lawful trading, that is, in the absence of unforeseen circumstances. If, on the other hand, the transacting partner were to violate the restrictions imposed upon him, all his credit purchases in excess of the capital of the firm would be on his own account.

Is it, then, possible for us to say that if the transacting partner were to abide by the restrictions, we have what is in modern times called the concept of limited liability? Unfortunately, the answer is no. The only statement we can make is that the liability of the partner in the absence of *istidānah* is limited to the extent of his share if all goes well (in which case the issue of liability is not even relevant). This can be visualized in the state prior to the authority of *istidānah* when the partners have total and unlimited liability even when the transacting partner has followed the restrictions imposed. This situation arises when the partner has purchased on credit, while he was in possession of substantial capital to back up this purchase, but the capital is destroyed or lost due to an unforeseen circumstance, like fire. Al-Sarakhsī explains this as follows:

> If a person gives to another a thousand *dirhams* by way of *muḍārabah* on a 50:50 ratio, and he (the *muḍārib*) purchases something with this amount, but the thousand are lost before the *mudārib* was able to pay the seller, the *muḍārib* will have a right to recover this (lost) amount from the *rabb al-māl*.... If he takes them (a second time) from the *rabb al-māl* and he has not made payment to the seller when the amount is lost (again), he is to recover the same amount (again).... He is to have recourse (to the *rabb al-māl*) again and again till the amount reaches the seller.[6]

This is the case in *mudārabah,* and it is obvious that in *sharikat al-'inān,* he will have recourse to the partners in proportion to their contributed capitals, and he will pay his own share too. This is unlimited liability, loud and clear, and we cannot say that imposing restrictions upon those undertaking transactions is likely to yield the concept of limited liability.[7]

---

[6]Ibid., vol. 22, p. 179; al-Kāsānī, *Badā'i' al-Ṣanā'i'*, vol. 8, p. 3665. This situation occurs prior to the emergence of profit.

[7]Although we will use the same idea to create some kind of imperfect limited liability for modern applications, it will be supported by other measures.

Liability after *istidānah*

Istidānah is the process of raising credit (not loans) during trading. The authority of *istidānah* given by one partner to another is called *wilāyat al-istidānah.* In *muḍārabah* and in *sharikat al-'inān,* if the *rabb al-māl* or the partners, as the case may be, grant *wilāyat al-istidānah* to the transacting partner, then, a new contract is born, which is one layer above the existing *muḍārabah* or *'inān.* This is a contract for *sharikat al-wujūh* based on the *'inān* form. It has its own new conditions that are different from the first contract. The liability for the credit purchases arising from this new contract after *istidānah* is distributed among the partners in accordance with their share of ownership in the goods purchased. If such ownership is not stipulated and the *istidānah* is unqualified, the partners are deemed to have equal ownership in the goods purchased and hence equal liability. This is based upon the principle that **the basis of all partnerships is equality, unless modified.** In this situation, the liability of both partners will be unlimited in accordance with the ratio of ownership, whether the partner is a *muḍārib* or a regular partner.

The description above gives rise to two situations. First, if the person concluding the transaction is acting with permission from his partner, then, they are both liable for the debts of the partnership, and their liability is unlimited, that is, till payment is made to the seller-creditors. Secondly, if the partner concluding the contract is acting without permission from his partner, the other partner has no liability for such a transaction, but the person concluding the contract has unlimited liability and his transaction has nothing to do with the partnership.

In both cases, however, the person who will be asked to perform the contract or who will be sued for the price is the partner who made the transaction. This, in fact, applies to all the transactions in these two forms of partnership, because the *ḥuqūq* of the transactions revert to this person, as we have repeatedly emphasized. The transacting partner always has recourse to his partner. The result is that the creditor cannot sue the principal for the payment or for the restitution of property, in case the transacting partner refuses to perform the contract. This applies to *muḍārabah* as well as to the ordinary *'inān.*

9.1.2 Liability of partners in the Ḥanafī *mufāwaḍah*

The relationship that exists between partners in a contract of *mufāwaḍah* is based on agency (*wakālah*) as well as on the contract of surety (*kafālah*).[8] By virtue of the contract of surety, the partner concluding the contract for the firm is not only acting for his partner, but also has *wilāyat al-istidānah*. In other words, in a *mufāwaḍah* contract special permission is not required for *istidānah;* it is built into the contract. Thus, if the partner buys on credit and exceeds the capital limit imposed, the other partners are held liable for such debts as they have provided surety. This liability is shared equally by all the partners as that is a basic condition of the *mufāwaḍah* contract. In this type of partnership there is no need to say that a new contract of *wujūh* is born, because it exists already within the partnership. It is not treated separately due to the fact that the *mufāwaḍah* is based upon equality and the same terms apply to excess credit purchases.

The liability in this partnership is unlimited for all the partners. The distinction between this contract and *'inān* with *istidānah* is that of *muṭālabah,* that is, who will be sued for performance. The creditor here has a right to sue each partner severally or jointly.

We, therefore, conclude that **liability in Islamic law is unlimited** and the *muṭālabah* is of three types:

1. First: *Muṭālabah* is from the *mubāshir* alone, that is the person concluding a transaction. This is true for *'inān* as well as *muḍārabah.*

2. Second: *Muṭālabah* is from each one of the partners severally as in the *mufāwaḍah.*

3. Third: *Muṭālabah* from all the partners jointly as in *mufāwaḍah* again.

It is important to note that modern law does not recognize the first type of *muṭālabah* mentioned above, because it does not recognize the distinction between the *ḥukm* or the contract and its *ḥuqūq.* Further, the concept of agency in law is different from that in Islamic law. The second and third types are recognized and form the basis of partnerships in law. They are called several and joint liability. In certain legal systems several liability is avoided.

[8] See the discussion of *mufāwaḍah* in chapter 12 below.

9.1.3 Liability of partners in the *'inān* partnership based on *kafālah*

We have already stated, in the discussion of the types of partnership, that the Ḥanafīs permit the introduction of the contract of surety even in an *'inān* partnership.[9] This gives the *'inān* partnership all the benefits and liabilities of a *mufāwaḍah* and yet permits participation with limited capital. The Ḥanbalīs permit such a partnership too, but they call it *mufāwaḍah.*[10]

The liability of the partners in this type of partnership is both joint and several. This we conclude from the introduction of the contract of surety. The jurists themselves have not discussed this partnership in detail. The details can be easily developed in the light of the principles developed by the jurists. Perhaps, the details were left to the state (ruler) to determine in the light of the changing needs of the state and by employing broad and general principles. In our view, this partnership is quite similar to the modern partnership and is waiting to be developed by modern Muslim jurists.

9.2 Liability in Modern Law

In this section, we shall deal briefly with the liability of partners under partnership law and the liability of shareholders under the law of companies or corporation law.

9.2.1 Liability of partners in law

In modern law, we have two types of partnership. The first is what may be called a general or common partnership, while the second is called the limited partnership in which one or more non-working partners have limited liability.

In a general partnership the liability of all the partners is unlimited. The creditors have the right of recourse to the personal wealth of the partners besides the capital or assets of the partnership, when the capital of the firm is not sufficient to meet the liabilities. The right to sue is of two types. First, the creditor can sue all the partners jointly, and this is called joint liability, as we saw in the *mufāwaḍah* contract above. Secondly, the creditor has the right to recover all the debts from a single partner if he so chooses. This is called several liability.

[9] For a detailed discussion of the issue see sections 10.5 and 10.6 below.

[10] See chapter 15 below, especially section 15.4.

The creditor, therefore, can demand the satisfaction of his debt from each of the partners, that is, severally, or from them together, that is, jointly. Joint and several liability existed in the law applied in India, and now obtaining in Pakistan.[11] In English law, the liability has been joint.[12] The same has been true for American law.[13] The idea behind joint liability appears to be that the capital of the firm must first be exhausted before the creditor is permitted access to the personal assets of the individual partners. The law of partnership in Pakistan or in other common law systems does not recognize the concept of suing the transacting partner alone, because of different implementations of the law of agency, as explained earlier.

Limited liability partnerships have been available in the English law as well as the American law. The Pakistani law does not recognize them. These partnerships have been based upon the old concept of the *commenda,* which may be considered the exact opposite of the *muḍārabah.*[14] In such partnerships, a partner with limited liability does not participate in the management of the firm. The English law appears to have adopted these partnerships following the French law in 1908, which appears to be the source for the Egyptian law as well where it is called *sharikat al-tawṣiyah al-basīṭah.* In these partnerships, the creditors sue the partners who are managing the firm and not the partners with limited liability. When there is a single working partner, his liability is similar to that of the *muḍārib* insofar as he is the one who is the target of the *muṭālabah.* The similarity ends here, however. The *muḍārib* can recover all the debts from the *rabb al-māl* and has no personal liability, whereas the working partner in a limited liability partnership is personally liable for all the debts and he has no recourse to the non-working or limited partner beyond the capital contributed by him. When there are a number of working or general partners their liability is joint. Another distinction between a *muḍārabah* and a limited liability partnership is that a limited partner is entitled to profits from all the credit raised, even when this credit exceeds the capital of the firm, and yet he enjoys limited liability. This would violate the Islamic principle of *al-kharāj*

---

[11]The Pakistan Partnership Act, 1932, §25.

[12]Lindley, *Law of Partnership*, p. 237.

[13]Eisenberg and Carry, *Corporations* (1995) p. 351.

[14]Udovitch has equated *muḍārabah* with *commenda.* This is not correct as *commenda* is the prototype for the limited partnership, which is more or less the opposite of *muḍārabah* insofar as it is the investor who has no liability or his liability is limited to the extent of his capital contribution.

bi al-ḍamān. In the case of a *muḍārabah,* the *muḍārib* has no liability, but if loans are raised, he becomes a full partner in a *sharikat al-wujūh,* and has full liability for such credit.

When we compare the concept of liability in law with that in *fiqh,* we find that assigning of liability in the law is more or less arbitrary. The law may choose to assign liability to any of the partners or withdraw it whenever it likes. In the Islamic system, on the other hand, the assigning of liability is linked to the underlying contracts, to the concept of *ḍamān,* and to the concept of ownership of the assets of the firm. The assigning of liability in Islamic law is, therefore, based upon the logic of the principles employed, while in the law such assignment has evolved out of experience and is somewhat arbitrary; it is based on the whim of the legislator, his *hawā.* This feature of assigning liability is even more evident in the case of the law of companies or corporations.[15]

9.2.2 Liability of shareholders in joint stock companies and corporations

We cannot go into too much detail here about the liability of the shareholders in companies. One thing is absolutely clear though that the assignment of liability in the law is arbitrary and depends on the legislator's will rather than on legal principles and their application. Limited liability is in the nature of a priveledge that is withdrawn if abused.[16] There are basically three types of liability for the shareholders in companies:

1. Unlimited liability of the shareholders that may involve even their personal assets.

2. Liability of the shareholders limited to the extent of their shares.

3. Liability of the members limited by guarantee to the extent of the guarantee.

We shall briefly examine the first and the second type and compare them to understand the concept of liability. A company is a juristic person in the eyes of the law. This means that it can hold

[15]Thus, liability is limited or unlimited depending on the way the promoters of the company have chosen to register it.

[16]This is called "lifting of the corporate veil" or "piercing the corporate veil."

property in its own name, have the full right of disposal over such property, and sue for the recovery of such property or its claims and be sued in turn for what it owes to others. In short, it has a personality and legal capacity in the eyes of law like that of a human being. The members of shareholders give money to this person in return for which it promises to pay them the entire net profit that it earns on the money. Once this money is paid, the money becomes the property of this artificial legal person, and it holds the property in its own name and not in the name of the shareholders. Whether this money is called equity or something else is not of much consequence, but in terms of Islamic law the ownership is transferred to this person and the repayment of the money becomes a debt attached to the *dhimmah* of the corporation.

If the position of the shareholder is to be compared to someone in a modern partnership, it resembles the position a creditor sharing profits. This creditor is owed money by the partnership, but instead of interest he is paid a profit. In any case, the shareholder has nothing to do with the property any more. All that he now possesses is and instrument, like a *ḥawālah* (transferable debt), called a share. This instrument can be endorsed and passed on to another person for whatever the other person is willing to pay for it. Usually, the price of this instrument is determined in a market called the stock exchange. In practice, as long as the personality of the corporation exists, it never pays back this money taken from the shareholders.[17] It is only when the personality is erased at the time of winding up that the shareholder may get back his money or whatever is left of it. In such a case, the position of the shareholder is the same as any creditor, and it is only the priority of payment that differs. The distinction between debt and equity is, therefore, quite vague and it is likely to be erased completely in the modern times.[18] The reason is that real equity, as in a partnership, is always owned by the shareholder, but in this case it is owned by the debtor. It is usually said that the shareholders own the corporation.

The position described above becomes clearer when we examine the relationship between the shareholders and the corporation according to the rules that we have applied to partnerships. If the shareholders own the corporation, as is usually stated for the benefit

[17]In other words, it is considered non-redeemable capital.

[18]See generally, *Is the Distinction Between Debt and Equity Disappearing:* Proceedings of a conference held in Boston, MA in 1994.

of laymen, the relationship arising from the delivery of money to this artificial person must be shown to exist. Are there any underlying contracts here? To be more specific, is the corporation an agent of the shareholders? Are the shareholders sureties for the corporation? In other words, is the relationship based on *wakālah* and *kafālah?* The answer is no; there is no such relationship between the shareholders and the corporation. The subscription agreement is nothing more than a deposit agreement in return for the receipt of shares. By virtue of this agreement, the shareholders are merely creditors sharing the profits of the enterprise, as is done by creditors in a partnership, and they have the lowest priority for the satisfaction of their debts. In return for this they are entitled to all the net profits remaining with the corporation.

Logically, the liability of shareholders, as creditors, should be limited to the extent of their shares. As the corporation has no bonds with the shareholders based on *wakālah* or *kafālah*, and their position is that of creditors, the other creditors should have no right to seek satisfaction of their claims from the personal assets of the shareholders, just as the shareholders cannot satisfy their claims against the corporation from the personal assets of the other creditors of the corporation. If this artificial person, the corporation goes bankrupt like any other natural person, all creditors will have access to whatever property is left with it, in accordance with the priority determined for each; so also the shareholders. If nothing is left over, each creditor loses what he gave to the corporation and has no further remedy. As the shareholder has the lowest priority among the creditors, he sometimes gets nothing while the other creditors do. It is for this reason that Hans Kelsen, who examined the concept of limited liability rightly concluded that limited liability is born out of the concept of corporate personality.[19]

As compared to this Dias points out that some jurists think that assigning of limited liability has nothing to do with corporate personality.[20] What he is saying, in fact, is that assigning of limited liability is arbitrary and has been delinked from the concept of corporate personality in practice. The law, then, in violation of all logic may refuse to assign limited liability to companies that should logically be entitled to it by virtue of their legal personality, as has been

[19]Hans Kelsen, *General Theory of Law and State*, p. 93; *Pure Theory of Law*, p. 173.

[20]Dias, *Jurisprudence*, p. 265.

stated by Kelsen. Likewise, the law can as easily attempt to pierce the corporate veil or be inclined to deny the privilege of limited liability in the case of private companies, as is the case in Pakistan. The net result of this is that Kelsen is pointing out what the logic of the law requires or what should be the position in the law if the rules are applied logically and consistently, while the law is behaving in accordance with what Justice Holmes said: "The life of the law has not been logic, it has been experience." This is the crux of the matter. The law may for the sake of its convenience design rules that are devoid of all legal logic, but Islamic law, a system based upon religious norms, must ensure that the logic of its norms and principles be carried out as far as possible so that the intention of the Lawgiver is reflected in the law.

Islamic law will, therefore, require that some type of legal relationship reflected in a basic contract be established between the shareholder and the corporation. And if it is possible to assign limited liability to the shareholders of a corporation, it should be taken away only when another relationship is imposed; this would obviously be a relationship based upon the contract of *kafālah* (surety) or on the modern concept of agency.

The topic of limited liability is not exhausted here and we shall come back to it when we attempt to create limited liability of the Islamic limited liability partnership in the last part of this study.

THE FIRST PART OF OUR STUDY IS NOW COMPLETE. It has given us a general idea about the structure of the law of business organization in *fiqh* as well as in law. The first part has also highlighted for us certain basic principles of Islamic law that need to be implemented in the modern age. In the next two parts, we shall seen how the Muslim jurists applied these principles. The application of the principles in the next two parts should elaborate for us the facilities created by these principles as well as the constraints imposed by them. After the first four parts are completed, we should be in a position to apply the principles we have acquired to the modern law of partnership and to propose new forms wherever these may be needed.

Part II

The First Category of Partnerships in *Fiqh*: Ḥanafī School

This part is devoted to the study of the first category of the contract of partnership in *fiqh.* Wherever possible, a comparison will be undertaken with the modern law of partnership. The third part will deal with the first category of partnerships according to the majority schools, while the fourth part will deal with the second category of contract partnerships in Islam; namely, *muḍārabah, muzāra'ah,* and *musāqāh.* In the fifth and final part some proposals will be made for the modern applications of the law of partnership. As for companies or corporations, they have been dealt with in a separate study entitled *Corporations and Islamic Law.* In each of these parts, we shall undertake our analysis in the light of the legal principles operating in the Islamic law of business organization.

We have divided this part into three chapters. The first chapter deals with the general conditions of *'inān.* The second chapter analyzes the conditions specific to the different types of *'inān* partnerships depending on the subject-matter. The third chapter deals with the *mufāwaḍah* partnership as developed by the Ḥanafī school.

The first category of the contract partnership (*sharikat al-'aqd*) in *fiqh,* as pointed out in the first part, has two types: *'inān* and *mufāwaḍah.* These are further divided into sub-types according to the subject-matter. These types and the sub-types, as they exist in the Ḥanafī school, will first be subjected to a detailed analysis. The results arrived at will then become the criteria for judging and measuring the views of the majority schools. During this study, we will have occasion to refer to the conditions and rules laid down for partnerships in modern law, especially in the Pakistani law and its source, the English common law. We shall not refer to the Egyptian law or the the law of the Arab countries in general for this comparison, because this law does not divide the *sharikah* on the basis of personality. This will avoid unnecessary complication in treating an already complex subject.

We begin with the Ḥanafī school by first considering the *'inān* contract and then the *mufāwaḍah* contract. It should be remembered that in the Ḥanafī school, there are only two contracts of partnership, and the rest are sub-classifications of these contracts.

Chapter 10

Ḥanafī School: General Conditions of *'Inān*

This chapter contains the following five sections:

1. The meaning of *'inān* and its legal validity.
2. The *rukn* of *'inān* and its formation.
3. The implication of the term *'inān* and its types.
4. The capacity of the parties and associated conditions.
5. The termination of *'inān* and its vitiation (*fasād*).

10.1 The Meaning of *'Inān* and its Legal Validity

Al-Ṭaḥāwī says in his book, *al-Shurūṭ al-Ṣaghīr:*

> We have based our book on the *'inān* partnership to the exclusion of *mufāwaḍah,* because of the distinction between them and also because of the differences between their rules according to more than one jurist. Some of them, however, considered them similar.... Abū 'Āsim al-Nabā was asked about the views of his companions, that is, Abū Ḥanīfah and his companions with respect to *'inān,* and he said: "This term is employed by the jurists of Kūfah, because in effect *'inān* and *mufāwaḍah* are the same thing and there is no distinction between them." I mentioned this to Abū 'Imrān, but he denied this and said: "*'Inān* is different from *mufāwaḍah,* because *'inān*

> does not involve personal wealth, while *mufāwaḍah* involves the entire personal assets. The use of the term *'inān* for such a form is based upon the meaning of the reins (*'inān*) of a riding animal that prevent it from doing certain things."[1]

The power of al-Ṭaḥāwī's legal analysis is obvious here. In a few lines, he not only captures the different views, but reaches the heart of the matter. We will see later that the *'inān* is constituted with the contract of *wakālah* and the *mufāwaḍah* with *wakālah* as well as *kafālah*. This gives the *mufāwaḍah* partner full and unhindered authority to deal with the assets of the partnership as he likes. It is, however, possible to extend the *'inān* by expressly including the contract of *kafālah* in it. It is for this reason that some jurists in the above quotation hold them to be similar in legal form. The real distinction, then, lies in the fact that in the *mufāwaḍah* all the assets of the partner that are eligible to serve as capital are involved, even when such assets are meant for personal use.[2] The *mufāwaḍah* partner is at liberty to play havoc with these assets if he likes. In the *'inān* contract, even if it incorporates *kafālah,* the assets involved are those contributed to the partnership. The remaining assets of the partner are not involved in the business directly. The *'inān* partner is restrained, as if by reins, from using up all the wealth owned by the partners. The reader must keep these useful distinctions in view. After having said this, we may turn to the more usual description of the *'inān* contract. Al-Sarakhsī says:

> As for *'inān,* it is derived from the statement, "*'anna lī kadhā,*" that is, he presented (he then quotes a verse in support)... and it is said that it is derived from the reins of a riding animal. This portrays the rider holding on to the reins with one hand, while doing something with the other. Again, each one of the partners hands over the reins (right) of transaction in some wealth to the other and not in the rest. Further, the animal has two reins, one longer and the other one shorter. Thus, it is permitted in

[1] Al-Ṭaḥāwī, *al-Shurūṭ al-Ṣaghīr,* vol. 2, p. 737.

[2] This point will be clarified later, in chapter 12 below, where it will be explained what kind of assets are meant by this and why they are to be included in the partnership.

> this partnership to have equality in capital and profit or inequality. We, therefore, called it *'inān*.[3]

This is the brilliant al-Sarakhsī, without reins if we may, trying to include all the characteristics of this partnership into the meaning of the term *'inān*. He succeeds very well.

10.1.1 The definition of *'inān*

When we seek a comprehensive definition of the *'inān* partnership in the Ḥanafī manuals, we do not find one. The only definition we find for *'inān* is for one of its types called *sharikat al-amwāl*, that is, the *'inān* based on wealth. It is possible to say that the reason for the absence of such a definition is due to the method adopted by the jurists for the study of contracts, that is, examining them as individual contracts without building up a theory.[4] The real reason, however, appears to be that as the rules are meant for traders, the jurists gave priority to what was foremost in their minds. Thus, they said that a partnership could be concluded with wealth, with work, and with credit-worthiness, and then each of these could take the form of the *'inān* or *mufāwaḍah* for the detailed conditions and rules. This would be more meaningful for traders and businessmen. Thus, al-Kāsānī, defining the *sharikat al-wujūh* and *sharikat al-a'māl,* says:

> As for the *sharikat al-a'māl,* it is participation in work as tailors or as butchers or as something else, by saying that we have become partners to undertake this work so that whatever sustenance is given to us by Allah, the Mighty, the Exalted, as wages will be shared on the following conditions. As for *sharikat al-wujūh,* it is participation without having wealth, but they have credit-worthiness among the people. They would say: We have become partners to buy on credit and sell on cash, so that the sustenance given to us by Allah, the Glorious, the Exalted, by way of profit would be shared among us on the following conditions."[5]

---

[3]Al-Sarakhsī, *Mabsūt,* vol. 11, p. 14.

[4]Ḥusayn Ḥamid Ḥassān, *al-Madkhal li Dirāsat al-Fiqh al-Islāmī*, p. 233. This assertion is questionable in itself, but the issue belongs to the Islamic theory of contracts.

[5]Al-Kāsānī, *Badā'i' al-Ṣanā'i'*, vol. 7, p. 3531.

It is obvious that the "following conditions" in this statement, which is made from the point of view and for the convenience of traders, would either incorporate *'inān* or *mufāwaḍah*.

In our study, however, which is basically a search for legal principles, we shall focus on the contract of *'inān* and on the relationships between the partners emerging from such a contract. Thus, if we want a comprehensive definition for *'inān* that highlights what the jurists want to highlight, we would say: "It is participation of two or more persons, with the permissibility of stipulating equality, through their work on their wealth, or through their work on the wealth of another, or through their credit-worthiness without wealth, so that the profit can be shared by them as agreed."[6] If, however, we wish to highlight the underlying contract of *'inān*, we may define it as follows:

> *'Inān* is a contract, based either on *wakālah* or on *wakālah* as well as *kafālah,* that permits participation from both sides with wealth, work, or credit-worthiness and the sharing of profits in an agreed upon ratio.

We may wish to recall, for purposes of comparison, a definition of partnership in law given by Parsons. He said: "Partnership is the combination of two or more persons of capital, or labor, or skill for the purpose of business for the common benefit."[7] This definition shows that in law the combination may take any form without restriction. Thus, it is possible that *māl* may be contributed from one side, and skill from another and so on. This is not permitted in *sharikat al-'inān* according to the apparent statements in the books of *fiqh* at least for the *'inān* based on *wakālah*. Wealth must be contributed from both sides, labour from both, and credit-worthiness from both or all these things combined from both sides.

When we examine the issue on the basis of the underlying contracts, we find that this stipulation may be fruitful in the case of

---

[6]This definition may be stated in Arabic as follows:

هي أن يشترك إثنان فأكثر مع جواز شرط التفاوت بعملهما في مالهما، أو بعملهما في مال الغير، أو بوجوههما دون المال على أن يكون الربح بيهما حسب الاتفاق

The author of *al-'Ināyah* says that participation through work on the wealth of another is the partnership of artisans, while not in the wealth of another means *sharikat al-wujūh*. *Al-'Ināyah* on the margin of Ibn al-Humām, *Fatḥ al-Qadīr,* vol. 7, p. 5.

[7]As quoted by Lindley, *Law of Partnership,* p. 15.

'inān based on *wakālah* alone. Even here, it may be mentioned that, the Ḥanafīs do not insist on actual work by a partner, but they do insist that it be stipulated in the contract. In the *'inān* contract that includes the *kafālah* as well, the utility of such a strict stipulation does not appear to be effective. Supposing, in such a contract, if one partner joins in with wealth, but does not actually work, and the other participates with work alone. What will be the difference between this type of *'inān* and *muḍārabah,* in which the *muḍārib* is not responsible for loss? The difference is obvious: the *muḍārib* is not a surety for the *rabb al-māl,* but the working partner (or the partner contributing work alone) is also a surety for his partner; he is, therefore, liable for the loss as well. He is sharing profits on the basis of work as well as on the basis of his *ḍamān* as a *kafīl.* This is an area on which the jurists are silent, and it has to be developed in the light of the available legal principles. We shall, therefore, return to it later.

10.1.2 Legal justification of *'inān*

The jurists cite the general approval for the contract of *sharikah* granted by the Prophet (peace be upon him) as justification for this type of partnership. In addition to this, they cite the *ijmā'* of the jurists, which in turn appears to be based on the fact that this contract is structured upon *wakālah,* and *wakālah* is permitted. Further justifications are provided on the basis of the interest (welfare) of the people and the need to promote growth in wealth. Thus, for example, al-Kāsānī states:

> As for the discussion of *sharikat al-amwāl,* the *'inān* contract is valid by the consensus of the jurists of the provinces and the practice of the people in this. [He then quotes a few traditions from the Prophet (peace be upon him) in support and says:] He approved their actions insofar as he did not proscribe them or deny it to them, and *taqrīr* (tacit approval) is one form of the *Sunnah.* Further, these contracts were declared legal for the welfare of the people, and for their need to cause their wealth to grow. He, therefore, confirmed this (partnership), and this method (of business) is suitable for growth and is thus legal. Finally, because it includes *wakālah,* and *wakālah* is permissible by consensus (*ijmā'*).[8]

---

[8] Al-Kāsānī, *Badā'i' al-Ṣanā'i',* vol. 7, p. 3535.

This is proof of the validity of *'inān* when it is formed with wealth (*māl*). When the *'inān* is based upon work or upon credit-worthiness, al-Kāsānī states:

> We hold that the people practiced these two types in all ages without there being a single denial for them from anyone. The Prophet (peace be upon him) has said, "My *ummah* will not agree upon a falsehood." Further, they are both structured upon *wakālah* and *wakālah* is permitted; what is structured upon a permissible act is permissible too.... We, therefore, hold that *sharikat al-amwāl* is legal for growth in wealth. As for *sharikah* with work or credit-worthiness, they have not been declared legal for growth in wealth, but for the acquisition of wealth itself, and the need to acquire wealth has priority over the need to make it grow. If a thing can be declared legal for an attribute rather than the essence, then, the essence itself has greater priority.[9]

This is the clear ruling of the Ḥanafī school. What is noteworthy here is that the underlying contracts such as *wakālah* and *kafālah* not only elaborate the fundamental relationships between the partners, they are also used for gaining support for the validity of partnerships. The main argument in the above statements is: *'inān* is legal, because it is based on *wakālah*.

10.2 The *Rukn* of *'Inān* and its Formation

The solitary *rukn* (element) of the *'inān*, like all other contracts according to the Ḥanafī school, is the *ṣīghah* (form)—offer and acceptance.[10] This is different from the approach of the majority, who consider some of the conditions as elements too. The Ḥanafīs maintain that all other conditions, like the parties to the contract and the subject-matter, are implied by offer and acceptance.[11] As indicated earlier, a defect in the *rukn* makes the contract *bāṭil*, while one in the conditions makes it *fāsid*. We will focus here on what is specific to the *'inān* partnership.

---

[9]Ibid., vol. 7, p. 3536.

[10]Loc. cit.

[11]Ibn Rushd, *Bidāyat al-Mujtahid*, vol. 2, p. 179; al-Ramlī, *Nihāyat al-Muḥtāj*, vol. 5, p. 219.

When the parties conclude a partnership without mentioning which type of partnership it will be the partnership formed will be *'inān*. This means using the word partnership (*sharikah*) alone and by itself in the offer and acceptance. This is not possible in a *mufāwaḍah* contract, in which the term *mufāwaḍah* must be used, or at least the conditions should be spelled out to eliminate all ambiguity. What if the word *sharikah* is used by itself and it is stipulated that the contract of *kafālah* is also to be included in it? This would still be concluded as an *'inān* partnership with the contract of *kafālah* included by stipulation. The jurists, however, are silent on this last point. Nevertheless, a purely unqualified and absolute use of the term *sharikah* leads to the simple or ordinary *'inān* based upon *wakālah* alone.[12]

If the offer and acceptance just use the term *tijārah* (trade) and do not specify what type of trade it will be, the *'inān* concluded will be general for all trades, and the contract of agency underlying it will also be general. About the formation of the general *'inān*, al-Kāsānī says: "If they intend thereby *sharikah* alone, it will be *sharikah* in all trades in general, because **the basic rule for *sharikah* is generality.** The objective of the *sharikah* is the acquisition of profit and this objective is not attained without the repetition of trading transactions again and again."[13] He then elaborates upon the distinction between a general and special partnership as well as upon the contract of agency underlying it. He says: "If they intend thereby *wakālah* alone, the agency would be constituted and its validity would depend upon its conditions whether general or particular. **The primary rule in agency is that it is special, because the purpose of agency is the acquisition of ownership not profit.**"[14] We understand from this that if an agency is being granted, the use of an absolute *ṣīghah* would lead to a special agency, but when this is granted as part of *sharikah* and the meaning of trade is not restricted, it leads to a general partnership of *'inān* based upon a general agency.

10.2.1 When the *ṣīghah* is restricted by duration—*tawqīt*

The contract of partnership can be restricted to a period of time according to the Ḥanafīs, because it is based on *wakālah*, and *wakālah*

---

[12]Ibn Nujaym, *al-Baḥr al-Rā'iq*, vol. 5, p. 182.

[13]Ibid., vol. 7, p. 3532.

[14]Loc. cit.

accepts *tawqīt*. Al-Sarakhsī says: "Likewise, if he says, 'It is for a month,' because this is *tawqīt* in an agency, and *wakālah* accepts restriction (*takhṣīṣ*) with respect to time as well as work."[15] Ibn Nujaym comes up with two narrations in the school on the authority of al-Ṭaḥāwī about *tawqīt,* but none of these views is preferred.[16] Ibn 'Ābidīn notices this and says: "Then if he restricts it with respect to time, does it accept such restriction so that it no longer exists after the passage of this time? There are two views (narrations from the earlier Ḥanafīs) about this and the details are in *al-Baḥr* relying on *al-Muḥīṭ.* Nor is a *tarjīḥ* mentioned with a certainty in *al-Khānīyah* that it can be restricted insofar as it is said that *tawqīt* is not a condition for the validity of this partnership or of *muḍārabah*."[17] From all this we gather that though a partnership can be formed for a specific period, every partnership does not have to stipulate a time period.

10.3 Formation of *'Inān* by Conversion of *Mufāwaḍah*

The *'inān* partnership is formed by default, so to say, by the conversion of *mufāwaḍah*. This takes place when some of the conditions of *mufāwaḍah* are found lacking. Al-Kāsānī, elaborating the causes of such conversion, says: "On each occasion that a condition of *mufāwaḍah* is not met, the partnership formed is *'inān*. The reason is that the *mufāwaḍah* includes the *'inān* within it and more. The *buṭlān* (nullity) of the *mufāwaḍah* does not imply the *buṭlān* of the underlying *'inān,* because a contract becomes void on the lack of conditions when its validity depends on such conditions, and the validity of the *'inān* does not depend upon the lack of such conditions. The lack (of the conditions of *mufāwaḍah*), therefore, does not lead to the vitiation of the (included) *'inān*."[18]

The type of *'inān* that is formed by this conversion is the general *'inān*. Al-Sarakhsī points out that: "The *mufāwaḍah* is not valid due to the lack of equality between them. ... The partnership between them, then, is *'inān,* because it is obligatory that the objectives of the partners be achieved to the extent possible. *'Inān,* however, is general or special. This *'inān* is the general *'inān,* and if it is designated by

[15] Al-Sarakhsī, *al-Mabsūṭ,* vol. 11, p. 168.

[16] Ibn Nujaym, *al-Baḥr al-Rā'iq,* vol. 5, p. 174.

[17] Ibn 'Ābidīn, *Ḥāshīyah,* vol. 4, p. 312.

[18] Al-Kāsānī, *Badā'i' al-Ṣanā'i',* vol. 7, p. 3544.

the title of *mufāwaḍah,* it is a false title due to the lack of the (vital) condition of *mufāwaḍah.*"[19] This view is based upon the case where the *mufāwaḍah* was general too. It is stated in *al-Baḥr al-Rā'iq* that: "In *al-Tātārkhānīyah:* among the conditions of the *mufāwaḍah* is the stipulation that it be general for all kinds of trade, towards which Muḥammad (al-Shaybānī) has pointed in his book. The Shaykh al-Islām has mentioned at the end of the chapter on *mufāwaḍah* that it is permissible in special trades as well."[20] This shows that the *'inān* will be formed by conversion for a special trade if the *mufāwaḍah* was being formed for that trade.

The conversion of the *mufāwaḍah* to *'inān* is conceived in two general situations:

1. The lack of equality in wealth of the partners, and this applies when the *mufāwaḍah* is based on wealth. This has three sub-cases:

   (a) When the term "*mufāwaḍah*" is used in the *ṣīghah* (offer and acceptance), but an actual equality in wealth of the partners is not found. Here the partnership formed is *'inān.*[21]

   (b) When the wealth of one of the partners, after the formation of the partnership, grows and becomes more than the wealth of the other partner, before they have started trading with their joint capital. The *mufāwaḍah* in this case is declared vitiated and is converted into *'inān.* When this growth occurs after transactions begin, the *mufāwaḍah* will continue, because the goal is achieved when they begin transactions with the joint wealth.[22]

   (c) When one of them inherits wealth in which *sharikah* is possible, and he takes possession of it, the *mufāwaḍah* is void and reverts to *'inān.* This rule applies even in the case of *hibah, ṣadaqah* and *waṣīyah* to one partner or even in the case of possession of debt by him.[23]

---

[19] Al-Sarakhsī, *al-Mabsūṭ,* vol. 11, p. 178.

[20] Ibn Nujaym, *al-Baḥar al-Rā'iq,* vol. 5, p. 168.

[21] Al-Sarakhsī, *al-Mabsūṭ,* vol. 11, p. 178.

[22] Loc. cit.

[23] Ibn al-Humām, *Fatḥ al-Qadīr,* vol. 5, p. 12. From this it should not be concluded that the *mufāwaḍah* is a temporary or useless contract. The purpose of the *mufāwaḍah* will be obvious when we analyze it.

It is obvious that these conditions do not apply when the *mufāwaḍah* is being constituted on the basis of work or credit-worthiness, though in the latter case details can be conceived where this is possible. This cannot be explained, unless the entire concept of *mufāwaḍah* is understood, so we will return to this point later.

2. The lack of a condition of equality in the capacity of the parties or the total lack of contractual capacity. This situation applies to all cases of *mufāwaḍah,* that is, whatever their subject-matter. Al-Sarakhsī says:

> *Mufāwaḍah* is not permitted between a freeman and a slave, nor between two slaves, nor two minors, even if their fathers have granted permission to them, because the *mufāwaḍah* is based on *kafālah* and each partner becomes a *kafīl* for the other. The slave, the minor, and the *mukātib* are not legally capable of contracting a *kafālah.* It is for this reason that *mufāwaḍah* between them is not permitted.... The partnership among them will be *'inān* in this case, because they do have contractual capacity for partnership. The *mufāwaḍah* alone becomes *fāsid* and *'inān* remains.[24]

There is one case that does not fall under either of the two situations described above. This case is stated by al-Sarakhsī: "A partner in *mufāwaḍah* has the right to contract and *'inān* with another person with some of the wealth of the *sharikah.* This is permitted to him and to his partner, whether or not it is done with the permission of the other partner. If he forms another *mufāwaḍah* with the permission of his partner, it is permitted to both of them, but if he concludes it without his permission their partnership reverts to *'inān.*"[25]

The conversion of *mufāwaḍah* to *'inān* is a very important concept, because it explains the whole structure of the Islamic law of partnerships. It shows that on one extreme is the *mufāwaḍah* contract and on the other extreme is the ordinary *'inān* based on *wakālah* alone. As we go on placing layer upon layer on the simple *'inān* a

---

[24] Al-Sarakhsī, *al-Mabsūṭ,* vol. 11, p. 198.

[25] Loc. cit.

stage is reached when we have the extreme case of *mufāwaḍah.* Now, the *fuqahā'* have discussed the extreme cases alone, but there can be many layers in between depending on what conditions are imposed by the partners. One such layer in the middle is the *'inān* partnership that is based not only upon *wakālah,* but also includes the contract of *kafālah.* This also shows that the Islamic law of partnership conceived by the Ḥanafī school is quite flexible between the two extreme cases of *mufāwaḍah* and the simple *'inān.* Modern Muslim jurists, if they wish, can construct unique partnerships within this range to suit the new conditions.

10.4 The implication of the term *'inān*

We have mentioned, in what has preceded, that *sharikat al-'inān* is formed whether the word *'inān* is used in the contract or whether the word partnership is mentioned without the qualification of *'inān.* What kind of contract is contemplated, however, when the term *'inān* is specifically mentioned? In other words, what do we mean by saying that an *'inān* contract has been concluded? What are the terms of the implied contract? The minimum that an *'inān* contract implies are the following three things:

1. Each partner in a *sharikat al-'inān* is the agent of the other partner.
2. A partner in a simple *'inān* contract is not a *kafīl* (surety) for the other partner.
3. The undivided share of a partner (*mushā'*) is like a *wadī'ah* in the possession of the other partner and is governed by the rules of *amānah* (trust).[26]

From the above we conclude the following:

1. When a partner becomes the agent of another, he possesses all the rights of the agent. Further, he also possesses the right

[26] The author of *al-Hidāyah* says: "As for the *sharikat al-'inān,* it is formed with *wakālah* without *kafālah.*" He then says: "And his possession is the possession of *amānah,* because it is the possession of wealth with the permission of the owner." Al-Marghinānī, *al-Hidāyah,* vol. 3, p. 11.

to buy and sell for the partnership on credit by virtue of the simple *'inān* contract.[27]

2. A partner in the *sharikat al-'inān* is not a surety (*kafīl*) for his partner. He, therefore, does not possess the right of *istidānah,* because it arises through express permission or through the contract of *kafālah.*

3. The wealth in the possession of a partner is a kind of a deposit. What is destroyed (or lost) is a loss that is borne by both and falls within their liability.

4. The *'inān* contract does not imply or require equality with respect to capital, sharing of profits or other things. The author of *al-Hidāyah* says: "Because equality in wealth is not a condition for it as the word (*'inān*) does not require this."[28]

10.5 Stipulating Additional Conditions, Like *Kafālah,* in *'Inān*

All the above, then, is what we consider the contract of *'inān* to imply. The question that comes to mind here is: Is it permitted to stipulate additional conditions, beyond what is implied by the word, by stating these in the offer and acceptance?

This question is extremely important, because it leads to the widening of the concept of partnership in Islamic law. One major idea, which we have assumed more or less so far, is the stipulation of the contract of *kafālah* in the *'inān* partnership. If it is permitted, what changes is it likely to cause in the ordinary *'inān* contract and in the relationship between the partners?

Ibn al-Humām, the author of *Fatḥ al-Qadīr* has tried to answer this question. Commenting on the words of al-Marghinānī, he says:

> His statement, "As for *sharikat al-'inān,* it is concluded on the basis of *wakālah* and not *kafālah,*" means where

[27] Al-Sarakhsī says: "Each one of them acts according to his considered opinion. He sells on cash and on credit. In our view, this right belongs to each one of them by the absolute contract of *sharikah.* There are some jurists, however, who say that he does not possess this right, unless it is expressly stipulated in the contract." Al-Sarakhsī, *al-Mabsūṭ,* vol. 11, p. 156. By this he means that the Shāfi'ī jurists do not permit a credit sale without stipulation.

[28] Al-Marghinānī, *al-Hidāyah,* vol. 3, p. 11.

> two or more people trade generally and do not stipulate *kafālah,* because it is specific to *mufāwaḍah.* This implies that if it is stipulated and all other conditions are also met, it will be concluded as a *mufāwaḍah,* according to what has preceded about not mentioning the word *mufāwaḍah* in its formation after mentioning all the other conditions that it requires. If some of these conditions are not met it is necessary that it revert to *'inān.* In such a case, is the stipulation *kafālah* annulled? It is possible to say that it is annulled, because in the word *'inān,* the contract of *kafālah* is not included. It is also possible to say that it is not annulled, because not being included in the word *'inān* does not mean that it is negated. It is, therefore, a valid *'inān* [that is, with *kafālah*]. *Kafālah,* then, is an additional stipulation between them for the same *sharikah.* In the case of the first (conversion from *mufāwaḍah*) it may imply that it is a *kafālah* for an indeterminate act, therefore, it is not valid except by inclusion in a contract. Thus, when it is not part of a contract (like *mufāwaḍah*), it should not be assumed, except by special intent.[29]

This implies that the contract of *kafālah* should not be assumed in an *'inān* contract when it is converted from a *mufāwaḍah,* because it will not be clear what it is meant for. For *kafālah* to be valid in the *'inān* contract, it must be inserted with an express stipulation. There are jurists in the school whose texts are clearer on the validity of such an insertion into an *'inān* contract. Before we turn to their views, it will be better to look at what al-Sarakhsī has to say on the issue. He says first:

> As for *jahālah* in itself, it does not annul *kafālah,* but it does give rise to the possibility of disputes, which is not present in this case (that is, in *mufāwaḍah*), because each one of them becomes a surety for his partner in what he is liable for due to his trade. In such a case, the surety and what they stand surety for are known by necessity. The same cannot be said about the *sharikat al-'inān.* The agency for buying an unknown commodity is not valid as an objective. But the *sharikat al-'inān* is valid

[29]Ibn al-Humām, *Fatḥ al-Qadīr,* vol. 5, p. 60.

> even when it includes this, because what each partner purchases is not mentioned in the contract. Likewise, the *mufāwaḍah.*[30]

We understand from this that *jahālah* does not annul *kafālah* itself, but it may give rise to disputes, and such a dispute is not likely to occur in a *mufāwaḍah* contract. Yet, the *sharikat al-'inān* would be valid if the contract of *kafālah* is stipulated in it, because dealing in unknown products is not the objective of the partnership even if it is so in the nature of the contract. Even *wakālah* is not valid with this type of *jahālah,* but the *'inān* has been declared valid despite this. So why not with *kafālah.*

Al-Sarakhsī, then, says about the conversion of the *mufāwaḍah* into *'inān,* and this has been quoted earlier, that the *'inān* in such a case would be general.[31] He does not, however, mention the annulment of the implied *kafālah* contract, but it is obvious that a general *'inān,* unless qualified, does not include the contract of *kafālah* when it is concluded as *'inān.* In the case of *'inān* based on work, when the Hanafī school needed the permissibility of *muṭālabah* (demanding the satisfaction) of a debt from a partner who has not concluded the transaction in a *sharikah,* they permitted it through *istiḥsān* based on necessity rather than *kafālah.*

Despite the hesitations of the earlier jurists, the later jurists found no difficulty in admitting *kafālah* into *'inān.* In fact, they insisted that this is a natural requirement for any partnership. Ibn Nujaym recorded the entire statement of Ibn al-Humām in his *al-Baḥr al-Rā'iq.*[32] Ibn 'Ābidīn then followed up this statement and said in his *Ḥāshīyah:*

> This requires that the partner becomes a *kafīl* when *kafālah* is mentioned. This is based on the preference of the second possibility (as stated by Ibn al-Humām). Perhaps, one interpretation is that when *kafālah* is specifically mentioned it is established as an integral part of the partnership and not as an external intention, because *sharikah* does not negate the concept of *kafālah,* but in fact requires it. It is, however, not established unless the

[30] Al-Sarakhsī, *al-Mabsūṭ,* vol. 11, p. 153.

[31] Ibid., vol. 11, p. 178.

[32] Ibn Nujaym, *al-Baḥr al-Rā'iq,* vol 5, p. 174.

> word itself implies this, as in *mufāwaḍah,* or when it is mentioned as part of the contract. Ponder over it.[33]

He says in *Minḥat al-Khāliq 'alā al-Baḥr al-Rā'iq:* "About his statement, 'It is necessary that it be *'inān'*—it is stated in *al-Khānīyah:* In the *sharikat al-'inān,* each partner is not the *kafīl* of the other if *kafālah* is not specifically mentioned, as against the *mufāwaḍah.*"[34]

We, therefore, see that the later Ḥanafī jurists have no hesitation in including the contract of *kafālah* in the *'inān* contract when the parties wish to include it. As these jurists have not talked much about the *'inān* partnership that includes *kafālah,* it would be useful to understand as far as is possible, the impact of including *kafālah* in the *'inān.*

10.6 The Implications of Including *Kafālah* in *'Inān*

What happens when the contract of *kafālah* is included in the partnership contract? Perhaps, the only Muslim jurist who has really tackled this issue and explained it at some length is al-Sarakhsī. Part of the issue has already been considered in the course of our discussion of fundamental concepts as well as types of partnership in Islamic law. In the Ḥanafī system, the contract of *kafālah* is split up into the *ḥukm* of the contract and its *ḥuqūq.* This means that the partner who is dealing with a customer is the only person whom the customer can approach for the delivery of goods, for payments, and for the completion of the work, as the case may be. The reason is that he is the agent of the other partners and only the agent can be approached and not the principal.

When the relationship of *kafālah* is also established between the partners, the customers get the right to approach the other partners too, that is, they can sue the other partners as well. Liability, therefore, becomes joint and several. The only exception to this rule of *ḥuqūq* made by the Ḥanafīs is in the case of an *'inān* partnership formed on the basis of labour. This exemption is based upon *istiḥsān.* Al-Sarakhsī explains this as follows:

> If one of them accepts work, then, if they are *mufāwaḍah* partners there is no difficulty if the other partner is asked

[33] Ibn 'Ābidīn, *Ḥāshīyah,* vol, 4, p. 311.

[34] See Ibn 'Ābidīn on the margin of Ibn Nujaym, *al-Baḥr al-Rā'iq,* vol 5, p. 174.

> for the delivery (completion) of work. If, however, the partnership between them is left unqualified (absolute), there are some views in *al-Nawādir* about it that are based on analogy. By way of analogy (it is decided that) only that person is to be asked to deliver who accepted the work, because the partnership among them is *'inān,* and this partnership does not include *kafālah.* For instance, if one of them were to acknowledge a debt in favour of a third person, the other person would not be asked to satisfy it; likewise, when he accepts work.
>
> By way of *istiḥsān,* the other partner would be asked to deliver (or complete) the work, because such acceptance (of work) is the very purpose of the partnership, and for what is the purpose, each one of them stands in the shoes of the other, and they are considered to be the same as partners in a *mufāwaḍah* contract. Thus, if one of them does the work, a third party (customer) has the right to demand completion from the other partner, on the basis of *istiḥsān,* **because this is the objective of their contract.**[35]

Now if the contract of *kafālah* were introduced in the above partnership, the difficulty would disappear altogether. There is a catch, however, in the introduction of the contract of *kafālah.* The contract of *kafālah* implies the authority of *istidānah,* which means raising debts beyond the limits of the capital of the partnership. This too was explained by al-Sarakhsī and we have discussed it already.[36] In a simple *'inān* and in *muḍārabah,* the stipulation of *istidānah* gives rise to a second partnership based on *wujūh.* What happens in an *'inān* with *kafālah* with respect to *istidānah?* Are the partners liable for all the debts that a partner raises, even when these go beyond the capital of the partnership? The answer appears to be yes! The liability for the debts of the partnership will be the same as that in a *mufāwaḍah:* joint and several.

Another problem that arises because of *istidānah* accompanying *kafālah* is in the sharing of profits. In the *'inān,* the ratio of profit-sharing does not have to be equal. The exception is *'inān* based on credit-worthiness. It implies equality of profits, because of equal

---

[35] Al-Sarakhsī, *al-Mabsūṭ,* vol. 11, p. 215.

[36] See §9.1.3 in chapter 9.

ḍamān for loss. This is the reason why the granting of *istidānah* creates a second partnership in the case of the simple *'inān* as well as *muḍārabah*. Does the contract of *kafālah* inserted into the *'inān* cause a problem if the existing rate of profit-sharing is unequal. If profits are to follow the liability for loss, each partner here is liable now for his own share as well as the entire loss resulting from excessive credits. In other words, the contract of *kafālah* has made their liabilities equal.

The logical answer to this would be that a disparity in profit-sharing is still possible, because it is always linked to excessive work or some other skill. The jurists, however, do not go into these details. Perhaps, they assume that all this is valid. It is for this reason that the *Majallat al-Aḥkām al-'Adlīyah* confirms the earlier rulings and says: "*Sharikat al-'inān* includes the contract of *wakālah* specifically and does not include the contract of *kafālah*. Thus, when the contract is concluded, if *kafālah* is not mentioned, then, each partner is not the *kafīl* of the other. The contract of *sharikat al-'inān* is, therefore, possible for an authorized minor. If, however, the parties are majors and *kafālah* is mentioned when the *sharikat al-'inān* is concluded, each partner becomes the *kafīl* of the other."[37]

It has been stated repeatedly that this problem has been avoided in modern law by widening the concept of agency. Thus, a partner has *istidānah* as well as joint and several liability. A partner may be specifically prohibited from undertaking certain transactions, but if he does so anyway, the other partners will be held liable.[38] The law here appears to be quite arbitrary and defies organization according to rules. The rules themselves become quite arbitrary in such case.

10.7 Types of *Sharikat al-'Inān*

On the basis of the above discussion and the previous discussions about he types of partnerships generally, it is possible to list the complete classification of *'inān*. The types are first classified on the basis of the underlying contracts, that is, *wakālah* and *kafālah*. They are divided further on the basis of subject-matter with which partnership is formed. The first classification on the basis of contracts yields two main types:

1. Ordinary or Restricted *'Inān*.

[37] *Majallat al-Aḥkām al-'Adlīyah*, §1335; see also *Fatāwā 'Ālamgīrīyah*, vol. 2, p. 315.

[38] See §20 of the Pakistan Partnership Act, 1932.

2. *'Inān* with Full Powers (through *wakālah* and *kafālah*).

Each of these types is divisible into further three types on the basis of the subject-matter. Another qualification is based on whether *wakālah* is special for one type of trade or is general for all types of trade.

1. Ordinary *'Inān*—Special (with *wakālah*)
   (a) Capital is *māl*
   (b) Capital is labour
   (c) Capital is credit-worthiness
2. Ordinary *'Inān*—General (with *wakālah*)
   (a) Capital is *māl*
   (b) Capital is labour
   (c) Capital is credit-worthiness
3. *'Inān* with Full Powers—Special (with *wakālah* and *kafālah*)
   (a) Capital is *māl*
   (b) Capital is labour
   (c) Capital is credit-worthiness
4. *'Inān* with Full Powers—General (with *wakālah* and *kafālah*)
   (a) Capital is *māl*
   (b) Capital is labour
   (c) Capital is credit-worthiness

The most important point to note in the above classification about the use of the words special and general is that this does not mean special *wakālah* or general *wakālah*. The word special here means one type of trade and the word general means all types of trade. *Wakālah,* on the other hand, may be general or special for one type of trade. Thus, special here means a single trade, while general means multiple trades. This distinction is important for the discussion of *mufāwaḍah* that we will take up later.

Another point to notice is that there may be very little difference, within the special trade or within the general trade, between a partnership based on labour, because of *istiḥsān* used by the Ḥanafīs, as discussed above.

10.8 Contractual Capacity of Partners

Each partnership in Islamic law has to be based upon the contract of *wakālah*. It is, therefore, necessary that each partner have the legal capacity of being a principal as well as an agent. Al-Kāsānī says:

> As for the general conditions, they are of several types. Among them is the legal capacity for agency, because *wakālah* is binding in each type. This means that each partner becomes an agent of the other in transacting purchases and sales and the acceptance of work in accordance with the requirements of the partnership. An agent is a person who is transacting on authority, therefore, it is necessary to stipulate for them the legal capacity for *wakālah*.[39]

Among the conditions of *wakālah* stipulated are a sound faculty of reasoning (*'aql*) and the ability to discriminate as to what is beneficial and what is harmful (*tamyīz*). The *Majallah* points out: "Just as *'aql* and *tamyīz* are stipulated as conditions for *wakālah,* they require each of the partners to be in possession of the faculty of reasoning and the ability to discriminate and these are stipulated for partnership in general."[40]

The condition for the principal is that he be in possession of the same rights of transaction that he is delegating to the agent. This means that he must have the authority to perform the same acts himself irrespective of whether this arises from ownership or from *wilāyah* (guardianship). When a person does not possess a right to undertake an act on his own, he cannot possibly delegate authority for the act to another. Thus, an unauthorized minor, an insane person or one under interdiction (*ḥajar*) cannot delegate to another person acts that they cannot perform themselves, nor can another person delegate such acts to them, because they cannot perform them on their own account.[41] Like Islamic law, modern law imposes similar conditions for a partner. There might be a slight difference between the conditions for the minor. It is for this reason that the minor can only be permitted to the benefits of a partnership in law. Likewise,

---

[39] Al-Kāsānī, *Badā'i' al-Ṣanā'i'*, vol. 7, p. 3537.

[40] *Majallah,* §1333.

[41] Al-Sarakhsī, *al-Mabsūṭ*, vol. 11, p. 198.

there are restrictions for the insolvent person under interdiction.[42] It would be useful, however, to compare some of these conditions for the minor in the two systems.

10.9 The Minor as a Partner in *Fiqh* and Law

A minor and a slave, in Islamic law, do not have the right to grant an agency or to become agents, because of the lack of contractual capacity. This is the case when they are not authorized. A discriminating minor and a slave can be granted authority to transact, and in such a case they have this right. For obvious reasons, we shall talk about the minor alone, and about his rights as a partner.

The Ḥanafīs have divided the transactions of a discriminating minor, and also of persons who have a similar *ḥukm,* into three types: gainful transactions, transactions with a loss, and transactions with equal probability of gain and loss. The purely gainful transactions are permitted to a *ṣabī* and all such transactions are valid. The transactions of evident loss are void *ab initio,* and are not assigned any legal effects. The third type that have an equal probability of loss and gain, like sale, hire and partnership and other synallagmatic contracts are valid if the natural guardian has authorized the minor prior to the transaction. When he has not given such permission, such transactions are still presumed valid, but are subject to ratification by the guardian. Thus, the only transactions not permitted to an authorized discriminating minor are those that entail an evident loss. Al-Sarakhsī has the following to say on this:

> The *mufāwaḍah* contract is not permitted between a freeman and a slave, nor between two slaves. It is also not permitted between two minors even if they have been authorized by their fathers, because the *mufāwaḍah* is based upon *kafālah* and each partner in a *mufāwaḍah* is a surety for the other; the slave, the *mukātab,* and the minor do not have legal capacity for *kafālah*.... Thus, as each one of them is not entitled to transact (this way), the *mufāwaḍah* is not permitted between them. The partnership between them, then, is *'inān* in this case, because they are eligible for entering into a partnership."[43]

---

[42]For these details see Lindley, *The Law of Partnership,* p. 53, *passim.*

[43]Al-Sarakhsī, *al-Mabsūṭ,* vol. 11, p. 198.

This shows that minors do have contractual capacity for the *'inān* partnership, but not the *mufāwaḍah,* because their authorization grants them contractual capacity for *wakālah* and not *kafālah.* We may also conclude from this that minors cannot enter into an *'inān* partnership that is based upon *kafālah.*[44] The reason for this is obvious on the principle that there is apparent loss in standing surety for someone. On the same principle, can we assume that a minor cannot grant *istidānah* to another person, because this entails evident loss? Or, are gains and losses equally probable in this case? Let us compare the position of the minor in modern law, but very briefly.

The law in Pakistan does not grant contractual capacity to the minor. This is the position taken in §11 of the Contract Act.[45] A contract for necessaries, however, is allowed. The American law permits the minor to enter into contracts, but these contracts are voidable at the option of the minor, except under certain circumstances. This is called disaffirmance. The Pakistani law of partnership, therefore, does not permit a minor to conclude a contract of partnership, but once a partnership exists, the minor can be admitted to its benefits.[46] The differences between *fiqh* and law will become clear if the following points are examined (with reference to the law of Pakistan—the position in other laws may vary somewhat):

1. In law, the minor does not have the right to enter into a partnership contract. He can only be admitted to the benefits of a partnership, once the partnership is concluded or exists. The authorized minor may do so in *fiqh* as far as the partnership is based on *wakālah,* like the ordinary *'inān* and *muḍārabah.*

2. The minor in law can be admitted to the benefits of the partnership alone; he is liable only to the extent of his share, but his personal assets cannot be used to satisfy the debts of the partnership.[47] Thus, he enjoys limited liability. The minor in *fiqh,* once authorized, will also be liable for the losses. As for excessive debts, he will be liable as long as the partners did not buy on credit beyond the capital of the partnership. This may

[44]See §1335 of the *Majallah* and previous discussions about this type of partnership.

[45]The Contract Act, 1872, §11.

[46]See §30 of the Partnership Act, 1932. As compared to this, the English law permits a minor to enter into a contract of partnership.

[47]See section 30(3) of the Partnership Act, 1932.

involve his personal assets. What if the minor grants *istidānah* to the partners (assuming that this is permitted to him after authorization)? In such a case, the personal wealth of the minor may also be used to satisfy the debts of the partnership.

The only point that may be objectionable with respect to *fiqh* in the Pakistani law is that the minor is being permitted to enjoy the benefits of all the debts raised by the partnership, but he is not being made liable to the full extent for the losses. In *fiqh*, this would amount to consuming revenue without *damān* and the principle is *al-Kharāj bi al-damān.* By making the minor liable for losses, Islamic law attempts to avoid this in pursuit of this cherished principle.

Another observation that is general is that the Pakistani law does not allow the limited liability partnership. The English and other Western systems do. The limited partner is not permitted to interfere in the management of the partnership. Supposing a person wants to manage a partnership and the same time enjoy some benefits of limited liability, all he has to do is to keep a very small share for himself, transfer his personal assets to the minor and admit the minor to the benefits of the partnership.

10.9.1 Partnership among family members

Some persons may give shares to their family members to obtain tax relief, if the income of the parties is first divided and then taxed separately. This benefit arises in case of some registered partnerships (registered under the Income-tax Act) when there is a rising scale of taxation. The law tries to block this by considering all the members of one family as a single person. What does Islamic law have to say about this? Section 1398 of the *Majallah* states:

> If a man and his son, who is dependent on him, work in a trade, the entire revenue belongs to this man and his son is treated as a supporter, like a person being helped by his dependent son in planting trees. The trees in this case belong to this person and his son is not treated like his partner.

10.10 The Vitiation and Termination of the Partnership

10.10.1 Vitiation (*fasād*) of the partnership

Fasād in *fiqh* means that the contract has become unenforceabie. As partnership is terminable at will anyway, performance of the contract is not the issue here. It is the law that does not permit such a partnership to function. In other words, the partnership becomes *fāsid* (vitiated). The reasons for the *fasād* may be the following:[48]

1. The lack of contractual capacity for the contract of agency. In the case of *'inān* with *kafālah,* the lack of contractual capacity for *kafālah* as well, however, such a partnership will be converted to a valid *'inān,* based upon *wakālah* alone.
2. When the subject-matter of the partnership or its objective is not lawful. This happens when partnership is formed on the basis of goods, debts, or wealth that is not present at the time of the contract, or the partnership is based upon things that are *mubāḥ* anyway.[49] Further, when the subject-matter is work, it must be work that is eligible for compensation and for joint compensation.
3. *Jahālah* (uncertainty that will lead to dispute) in profit-sharing or its stipulation that will lead to the termination of partnership in it (like monopolization by one person).

There may be other cases in which the *sharikah* does not become *fāsid;* rather it is the stipulations that are treated as null and void.

10.10.2 The effects of a *fāsid* partnership

In the previous discussions we have said that the rules, in case of *fasād,* revert to those of *wakālah* and *sharikat al-milk.* The joint property of a *fāsid sharikah* becomes a co-ownership between the partners. As the contract of *sharikah* is no longer operative, the sharing of profits that existed because of it disappears, but *wakālah* still remains. This leads to the following effects:

[48]See al-Kāsānī, *Badā'i' al-Ṣanā'i',* vol. 7, p. 3580 for the details.

[49]We shall see later that the Ḥanbalīs permit a partnership in things that are *mubāḥ.*

1. An agent is not entitled to profit due to his agency, he cannot, therefore, participate in the profits.

2. It follows that the profits will not be divided according to the agreed upon ratio, but will follow the capital contributed. In the case of a labour partnership, the compensation will be based upon fair wages (*ajr al-mithl*), which in turn depends upon the work accepted and done. In the case of *wujūh,* the profits are shared equally and the co-ownership in the wealth now owned by the partnership will be based upon equality.

3. As the effects are based upon *wakālah,* the *ḥuqūq* will revert to the person who concluded the transaction, and it is the partner who entered into the transaction who will be sued for performance. This is the case of *'inān* without *kafālah.* In case of *kafālah,* the liability will be joint and several.

4. If the partnership was made in a subject-matter in which partnership is not allowed, the entire profit of the transaction will belong to the owner of such subject-matter. When the partnership was in free goods, the profit will belong to the person who acquired the goods and the other partner will be given wages if he performed some services.

10.10.3 Termination of the *'inān* partnership

The *'inān* partnership is terminated in two ways. In the first, termination depends on the will of the parties, while in the second, the will of the parties has nothing to do with the termination.

When the termination arises from the will of the parties, it may occur in one of the following four ways:

1. *Faskh* (rescission) by either party. A partnership is a *jā'iz* (permissible) contract that is also *ghayr lāzim* (terminable). Any of the partners can, therefore, terminate it at will.[50]

2. Denial of the existence of the *sharikah* by either party. The denial amounts to *faskh.* If the other parties continue the *sharikah* after this, the entire profit will belong to such other partners. According to Muḥammad al-Shaybānī, this type of profit is not healthy, and it should be given away as charity.[51]

---

[50] Al-Kāsānī, *Badā'i' al-Ṣanā'i',* vol. 7, p. 3582.

[51] Ibn al-Humām, *Fatḥ al-Qadīr,* vol. 5, p. 34.

3. When one of the parties decides to migrate to the *Dār al-Ḥarb* (the enemy lands) as an apostate. When a partner does this, he is assigned the *ḥukm* of a deceased person as far as Islamic law is concerned. The Ḥanafīs consider this as legal death (*ḥukman*).[52] This takes place when a judicial order follows his act, but when there is apostasy without a judicial verdict to the effect, whether or not the partner migrates to the enemy lands, it leads to suspension of the partnership. This means that if he comes back into the fold of Islam, the partnership is presumed to continue as it existed prior to the act of apostasy.

4. When a partner intentionally violates the conditions of the partnership and acts contrary to its purpose.

When the partnership is terminated without the will of the partners, the cases may be as follows:

1. Death of one of the parties. This leads to termination, because the underlying contract of *wakālah* becomes void (*bāṭil*) upon death, and the *sharikah* is structured upon *wakālah*.[53]

2. Insanity of one of the partners that is continuos. The jurists disagree about this. According to Abū Yūsuf, the period for this is one month, while according to Muḥammad it is a full year. The *sharikah* is not to be considered as terminated during this period.[54]

3. When the subject-matter of the partnership is wealth, it is terminated when the wealth is entirely destroyed, before transactions have commenced in it. This is the case when it is formed with standard currencies like *dīnārs* and *dirhams* that do not mix up by mingling. This will be explained when the stipulations of *'inān* based on *māl* are studied.

4. By the termination of the period when the *sharikah* was for a limited duration.

The term used for the *intihā'* of a partnership is dissolution and it is the termination of the relationship that existed between the

[52] Al-Marghinānī, *al-Hidāyah*, vol. 3, p. 12; al-Kāsānī, *Badā'i' al-Ṣanā'i'*, in the Book of *wakālah*, vol. 7, p. 3489.

[53] Al-Kāsānī, *Badā'i' al-Ṣanā'i'*, vol. 7, p. 3581.

[54] Ibid., vol. 7, pp. 3581, 3489.

partners. The inclusion of a new partner or the departure of an old one is not considered dissolution, but a change in the firm.[55] There are three ways in which the dissolution of a partnership can take place: by agreement; mandatory dissolution; dissolution by the court. Dissolution by agreement is an obvious case. Mandatory dissolution occurs due to the insolvency of all the partners, or all except one partner. It also occurs because of a happening like the declaration of war and some of the partners turn out to be enemies,[56] or when the purpose for which the partnership was formed turns out to be illegal, like the sale of liquor in Pakistan, for example, or when a license granted to the firm is terminated by the state. A partnership formed for a limited duration also falls under this case when its period is over. Dissolution by the court takes place when one of the parties becomes insane or is unable to perform his functions or when one of the partners is acting in a manner that is harmful for the partnership and the others want to prevent this or end the relationship. When all the details are examined we find that there are only a few cases under this heading that may need amendment for their Islamization. It is easier, however, to justify the cases of termination according to Ḥanafite principles than it is with those of the law.

[55] Compare the opinion of al-Shaybānī quoted above about the departure of one partner and the distribution of profits as charity.

[56] Compare the views about apostasy above.

Chapter 11

Ḥanafī School: Special Conditions of *'Inān*

In the previous chapter, we examined the rules that are applicable to all types of *'inān* partnerships whatever their subject-matter. In this chapter, we will examine the rules that are applicable to the subject-matter of such partnerships. It is important to note here that though the three types of subject-matter—*māl, a'māl* and *wujūh*—are being considered separately, all three may be found in a single partnership. Thus, an *'inān* partnership based on *kafālah* and *māl* includes *'amal* and *wujūh* within it. It is true that *'amal* in the sense used here is for artisanship or workmanship, but an *'inān* that is general for all trades is likely to deal with this area as well. Further, it is even possible in a partnership confined to a single trade to include two or more of these factors. After having said this, we shall take up the discussion of each subject-matter separately. We begin with the *'inān* that is based on wealth (*māl*).

11.1 *Sharikat al-'Inān:* When the Subject-Matter is Wealth (*Māl*)

This will, perhaps, be the lengthiest section in the entire study. It includes eight subsections. The subsections are as follows:

1. The concept of *māl* with respect to the *sharikah.*
2. The wealth must be present at the time of the contract.
3. Partnership in absolute currencies is completed by transaction in the currencies contributed.
4. Stipulations of profit and loss in *sharikat al-'inān* with wealth.

5. Conditions for work in *sharikat al-'inān* with wealth.

6. Transactions of the partners and associated conditions.

7. Liability of partners for credit purchases.

8. Liability of partners with the stipulation of *kafālah*.

11.1.1 The concept of *māl* with respect to the *sharikah*

The concept of *māl* in Islamic law, or what should be called the concept of property today, deserves an independent and exhaustive study, and is decidedly beyond the scope of this small subsection. The maximum we can do here is to provide a list of issues. The most important point in all this would be the inclusion of abstract and intangible rights within the concept of *māl*. This has implications not only for the entire law of contracts, but also for the law of torts and damages as well as for the law of property in general. We will, therefore, begin with what the jurists state and then expand the concept if possible.

Partnership with absolute currencies: *dīnārs* and *dirhams*

The Ḥanafīs stipulate that the *ra's al-māl* of a *sharikah* be currencies. Al-Kāsānī states: "As for *sharikah* with wealth, it has conditions and among them is the stipulation that the capital comprise of absolute currencies (*athmān muṭlaqah*). These are those that cannot be subjected to ascertainment (*ta'yīn*) in any way[1] in synallagmatic contracts and these are *dirhams* and *dīnārs*."[2] As for copper coins (*fulūs*) (change), there is disagreement among jurists. Abū Ḥanīfah and Abū yūsuf said that partnership cannot be concluded on the basis of *fulūs,* because "the *ta'yīn* of copper coins is similar in form to that of nuts and eggs."[3] The reason is that "the practice of the people in *fulūs* is an obstacle in this, which in turn is due to the change (in value) from moment to moment. Thus, if we permit *sharikah* in them, it would lead to uncertainty in the capital contributed and also in the calculation and division of profits."[4] According to Muḥammad,

[1]That is, by weight and measure, because they have been standardized at the mint.

[2]Al-Kāsānī, *Badā'i' al-Ṣanā'i',* vol. 7, p. 3536.

[3]Al-Sarakhsī, *al-Mabsūṭ,* vol. 11, p. 160.

[4]Loc. cit.

"The *fulūs* prevailing in the market are not to be subjected to ascertainment (*ta'yīn*), just like currency."[5] This implies that al-Shaybānī considers them currency and permits *sharikah* in *fulūs*. The obvious reason is that he considers *fulūs* prevailing in a locality as standardized currency that should be accepted at face-value and should not be subjected to weight and measure to determine their value.

The important point to note here is that the Ḥanafīs do not require any kind of *khalṭ* (mixing) for currencies, because they do not mix. This permission is for currencies alone, and the *ḥukm* for other things will be discussed later. The other important point to notice here is that currency is something that people are ready to accept at face-value, as it is, without feeling the need to subject it to some method of valuation, like measure or weight or some other method.

Formation of *'inān* with fungibles

This topic is approached in two ways by the jurists. First, when the fungibles offered are of the same species and quality. Second, when the fungibles are of different species.

Fungibles of the same species and quality. These are fungibles that will mix completely without a possibility of separation. Partnership in these is permitted by the Ḥanafīs. Al-Sarakhsī says:

> He did not mention in the book whether partnership between them after mixing will be co-ownership or direct *sharikat al-'aqd*. He did mention in *al-Nawādir*, though, that according to Abū Yūsuf, the partnership between them is co-ownership prior to transactions in the (joint) capital, while the partnership according to Muḥammad is *sharikat al-'aqd ab initio*. The benefit of this distinction is that if they stipulate excess profit for one of them, it is not permitted according to Abū Yūsuf's view, and each one of them is entitled to profit in proportion to his share. According to Muḥammad, they will take the share of profits as stipulated.[6]

---

[5] Loc. cit.

[6] Ibid., vol. 11, p. 161.

This passage indicates the difficulties that may be involved. If two persons mix wheat of the same quality for purposes of partnership, and the price of wheat doubles while their joint wheat is in storage, it can lead to a dispute as to why one partner should be given profit in excess of his actual ownership in the wheat. Al-Shaybnı states that once the wheat is mixed, a *sharikat al-'aqd* stands concluded irrespective of transactions in the mixed wheat. The goal according to the reasoning of both jurists is mixing (*khalṭ*). In the case of currencies, it is obvious that they do not mix by a simple mixing. The goal of mixing in fungibles of the same species and quality is not achieved, according to Abū Yūsuf, unless transactions take place as in the case of currencies. According to Muḥammad, the goal is achieved by a simple mixing as their is no possibility of their separation, whereas the possibility of separation in currencies always exist. In other words, Abū Yūsuf assigns such fungibles the complete *ḥukm* of currencies, while Muhammad does not.

When the fungibles belong to different species. It is not possible in this case to achieve a partnership through the mixing of the species, as mixing them might mean destroying them or reducing their utility substantially. Al-Sarakhsī says:

> The same difficulty arises when one of the commodities contributed is wheat and the other is barley. The *sharikah* here is not valid whether or not they mix the commodities. The capitals contributed are fungibles and these can be acquired at the time of division of profits. Muḥammad makes a distinction here and says that the contract of *sharikah* is established only after *khalṭ,* taking into account the value of the mixed product (i.e., its value). Thus, when there is a difference in specie, the mixed product is not a fungible and is more like *'urūḍ* (goods, property), but as compared to this the mixing of similar species leads to a fungible and one destroying it would be asked to compensate through a fungible."[7]

The problem here, we may add, is one of valuation and subsequent disputes arising due to it. Al-Shaybānī appears to be saying that even if a partnership is permitted in this case, the valuation of the capitals contributed should be based on the mixed product for accounting

[7]Ibid., vol. 11, p. 162.

purposes. Thus, if someone were to destroy the mixed commodities, he will be asked to compensate on the basis of the mixed product, that is, the value of the mixed product. The Ḥanafī jurists, thus, insist on maintaining the rule of mixing for the creation of co-ownership and the application of the subsequent rules of *ḍamān* and sharing of profits. We shall see later that the Ḥanbalī jurists permit the partnership on the simple valuation of the separate fungibles without the need to mix. How do they interpret the same rules will be discussed later.

Partnership on the basis of non-fungibles (*'urūḍ*)

Al-Sarakhsī says:

> As for partnership on the basis of non-fungibles (*'urūḍ*), like animals, dresses and slaves, it is not permitted in our view. According to Ibn Abī Laylā and Mālik (God bless them), it is permitted to facilitate transactions and the need of people to form such partnerships and because the contract partnership leads to co-ownership (mixing ultimately).[8] But in the book, the causes of *fasād* are listed.[9]

He proceeds to elaborate the causes of *fasād*. We may summarize them as under:

1. The value of the capital is uncertain. This means that *'urūḍ* are non-fungible property. Such property requires valuation to determine the ratio of the capital contributed and affects the consequent profit. As valuation is based upon general estimates, the result is uncertainty.[10]

2. The first transaction in a partnership based on currencies is a purchase, while the first transaction in a partnership based upon *'urūḍ* is a sale. Each partner, therefore, becomes an agent for the other and seeks to share profits of the sale proceeds. This is not permitted. A *wakālah* based upon such conditions is not valid. The reasoning is that an agent for sale is merely an *amīn*,

[8] We may mention here, that the Ḥanbalīs later adopted a similar opinion.
[9] Al-Sarakhsī, *al-Mabsūṭ*, vol. 11, p. 160.
[10] Loc. cit.

and if he is being given some profit, it amounts to a profit for something that he is not liable for. This is against the principle of *al-kharāj bi al-ḍamān*. It also shows that for a partnership to exist, a joint liability must have been created and this is only possible by creating joint ownership.[11]

3. The value of goods belonging to one partner may suddenly rise in value due to some reason. This generates a profit for the partnership, but if it is given to the other partners, it would amount to an earning without a corresponding liability for loss (*ḍamān*). It is also possible that the value of this person's goods may fall, in which case the profit generated by the goods of the partners would not be justified for him on the same grounds.[12]

For the above reasons, it is not permitted to form a partnership on the basis of goods or on the basis of fungibles belonging to different species, because this reasoning can apply to the latter case as well. To overcome this difficulty, the Ḥanafī jurists have used some *ḥiyal* (justifying devices). Before we give the examples, it is necessary to understand that *ḥiyal* have been portrayed in modern literature as legal fictions, which are usually used to evade the rigidity of the law.[13] This is not the purpose of the *ḥiyal*, at least in this case, as they are employed to follow the letter of the law and to achieve actual physical mingling (*khalṭ*).

1. ***Ḥīlah* for formation of the *sharikah* with non-fungibles or fungibles of different species.** Al-Kāsānī says: "The *ḥīlah* for the permissibility of partnership in non-fungible property and in each thing that is not ascertained through *ta'yīn* is that each one should sell half of his property for the half of the other partner, till the ownership of each partner is half in each property, and *sharikat al-milk* is achieved. After this, they may conclude a contract of partnership. This is permitted without dispute."[14] It is obvious in this case that both partners are offering property of equal value at the existing rates. If, however, the goods are of unequal value, and partnership will be

[11] Loc. cit.

[12] Loc. cit.

[13] For an explanation of the the real meaning of *ḥiyal*, see the Appendix I of the author's *Theories of Islamic Law* (Islamabad: IIIT & IRI, 1994).

[14] Al-Kāsānī, *Badā'i' al-Ṣanā'i'*, vol. 7, p. 3538.

created on the basis of unequal ratios, then, the *ḥīlah* adopted will be the one given by al-Shaybānī, in his book *al-Makhārij fī al-Ḥiyal.* It is recorded therein:

> I said, "What is the solution if in the case of two persons one of whom has property worth 5000 *dīnārs,* while the other has property worth 1000 *dirhams,* and they wish to form a partnership with this property." He said: "A partnership with goods is not permitted." I said: "What then is the *ḥīlah* for them so that they become partners with the property that they have." He said: "The owner of property worth 5000 *dirhams* is to buy five-sixths of the property of the other with one-sixths of his own property. When they do this, they are co-owners in the same ratio as the property they own. The person who had property worth 1000 *dirhams* now owns a sixth of the entire property, while the other owns five-sixths."[15]

2. ***Ḥīlah* for combining *dirhams* and property.** "The *ḥīlah* for permitting this is that the owner of the property should sell half his property for half the *dirhams* of his companion. They should exchange them and mix them both so that the *dirhams* and the property are jointly owned by them. Thereafter, they should conclude the partnership contract, which is then permissible."[16]

The reader may wonder why these jurists want the parties to go to such a lot of trouble. Is it not simply an accounting problem? To some extent this question is justified, but the jurists are concerned more with the principles of the law and their strict application, while being aware of the simplicity of accounting solutions. Their main goal is to create an actual co-ownership. Once co-ownership is actually and physically established, the rules of liability and those of sharing of profits can be applied in a very clean manner. The basic principles, as discussed in the general concepts, are two. The first requires the creation of joint ownership or co-ownership. Once this is done, the principle of joint liability follows from it. Not only is joint liability created, but the requirements of the principle, *al-kharāj bi al-ḍamān*

[15] Al-Shaybānī, *al-Makhārij fī al-Ḥiyal*, p. 59.

[16] Al-Kāsānī, *Badā'i' al-Ṣanā'i'*, vol. 7, p. 3538.

are satisfied and the partner as agent is enabled to share profits in whatever ratio that is agreed upon. In addition to this, all disputes that may arise as a result of the fluctuation of prices or value of the property prior to transactions in the joint capital can be resolved on the basis of the co-ownership established, without causing any ill-feeling or injustice. This appears important as partnership is a terminable contract and the partner seeing the emergence of profit in his capital may be tempted to terminate the contract and rescind it. This option would be lost to him once the properties are inseparably mixed. Further, the act of actual physical mixing helps avoid many likely disputes when the partnership becomes vitiated prior to transactions. Some of the cases in which these disputes may arise have been summarized above.

Rights in incorporeal property

In the modern world there are many kinds of property and associated rights that did not exist during the days of the jurists. Some of these are rights in intellectual property (copyright, patents, trademarks, and trade secrets), goodwill, and a huge number of options. The concept of *māl* in Islamic law needs to be expanded to accommodate all these or most of these rights. This will naturally affect the Islamic law of contract, particularly the law of business organization.

The Islamic Fiqh Academy of the OIC has issued rulings with respect to most of these rights and has suggested that they be considered property. Most of these rights are marketable and are available for transactions, which is an issue discussed in the following section. If Islamic law has to function smoothly in the modern world, then, these rights must be deemed valid property and made eligible for all transactions including partnerships.

Out of these, the issue of options is somewhat complex and needs separate treatment, although by making sale with earnest money permissible, the Islamic Fiqh Academy has recognized an option as a financial asset or property that may be sold. Other issues that also need to be discussed and analyzed in the light of Islamic principles are those of damages in contracts and questions of product liability. Most of these are issues for the theory of contract and should be discussed there.

As far as partnerships are concerned, the only stipulation that is required for intellectual property is that of creation of co-ownership in these rights before a partnership is formed. This should satisfy the requirements of Islamic law. Another suggestion in this regard is made in the next section.

11.1.2 The capital contributed must be present

The Ḥanafīs stipulate that the capital of the *sharikah* must be an *'ayn* and not a *dayn* nor wealth that is absent. Present wealth, in their view, is wealth available for transactions, and not necessarily present physically on the spot. The formation of a partnership with a *dayn* (receivable) or wealth in which immediate transactions are not possible is not permitted. Al-Kāsānī says:

> Among these conditions is the availability of the wealth in the form of an *'ayn* (ascertained commodity). It should neither be a receivable (*dayn*) nor absent wealth. If it is so, the partnership is not permitted, neither as *'inān* nor as *mufāwaḍah.* The reason is that the purpose of the partnership is profit and this is achievable through transactions in the capital. Such transactions are not possible in a *dayn* nor in wealth that is absent. The purpose cannot be achieved. The presence (availability) of the goods, however, is stipulated at the time of the transaction and not at the time of the contract. The contract of *sharikah* is completed with the purchase transaction. The availability of the goods comes into operation then."[17]

This means that the partners can go ahead and conclude the contract even if the capital consists of receivables or wealth that is not available immediately, but the contract will have its legal effects only when the transactions in such property are possible. This brings us to the next condition, but before we deal with that a word about incorporeal rights.

In the previous section we have mentioned issues pertaining to incorporeal rights and their valuation. Here, it is suggested that these rights should considered *'ayn* for the purposes of the formation of partnership and their *ta'yīn* should be undertaken by ascertaining their market-value.

[17] Al-Kāsānī, vol. 7, p. 3540.

11.1.3 Partnership concluded with currency is effective after transactions in the currency

The Ḥanafīs do not stipulate mixing of capitals (*khalṭ*) prior to the conclusion of the contract, except in the case of *'urūḍ* (non-fungible property) as well as fungibles of different species. Al-Sarakhsī says:

> In our view, the basis of *sharikat al-'aqd* is *wakālah* in the sense that each partner is an agent of the other partners in purchasing things with ascertained wealth. It is for this reason that we stipulate ascertainment (*ta'yīn*) of wealth at the time of the contract or at the time of purchase, because *wakālah* with the wealth of a partner is not valid without it. Without ascertainment of this wealth, the agent would be buying on his own (credit) liability. Agency, however, is valid without the *khalṭ* (mixing) of the contributed wealth. The meaning of mixing that a *sharikah* requires is in the wealth purchased (for the partnership) and in the ensuing profit, not in the capital itself. This is achieved without mixing (of the capital). On the basis of this principle, if the wealth of one of them was in *dirhams* and that of the other in *dīnārs*, the partnership concluded by them would be valid in our view.[18]

The position attained by a prospective partner after the contract, and prior to the purchase with cash, is that of an agent. He becomes a partner with purchase alone, that is, with transactions in the cash, because these transactions by mixing the capital achieve joint liability and joint *damān*. Prior to a transaction, if the wealth is destroyed the loss is borne by the owner of the unmingled wealth that is destroyed. The other partners are merely agents and trustees up to this point. A major reason for this is that currencies cannot be mixed. Al-Sarakhsī elaborates further:

> If one of them has a thousand *dirhams* and the other has a hundred *dīnārs,* then, whether they mix them or they do not mix them it is the same, because they will not mix. We have already explained that the mixing of currency is not a condition for the validity of the contract of *sharikah.* Each one of them is an *amīn* with respect to the

[18] Al-Sarakhsī, *al-Mabsūṭ*, vol. 11, p. 152.

> capital of his partner, whether it is destroyed in his possession or in the possession of his partner, the loss is to be borne by him (for his own currency). Further, the partnership becomes void with the destruction of one of the contributed capitals, because the purpose of a *sharikah* is joint transaction not *sharikah* itself. Thus, if there is an obstacle after the contract and prior to the attainment of the objective, following the contract, it becomes a barrier for the *'aqd* (taking its effects).[19]

If the partnership becomes void, as explained by al-Sarakhsī, with destruction of part of the capital contributed, what is left is *wakālah*. If some of the capital was used up for transactions, what was purchased exists in the form of co-ownership between the partners. In case the partners want the loss to be joint before transactions, they have to legally mix the currencies and create joint ownership in them. This is explained by al-Shaybānī in *al-Makhārij fī al-Ḥiyal:*

> I said: "What do you think of two persons, one of whom contributes 100 *dīnārs* and the other 1000 *dirhams,* and they purchase with this amount." He said: "This is valid." I said: "What do you think, if one of the capitals is destroyed after the *sharikah?*" He said: "What is destroyed is the liability of the contributor of the capital alone, and his companion is not liable for any of the loss." I said: "What do you think, if they form a *sharikah* with the intention that if one of the capitals is destroyed it should be a joint loss. What is the *ḥīlah* for this?" He said: "The owner of the *dirhams* should buy from the owner of the *dīnārs* half his *dīnārs* with half of his *dirhams* and they should take possession of them and then form the *sharikah* as stated."[20]

In case of differing currencies, the mingling of capitals and, therefore, the creation of joint ownership and liability are achieved in the above manner. This also shows us that if the currencies are the same on both sides, that is, *dirhams* contributed by all or *dīnārs* contributed by all, mixing is natural and the *sharikah* is complete by mere contribution. The liability for the loss of capital, before transactions,

---

[19]Ibid., vol. 11, p. 163.

[20]Al-Shaybānī, *Kitāb al-Makhārij fī al-Ḥiyal*, pp. 57–58.

will be joint. Will the partnership be annulled due to such destruction? Al-Sarakhsī says: "If each one of them contributes a thousand *dirhams* to form a partnership and they mix the capitals, then, what is destroyed is a joint loss, and what is left is (joint capital) between them. The reason is that the mixed capital is common, and what is lost is a loss for the partnership."[21]

Today, partnerships are formed in a single currency. All that would be needed to achieve the mingling of capitals would be the opening of a joint bank account.[22]

11.2 Sharing of Profit and Loss in *Sharikat al-'Inān* Based on *Māl*

The *sharikat al-'inān* does not require equality among partners. It is, therefore, possible for partners to form partnership with unequal capitals. Further, no partner is required to contribute his entire wealth to the partnership, as may be required in a *mufāwaḍah* contract.[23] The contribution of capital is left to the discretion of the partners in the *'inān* contract.[24] In addition to this, the delivery of the capital by one partner to the other partners is not a condition for the formation of *'inān*.[25] The above statements are valid whether or not *kafālah* is stipulated in a partnership.

11.2.1 Conditions pertaining to profit sharing must be expressly stipulated

There are several conditions that are specific to the sharing of profits and these conditions must be expressly stated in the contract, otherwise the *'inān* contract will become *fāsid.* The conditions are given below:

1. The ratio of profits must be stated specifically. If this is left vague, it leads to the vitiation of the partnership. The reason is that the main object of the contract is the sharing of profits,

---

[21] Al-Sarakhsī, *al-Mabsūṭ,* vol. 11, p. 167.

[22] This is the opinion of this writer, and others may have objections to it.

[23] This needs some further explanation, which will be taken up under the discussion of the *mufāwaḍah* contract in the next chapter.

[24] *Majallah,* §1365.

[25] Al-Kāsānī, *Badā'i' al-Ṣanā'i',* vol. 7, p. 3541.

and if this is left vague, vitiation of the contract is the natural consequence.[26]

2. The profit should be an undivided share in every particle of the whole (*juz' shā'i'*). It should not be associated with a particular part of the profit, like so many bags of wheat. This is the meaning of the term *mushā'*, that is, undivided share in each particle of the entire profit. This is clear when the profit is in the form of property, fungible or non-fungible. When it is available in the form of standardized currency, it should not be a determined amount of such currency, like 100 or 1000, but a percentage of the whole. This may also be expressed as one-half, one-third or one-fourth. If this condition is violated the *sharikah* is *fāsid*.[27]

11.2.2 Conditions of profit that are permissible

In the chapter on fundamental concepts, we have studied that the bases for entitlement to profit are three: wealth, labour and *ḍamān*. We also qualified this by saying that co-ownership and *ḍamān* underlie the idea of wealth and are implied when wealth is deemed the capital of the firm.

When the parties stipulate profit in proportion to the capital contributed or in excess of it or loss, it is permitted whether work in the partnership is stipulated for one partner or for both.[28] If the capital contributed from both sides is equal and excess profit is stipulated for one of the partners, it is permitted even when work is stipulated for both partners. This condition, however, is opposed by Zufar.[29] Further, entitlement to profit on the basis of wealth becomes valid by merely stipulating work for the partners, but this stipulation does not require that the partners should actually work for the partnership. Thus, in whatever form the division of profits is stipulated in a valid partnership, the stipulation is to be followed.[30] The stipulation of excess profit for a partner is possible in several ways:

[26] Loc. cit.

[27] Loc. cit.

[28] Ibid., vol. 7, p. 3545.

[29] Ibid., vol. 7, p. 3546.

[30] *Majallah*, §1367.

1. When the contributed capitals are equal or are unequal, and excess profit is stipulated for one of the partners, the stipulation is valid.

2. When the capitals contributed are unequal and proportional work is stipulated for the partners, that is, more work for the partner with more capital, and thereafter excess profit is stipulated for the other partner who contributes less capital and work, then, this stipulation is not valid. Whether superior skill of this partner is being taken into account or work is based upon the man hours put in is not very clear. It appears that superior skill should be taken into account and not only the man hours contributed.

3. When the capital ratio is unequal and work is stipulated for one of the partners alone, while the sharing of profits is proportional to the capital, then, this stipulation is valid. The relationship, however, is no longer that of *sharikat al-'inān,* but that of *biḍā'ah.*[31] If, on the other hand, excess profit is stipulated for the partner who is a sleeping partner, then, this stipulation is not valid, because he would be enjoying *kharāj* without a corresponding *ḍamān* or liability for loss.

4. If work is stipulated for one of the partners alone, whether the capitals are equal or unequal, and excess profit is stipulated for the worker, then, this relationship will take the *ḥukm* of *muḍārabah,* and will no longer be considered *sharikat al-'inān.*[32] About this condition, the author of *Fatḥ al-Qadīr* says: "If the entire profit is stipulated for one of them, it is not permitted, because the contract then moves out of the domain of *sharikah* as well as *muḍārabah* and becomes a *qarḍ* if the profit is stipulated for the worker. It is as if he has given him his wealth as a *qarḍ* so that he (the worker) may have the entire profit, and it becomes a *biḍā'ah,* if it is stipulated for the *rabb al-māl.*"[33]

This discussion shows that wealth alone is not sufficient for profit and work must be stipulated, even if a partner does not

[31] *Majallah,* §1370.

[32] Ibid. §1371.

[33] Ibn al-Humām, *Fatḥ al-Qadīr,* vol. 5, p. 22.

actually work. It is, therefore, permitted to prevent a partner from work. The details of this are to follow.

The situations listed above are exceptionally useful for analyzing the contract between the shareholder and a corporation.

11.2.3 The stipulation of loss

The bearing of loss always follows the ratio of capital contribution. Stipulating this in a contract would be superfluous. If, however, an unequal ratio for sharing loss is stipulated, the stipulation is valid absolutely. This point is extremely important for understanding the problem of limited liability of the shareholders of a corporation as well as the limited partner in a limited liability partnership. Limited liability actually boils down to a violation of this condition of losses following capital contributed. This will be taken up in detail later.[34]

11.3 Stipulation of Work in *'Inān* Based Upon Wealth

Sharikat al-'inān requires that work in the capital of the partnership be stipulated for all the partners, but again it does not require all the partners to actually work. A partner has the right to give up work in the partnership with an excuse or even without an excuse. This act of the partner, if committed, has no bearing on the ratio of sharing profits stipulated in the contract. If work is stipulated for one partner alone, the contract will not be considered a *sharikat al-'inān,* because of the lack of the requisite conditions, and the relationship between the parties will become a *muḍārabah* constituted with the work *sharikah,* if the working partner is allocated a higher ratio of profits. Otherwise, it will become a *bidā'ah* if the worker contributes his work without profit (that is, when the profit stipulated is proportional to capital).

The Pakistani law, and its parent legal system, permits a sleeping partner who does not work, though his liability for the debts is like that of any other partner, unlike a limited partner in a limited liability partnership, where that is permitted. Such a partner though has the right to work in the partnership if he chooses. This is the position with respect to a general partnership recognized by Pakistani law. According to Islamic law, on the other hand, the stipulation that one

[34]Part of it will be discussed in *Corporations and Islamic Law.*

of the partners will be a sleeping partner is not valid. The provision of the Pakistani law should be changed to say that one may choose to become a sleeping partner by agreement of all the partners after the partnership is concluded. As for the limited liability partnership called *al-Sharikah al-Tawṣiyah al-Basīṭah* in Arab law, it is void, not only on this ground, but several others.[35]

11.4 Powers of the Partners in a *Sharikat al-'Inān* Based Upon Wealth

The Ḥanafī contract *wakālah* requires that the *ḥuqūq* (rights of performance) of a contract undertaken by a partner should revert to him. Thus, if one of them purchases something, or rents services, or takes possession of a receivable, then he is the one who has to be sued with respect to claims arising from such transactions. Likewise, it is he who has the right to sue third parties for all claims connected with the contract he concluded, and his other partners are not to be involved in this.[36] This is the case when the *sharikat al-'inān* is based upon *wakālah* alone. If the contract is based upon *kafālah* as well, then, the rest of the partners can also be sued as sureties, but they will have no right to sue third parties. The exercise of options (*khiyārāt*) and the returning of goods on the basis of defects (*radd bi-al-'ayb*) are rights that belong to such a partner. Likewise, what one of them has sold cannot be returned to the other for defects.[37]

The rules for transactions in an *'inān* based upon a special *wakālah* alone are as follows:

1. Each partner has the right to sell the goods of the *sharikah* for cash as well as for credit. Likewise, he has the right to purchase for cash or for credit. He possesses this right without qualifications, that is, it is unrestricted, by virtue of the contract of *sharikah* itself and does not need special permission from the other partner(s) for doing so. If, however, the other partner specifically denies him this right to buy and sell on credit, then, he cannot do so, otherwise he would be held liable for his personal account.[38]

---

[35] The details are to be found in the study mentioned above.

[36] *Majallah,* §1377.

[37] Ibid. §1378.

[38] Ibid. §1373–75, 1383.

2. Each partner has the right to grant an agency for sale and purchase, as well as for all other transactions.

3. A partner has the right to enter into contracts of *ijārah* and the hiring of all services.

4. A partner also has the right to invest the wealth of the *sharikah* by way of *muḍārabaḥ*, because *sharikah* is the major form of business organization, while *muḍārabah* is its offshoot, or a *muḍārabah* is less than a *sharikah* and is, therefore, included in the latter.[39]

5. Each partner has the right to give the wealth of the partnership on the basis of *biḍā'ah*.

6. A partner has the right to travel on account of the *sharikah* and to charge his expenses to the account of the *sharikah*.

7. A partner has the right to enter into *iqālah* with respect to the goods of the *sharikah* sold by him.[40]

8. A partner has the right to conclude contracts of *murābaḥah*.

9. He has the right to give the goods on deposit and enter into bailment contracts.

A partner does not have the following rights in an *'inān* partnership:

1. A partner cannot enter into another partnership with the wealth of the partnership.

2. He cannot mix up his goods with the goods of the *sharikah*, otherwise he will be liable for any resulting loss.

3. A partner cannot give a *qarḍ* to someone from the wealth of the partnership, nor can he accept a *qarḍ* for the partnership. It is to be noted here that the term *qarḍ* applies to a loan without interest and without a fixed period of repayment. This is called a *qarḍ ḥasan*. No other category of loans is acknowledged or permitted by Islamic law.[41]

---

[39] Al-Kāsānī, *Badā'i' al-Ṣanā'i'*, vol. 7, p. 3561.

[40] Loc. cit.

[41] For a detailed analysis of the issue, see Imran Ahsan Khan Nyazee, *The Concept of Ribā and Islamic Banking*, 61. For a clear statement of al-Sarakhsī on the issue in the context of partnerships, see sections 9.1.1 & 17.4.5 in this study.

4. He cannot purchase on credit beyond the limit imposed by the assets of the *sharikah,* as this would amount to *istidānah* for which special permission is required from the other partners.

In the general *'inān* partnership based upon a general *wakālah,* a partner has the following additional powers:

1. He can pledge/mortgage the assets of the partnership and also accept such pledges (*rahn* and *irtihān*).

2. He can enter into a contract of partnership with another on account of the *sharikah.*

3. He can mix his wealth with the wealth of the partnership.

He cannot do the following:[42]

1. He cannot give a *qarḍ* or accept one for the partnership.

2. He cannot destroy the property of the partnership or act in an injurious way.

3. He does not have the right to gift the property of the partnership. This is similar to the stipulation of *qarḍ,* which is also an act of *tabarru'* or the gifting of the use of money for an undetermined period.

4. He does not have the authority of *istidānah,* that is, purchase on credit beyond the assets of the corporation.

In an *'inān* that is based on *kafālah,* all the above stipulations apply to the partners, except that the partners have the authority of *istidānah* as well.[43]

Now all the stipulations about what a partner cannot do, that is, authorities, can be granted to a partner, but through special permission or express stipulation at the time of the contract, unless the act is prohibited by the Islamic law of contract in general.

---

[42] Al-Kāsānī, *Badā'i' al-Ṣanā'i',* vol. 7, 3561.

[43] This is based on an application of the principles used by the jurists, who have not revealed too many details about this form.

11.5 Liability of *'Inān* Partners for Debts

In the fundamental concepts, we have already discussed the distinction between the right of a partner to raise debts through credit purchases when he does not have authority of *istidānah,* and also when he does have such authority. We also discussed there the distinction between *istidānah* and the additional powers arising through *kafālah.* Let us reiterate briefly what we said earlier.

In an *'inān* partnership:

1. **When the partner does not possess the right of *istidānah.*** When the partner does not possess *istidānah,* he is not permitted to go beyond the limit imposed by the assets of the partnership. The assumption is that the liabilities will never exceed the assets. In such a case, the liability is limited to the extent of the capital contributed by each partner. This, however, is not to be construed as limited liability. The point becomes obvious when due to some reason the assets are lost and the liabilities are still outstanding, that is, payments for goods purchased are still to be made. The partners here will have to contribute more funds in proportion to their capitals to meet these liabilities. The liability in such an eventuality will be joint not several. By several liability we mean that each partner can be sued separately for the entire liability. This is not the case in Islamic law in *sharikat al-'inān* based on *wakālah* alone. As the *ḥuqūq* revert to the partners dealing with the parties, they are the only partners who can be sued. If only one partner, like a managing partner, had been dealing on behalf of the firm, only he will be sued. This partner will, then, have recourse to all the other partners, who will then be jointly liable.

2. **When the managing partner assumes *istidānah.*** It may happen that the partner sighting an opportunity for making profits buys in excess of the limit imposed by the assets. If there is a loss, it is this partner alone who will be liable for the excess amount. All the profits made due to the excess purchase will also belong to this partner. What if there is a loss and the liabilities exceed the entire assets of the partnership? All the assets will be used up for meeting the liabilities of the *sharikah* and what is left over will be borne by the partner who made the transactions.

The other partners will not be asked to pay anything more. Is this limited liability? The answer is yes and no. Yes, it is limited liability **with the condition that the firm still holds the assets equal to the original capital contributed by the partners.** This means that the partners actually pay through the firm what they originally contributed. If the firm has no assets left, the partners will have to pay more in proportion to a ratio that is determined between liabilities based on legal acts and liabilities based on unauthorized acts. A further complication is added when the actual meaning of *istidānah* is analyzed. Suppose that Microsoft started with a capital of 3 million dollars. Today, it owns assets worth billions. Is *istidānah* limited to purchases worth 3 millions always or does it extend to the net assets shown at any time in its balance sheet. One would assume it is the latter.

This is a somewhat complex problem and it may be the only way in which the concept of limited liability can be accepted in Islamic law. It is, therefore, in need of *ijtihād.* The ruling given by the Islamic Fiqh Academy of the OIC on limited liability is one such *ijtihād,* but it is not clear how they have arrived at the decision.[44] The proper thing to do would be to lay down certain principles that explain and systematize the concept. The need for such principles is obvious, because the courts need to decide cases based on such principles and to develop the principles further. Further, businessmen and their legal advisers need to design new forms of transactions and institutions and it is these principles that will come in handy not simple statements about limited liability being valid or acceptable. The following broad principles are, therefore, suggested on the principles of limited liability.

(a) When a legal or natural person hands over property to his agent for business purposes with the express stipulation that the liabilities raised in the business should not exceed the amount delivered, there will be no further liability for such principal beyond the amount delivered. This principle is a limitation on the existing law of agency and will be operative only when a relationship of *kafālah* is not coexisting with the agency relationship.

---

[44] *Majallat Majma' al-Fiqh al-Islāmī* (1992) 7:1.

(b) If the agent violates this stipulation, all profits resulting from the illegal part of the act will belong to the agent and the principal will be entitled to profits from such a transaction to the extent of the amount delivered.

(c) When such a stipulation is made by the principal, it will be accompanied by an additional presumption that any loss of the capital or assets delivered due to a natural calamity (*force majeur*) or other reason is a business hazard arising from the negligence of the agent. The principal will, therefore, not be responsible for the liabilities arising as a result of such loss beyond the amount delivered, however, the agent will not be required to compensate the principal for such loss through *ḍamān*.

(d) The above principles will apply only when a dual ownership is created in the wealth, that is, the agent will hold the wealth in his own name on behalf of the principal.

3. **When the partners grant *istidānah* to the managing partner.** The granting of *istidānah* is an authority for the managing partner to exceed the limit imposed by the capital of the firm (or its assets if that is possible) and to purchase on credit beyond this limit as well. When the partners grant this authority, they assure the managing partner that they will be liable for the debts in excess of the capital limit. Beyond this limit, then, as already explained, the relationship between the partners is governed by *kafālah*. The liability created here is joint and several. This means that the transacting partner can be sued in any case, because the *ḥuqūq* revert to him, but the other partner(s) can also be sued individually now as they are sureties for the transacting partner. Further, the creditors can sue all the partners jointly as well, which is joint liability. The liability in this case is unlimited.

11.5.1 Liability when the *'inān* is based upon *wakālah* as well as *kafālah*

In an *'inān* based upon *kafālah* along with *wakālah,* we have indicated that the partner has the right of *istidānah* by virtue of the contract itself. The liability created in this type of partner is joint as well as several. Whoever out of the partners pays the debt will have recourse to the other partners.

11.5.2 Conclusion about liability of partners

The main conclusion we may draw from the above discussion is that the liability of the partners in a contract of *'inān* is unlimited in each case. They are liable for the debts of the *sharikah* when the partners are acting according to and within the authority granted to them. The only case of unlimited liability is one in which the transacting partner has acted in contravention of the authority granted to him. In other words, when such a partner abuses his authority, the liability of the other partner is limited to the extent of their shares. In fact, they have no liability for the debts arising out of the unlawful transaction. If this case of limited liability is extrapolated and applied to the modern corporation, there will be severe limitations. Further, new general principles will have to be laid down through *ijtihād.* Some modern scholars have, in fact, tried to do exactly this by quoting the example of an unauthorized slave, who acts unlawfully in a master's business.[45] This analogy is defective, and it appears that the concept of limited liability can be introduced only in a new Islamic design of the corporation.

11.6 *Sharikat al-'Inān* When the Subject-matter is Work

Al-Sarakhsī says: "*Sharikat al-taqabbul* is found when two workmen participate in the acceptance of work, like tailors or butchers and so on. It is called *sharikat al-abdān,* because they perform manual labour, and it is (also) called *sharikat al-ṣanā'i',* because their capital is their skill."[46] This partnership, as explained in the classification of partnerships, may be *'inān* and it may be *mufāwaḍah.* In this section, we will examine its conditions when it is constituted as *'inān.*

11.6.1 Work for which this partnership is not permitted

We will seek al-Kāsānī's help in explaining this point. He says:

[45] S. M. Hasanuzzaman, "Limited Liability of Shareholders: An Islamic Perspective," *Islamic Studies* 28:4 (Islamabad: IRI, 1989) 353–61; Muhammad Taqi Usmani, "The Principle of Limited Liability From the Shariah Viewpoint," *New Horizon,* Aug.–Sept., 21–22. This opinion has been analyzed and rejected with reasons in *Corporations and Islamic Law* by this author.

[46] Al-Sarakhsī, *al-Mabsūṭ,* vol. 11, p. 152.

> As for *'inān* (with labour), none of the above stipulations is made for it. The only stipulation made for it is that of legal capacity for agency. This is what Abū Yūsuf related from Abū Ḥanīfah, saying, "This *sharikah* is valid in each thing in which agency (*wakālah*) is valid, and it is not valid in things in which agency is not valid." This excludes *sharikat al-a'māl* in free (*mubāḥ*) commodities, as in hunting, gathering firewood or dry grass in the wilderness, as well as wild fruit in the mountains, and also prospecting for minerals in the land, and whatever resembles these. If they participate with the condition that the hunt, the firewood, or the water gathered, would be sold and the sale proceeds would be shared by them, the partnership is *fāsid.* The reason is that an agency cannot be granted in these things.... If they do participate in this manner and each one acquires something (with labour) individually, he is acquiring ownership for himself, because the basis for establishing ownership in permissible (free goods) is acquisition and possession. Each one of them here has acquired these individually.[47]

It is possible, however, that in the *mubāḥ* category there is something that requires joint work, for example, hauling a huge log that one person cannot move. In such a case, it is obvious that what is taking place is *sharikat al-milk* in equal shares and not *sharikat al-'inān.* Ibn Nujaym explains further that "a partnership between workers is not valid nor that of reciters in recitation nor a partnership in begging, because agency for begging is not valid."[48]

This shows that the partnership is valid in almost everything except those things that are dependent upon a purely individual effort and do not accept agency.

11.6.2 Partnership is valid in the benefits of property and implements

Al-Sarakhsī says:

> If the owner of a shop concludes a partnership with a workman that he will give him work and the profit will

[47] Al-Kāsānī, *Badā'i' al-Ṣanā'i'*, vol. 7, p. 3547.

[48] Ibn Nujaym, *al-Baḥr al-Rā'iq*, vol. 5, p. 181.

> be shared equally between them, the partnership is *fāsid* according to analogy, because the capital of the owner of the shop is the utility (*manfa'ah*) of the shop and *manāfi'* are not suitable as capital for partnership. Further, if the person accepting work is the owner of this shop, then, the worker has been hired by him for one-half profits. This is indeterminate and uncertainty renders the *ijārah* vitiated. If the person accepting work is the worker here, then, he has hired his sitting place in the shop for one-half profits of his work, and this too is indeterminate (*majhūl*). He (Muḥammad) undertook *istiḥsān* in this case and permitted it as this is a common practice among the people without any disputation. Denying the people what they are used to leads to hardship. In order, therefore, to repel this injury, this contract is permitted, because there is no text that declares it void. In addition to this, the people are in need of such contracts. Thus, a worker may be new in town where the people do not know him and are not ready to trust him with the their goods, but they would trust the owner of the shop with their goods whom they do know. The owner of a shop does not in practice provide such a free voluntary service to the workers. In validating this contract, then, the objective of both is attained, as the worker is able to get compensation for his work and the people are benefited by the value of his labour. The owner of the shop is able to receive the compensation for his shop. The contract is, therefore, valid. Even an excess compensation for the owner of the shop is good in this case, because he agreed with him fo the use of his shop and supported him with his goods. Perhaps, he will also contribute something in terms of labour, like a tailor accepting goods and cutting them (by pattern) and then handing them over to someone else for half wages. It if for this reason that he may be entitled to more. The permissibility of this contract is identical to the permissibility of the *salam* contract. The *shar'* permitted it due to the need of the people for it.[49]

This lengthy passage not only explains a basic point in *'inān* based upon labour, but also the methodology to be used in employing *'urf*

[49] Al-Sarakhsī, *a-Mabsūṭ*, vol. 11, p. 161.

as a basis for commercial law. The contract based upon *'urf* has been permitted here not merely upon the basis of *'urf,* but after justification through *istiḥsān* based upon necessity and need. Those who plan to use *'urf* by itself as a source of law should read this passage very carefully.

Coming back to *'inān* based upon labour, we note from this passage that *'urūḍ* (property, like shops) or tools and implements are entitled to part of the profits in a partnership based upon labour, as compensation for the use of such property. Does this provide us with an independent basis for entitlement to profit? Is *manfa'ah* to be included in the concept of *māl* that is acknowledged as a basis for profit. We would suggest that it be treated as an independent basis for entitlement to profit. This will enable it to be compensated separately from profit in a *sharikah* based on wealth (*māl*). If it is merged with the concept of *māl,* it will give rise to problems of *khalṭ* and the creation of joint liability. Treating it as an independent ground will deem it to be a subservient basis for a higher ratio of profits, just like labour with wealth is deemed a subservient basis.

The *Majallah* makes a further distinction between partnership in the acceptance of work and partnership in wages earned. The former is permitted, while the latter is not. Section 1395 of this book says: "If two persons form a partnership on the condition of accepting work when a shop belongs to one of them and the implements and tools to the other, the partnership is valid. As for riding animals, if the partnership is formed on the condition of acceptance of work, the partnership is valid, but if it is formed for sharing wages it is not valid. Wages belong to the owner of the animal alone."[50] The principles operating here again are those of *ḍamān* or the creation of joint liability and *khalṭ* or the mixing of capitals. An animal, however, is not subject to *khalṭ,* and belongs to the owner alone. As it belongs to the owner alone, he is the one who is liable for loss of the animal. The wages must, therefore, go to him. If the animal here is relegated to the status of subservient capital and joint liability is created through the acceptance of work, the problem is solved. This is what the *Majallah* appears to be saying; namely, that partnership in acceptance of work creates a joint liability for the performance of contracts undertaken by the *sharikah*.

---

[50] *Majallah,* §1395.

11.6.3 Similarity of profession is not necessary

Al-Kāsānī says:

> Zufar said that this partnership is not valid, unless the profession is similar, like two butchers or two tailors. This is based on the issue whether partnership is permitted in two different types of wealth, as it is in our view, and also on whether it is permitted in two types of labour. It is not permitted in his view in two different types of wealth or in two different types of labour. The correct view is ours, because entitlement to compensation in this type of *sharikah* is based upon *ḍamān al-ʻamal* (being liable for performance of work accepted). They are both liable for *ʻamal,* whether the work is identical or different. Allah, the Mighty, the Powerful, knows best.[51]

The principle in the previous paragraph, which was called acceptance of work (*taqabbul al-ʻamal*), is given a more precise meaning here by al-Kāsānī. He calls it *ḍamān al-ʻamal,* which means liability for the performance of work accepted, or liability for the performance of contracts made by the partnership. This is the real basis for entitlement to profit, as has already been explained in the fundamental concepts.

11.6.4 Conditions for acceptance and performance of work

The conditions for acceptance of work in an *ʻinān* partnership based upon labour are divided into acceptance of work by a partner, delegating it, and the liability of a partner. These are explained separately in three subsections.

The first condition: each partner has the right of accepting work and of performing it

Each partner has the right to accept work on behalf of the *sharikah* and then to perform this work himself on behalf of the *sharikah.* It is also permitted that one of them accepts work, while the other performs it. In a business that requires mixed labour, the work may be accepted by one and then performed jointly by both. For example, in the tailoring business, it is permitted to one person to accept

---

[51] Al-Kāsānī, *Badā'iʻ al-Ṣanā'iʻ*, vol. 7, p. 3551.

work, cut the cloth according to pattern, and then hand it over to his partner for stitching and completion.[52]

The second condition: a partner has the right to delegate the work accepted by him

No partner can be forced into personal performance of the work that he accepted. If he wishes, he may do the work personally or he may delegate it to another. If the customer stipulates performance of the work by a particular partner, in that case the partner has to perform it (because the customer is always right).[53]

The third condition: performance of the work is the liability of each one of the partners

We have discussed in the topic of fundamental concepts that the *ḥuqūq* of a contract revert to the person making the transaction. According to this, only the partner accepting the work should be sued for its performance. We also discussed the statement of al-Sarakhsī where he elaborated that this rule has been changed for the *sharikat al-ʿinān* based on *māl* through *istiḥsān*. Thus, one partner may be required to perform the work accepted by his partner. If we ponder over this problem, we realize that this would be a requirement of the principle of *ḍamān al-ʿamal*. This, then, is a clear case of reasoning from principle, that is, giving up of strict analogy for a general principle.

The operation of this principle also shows that if the other conditions are ignored there would not be a major difference in a partnership based on labour whether it is concluded with *kafālah* or without *kafālah*, or even as a *mufāwaḍah*. The reason is that by virtue of the *istiḥsān* based on the principle of *ḍamān al-ʿamal*, each partner has become more or less a *kafīl* for the other in the performance of work accepted.

The *Majallah*, in section 1387, has indicated this at some length:

> Each partner is the agent of the other in the acceptance of work. For the work that is accepted by one of them, performance is binding upon him as well as his partner. *ʿInān* by way of *sharikat al-aʿmāl* has the same *ḥukm* as

[52] *Majallah*, §1386.

[53] Loc. cit.

> *mufāwaḍah* with respect to *ḍamān al-'amal.* Thus, the work accepted by one of the partners may be demanded by the customer from either one he chooses. Each partner is (legally) bound for the performance of such work. He does not have the right to say: "This work was accepted by my partner and I have nothing to do with it."[54]

Section 1388 further states that: "*'Inān* by way of *sharikat al-a'māl* takes the *ḥukm* of *mufāwaḍah,* in the demand for compensation from the customer for full satisfaction of the claim for wages. The customer is absolved of this liability by paying to either one of them."[55]

11.6.5 Conditions for sharing profit and loss

The first condition: division of profits by stipulation

The partners divide the profits among them in accordance with the ratios stipulated, whether equal or unequal. If they stipulate equality in work and inequality in profits, it is permitted, because one of the partners may be more qualified in his profession and does better work.[56]

The second condition: no requirement of direct work

If one of the partners does the work and the other cannot work due to some excuse, for instance illness or journey, or even without an excuse, the profit will be divided according what they have stipulated. In other words, this lack of work will not affect the sharing of profits. Al-Sarakhsī says:

> In the case of partners in work, if one of them is absent, or is ill, or does not work, while the other is working, the profit is shared by them as stipulated. This is due to the tradition from the Messenger of Allah (p.b.u.h.) that a person came to his and said: "I work in the market and I have a partner who prays in the mosque." The Messenger of Allah said: "Perhaps your work is blessed because of him." The meaning here is that entitlement to

[54] *Majallah,* §1387. See also al-Marghinānī, *al-Hidāyah,* vol. 3, p. 10; Ibn Nujaym, *al-Baḥr al-Rā'iq,* vol. 5, p. 182.

[55] *Majallah,* §1388.

[56] Ibid. §§1391–92.

> profit is due to acceptance of work and not in its direct participation. The acceptance is (presumed to be) from both, even if one of them works."[57]

The underlying principle here too is that of *ḍamān al-'amal.*

The third condition: bearing loss through *ḍamān*

This conditions arises from the direct application of what al-Kāsānī has called *ḍamān al-'amal.*[58] If the goods delivered to the partnership are rendered defective or are destroyed by the act of one partner, he is liable for these goods along with his the other partner in accordance with the ratio of liability. The customer utilizing their services sues either partner he chooses. The loss will be a loss for the partnership and will be divided in proportion to the *ḍamān* borne. For example, if they participate in the acceptance of work and stipulate performance in an equal ratio, the loss will be borne equally.[59] This shows that unlike partnership in wealth, where loss follows the capital contributed, the liability for the performance of work must be stated explicitly in the contract. The ratio fixed for the liability for performance is what will determine the ratio for sharing profits. It is obvious that if such a ratio for *ḍamān al-'amal* is not fixed, it will be presumed to be equal.

11.6.6 Legal capacity, relatives as partners, and duration of partnership

Contractual capacity

We have stated above that *sharikat al-'inān* based upon work takes the same *ḥukm* as *mufāwaḍah* or that of *'inān* concluded with the contract of *kafālah.* This pertains to contract performance (*īfā'*), suing for performance(*muṭālabah*), work, and *ḍamān al-'amal.* Is it, therefore, necessary that the parties to such a contract have contractual capacity for *kafālah?* We have not been able trace this in *fiqh* books, but it is evident that if the partner is being considered a *kafīl,* it is necessary that he have such legal capacity. This would exclude the minor who does not possess legal capacity for *kafālah.*

---

[57] Al-Sarakhsī, *al-Mabsūṭ,* vol. 11, pp. 157–58.

[58] See section 11.6.3.

[59] *Majallah,* §1393.

Partnership among relatives

Section 1398 of the *Majallah* states that this type of *sharikah* is not possible between a person and his immediate family member, who is in his charge or is dependent upon him. It says that if a person and his son work together in a similar profession, then, the entire earning belongs to this person and his son will be deemed his supporter.[60] The reason appears to be *ḍamān al-'amal*, and the performance of the contract will revert to this person, his son being dependent upon him for such performance. Thus, the creation of a partnership here is pointless when the bonds between the two are much stronger.

11.6.7 Duration of the partnership

Ibn Nujaym, transmitting from *al-Khānīyah,* says that a duration for this partnership cannot be stipulated.[61] This appears to be logical, because as long as contracts that need to be performed are outstanding, *ḍamān al-'amal* would work against a stipulation of a fixed duration.

11.7 *Sharikat al-'Inān* with Credit-Worthiness (*Wajāhah*)

Al-Sarakhsī says:

> As for *sharikat al-wujūh* (that is, *sharikah* with credit-worthiness), which is also called *sharikat al-mafālīs* (*sharikah* of the insolvents or those reduced to a financial state of copper coins), it is a partnership of two people with capital upon the condition that they will buy on credit and sell (for cash). It has been called by this name on the grounds that they employ their credit-worthiness, because credit sales are made only to those who have a standing among the people (traders).[62]

[60] *Majallah,* §1398.

[61] Ibn Nujaym, *al-Baḥr al-Rā'iq,* vol. 5, p. 182.

[62] Al-Sarakhsī, *al-Mabsūṭ,* vol. 11, p. 152.

11.7.1 Conditions for sharing profit and loss

The conditions for sharing of profit and loss in this type of partnership are as follows:[63]

1. **The share of the partners in the goods purchased must be specified.** This is the primary condition for this type of partnership and the remaining stipulations are based on this condition.

2. **Entitlement to profit is based upon *ḍamān* (liability to bear loss).** The type of *ḍamān* mentioned in the labour *'inān* was called *ḍamān al-'amal.* The type of *ḍamān* involved here is *ḍamān al-thaman* (liability for the price of the purchased goods), and is based upon the share of ownership in the property purchased. This brings us closer to, or makes it similar to, the *ḍamān* for *sharikat al-māl* where the ownership in capital is the basis. The distinction between the two is that as there is no capital involved, the ownership is associated with the price of the thing purchased. Once something is purchased, it becomes the asset of the partnership and its value is based upon its price. The ratio in which this asset is owned by the partners is the basis and not the ratio of the debt owed. Thus, if the share of a partner is one-half in the purchased goods, he is liable for half the price owed for these goods. He is, therefore, entitled to half the profits.

3. **Equality of ownership in the purchased goods is not a requirement.** The ratio of ownership is to be expressly stated at the time of the *sharikah* contract. The ratio may not be based upon equality and a partner may opt for two-thirds or one-third, as agreed. Whatever the ratio of ownership, the profits must be distributed in the same ratio.

4. **Stipulation of profits contrary to ownership in price is of no consequence.** If an additional profit is stipulated for any partner, the ratio of ownership is violated; the condition is, therefore, ignored. If the liability for the price is equal, it is not permitted to give 60% of the profits to one partner.[64] The

[63]For a detailed discussion see al-Kāsānī, *Badā'i' al-Ṣanā'i'*, vol. 7, p. 3551 *passim.*; *Majallah,* §§1399–1403.

[64]Al-Sarakhsī, *al-Mabsūṭ,* vol. 11, p. 68.

reason appears to be that the skills, reputation and good work of one partner are already tied in with the amount of credit a partner can raise. The ratio of ownership in the price has already taken all those things into account. This leads to the next condition.

5. **Excess work in the partnership is of no consequence for entitlement to profit.** We have already discussed this issue, while discussing the stipulation of *kafālah* in *'inān.* It will, therefore, suffice to quote al-Sarakhsī here. He says:

> In this contract, a stipulation of profits in excess (over the ratio of ownership) is not valid when there is equality of ownership in the thing purchased. The reason is that this excess is not linked either to the share of the partner in wealth or to his work or to *ḍamān.* Stipulating such a part of the profits will amount to something that is not supported by liability. The Messenger of Allah (peace be upon him) has proscribed this. If an excess of the profits is desired, it is necessary to stipulate a corresponding excess in ownership of the purchased goods (and thus in the liability to bear loss). This way, it may be, that a third is for one partner and two-thirds for the other, and thereafter the other profits may be shared in proportion to the ownership.[65]

11.7.2 Liability of partners in this partnership

When this partnership is formed as *'inān* based upon *wakālah* alone, the liability of each partner is for his own share of ownership in the thing purchased. One partner is not held liable for the share of the other. The creditors, however, will sue the partner they have dealt with in accordance with the Ḥanafī stipulation of *ḥuqūq* reverting to the agent. The liability here is joint alone.

When this partnership is generated by the authority of *istidānah* granted in the *'inān* with *wakālah* or in *muḍārabah,* the additional liability due to this partnership will be equal, and so will be the ownership in the property bought, if no stipulations are made about *ḍamān* and ownership. If, however, the partners grant *istidānah* and

[65]Ibid., vol. 11, p. 154.

mention a ratio of ownership, then, the additional liability will be based upon such a ratio.

When the *sharikat al-wujūh* is based upon *wakālah* as well as *kafālah,* each partner becomes liable for the share of his partner in addition to his own. In other words, each partner will become liable for the entire debts of the *sharikah. Muṭālabah* may be made from the dealing partner or from his sureties. Consequently, the liability in case of *kafālah* will be joint as well as several.

Chapter 12

Ḥanafī School: The *Mufāwaḍah* Partnership

The *mufāwaḍah* form of partnership has been a victim of neglect in the modern age because of some hasty conclusions drawn about it by a few influential scholars. The main reason for such conclusions has been the requirement of this partnership that a partner participate with his entire wealth. Yet, this partnership is the basis for constructing the *'inān* with *kafālah* in Ḥanafī law. In addition to this, the partnership is based upon a vital principle of commitment to the business undertaken that needs to be appreciated, because the principle is operative to this day.

The discussion of the *mufāwaḍah* partnership will be undertaken in the following sections:

1. The meaning of *mufāwaḍah* and its legal justification.
2. The implication of the absolute term *mufāwaḍah*.
3. The contractual capacity of the partners.
4. Conditions of *mufāwaḍah* according to subject-matter.
5. Termination of the contract.
6. The need for the *mufāwaḍah* contract.

In discussing the above topics, we will try to focus on stipulations that are specific to *mufāwaḍah* alone. The reason is that most of what has been said about *'inān* applies to *mufāwaḍah* too. The *mufāwaḍah* contract, in a way, includes the *'inān* contract within it. This was explained in the formation of *'inān* through the *inqilāb* (conversion) of *mufāwaḍah,* in the earlier chapters. The statement we made earlier was that *mufāwaḍah* includes *'inān,* just as *'inān* includes *muḍārabah.*

12.1 The Meaning of *Mufāwaḍah* and its Legal Justification

Let us first deal with what the term *mufāwaḍah* means.

12.1.1 The meaning of *mufāwaḍah*

Al-Sarakhsī gives three meanings from which the term *mufāwaḍah* could possibly have been derived. The first is the term *tafwīḍ,* which means delegation. As each partner, in this partnership, makes a complete delegation of all acts to his partner in the entire stock of marketable goods, the meaning of *tafwīḍ* is realized.[1] The second meaning is in the term *intishār* in the sense of spreading, which is similar to *fawḍ.* As the contract spreads to all transactions, this meaning too is realized in *mufāwaḍah.*[2] The third meaning is that of equality. As this contract is based upon equality of wealth and profit, the meaning of *masāwāh* is realized as well.[3]

Ibn 'Ābidīn says: "In the dictionary, *mufāwaḍah* means the participation in each thing with equality, but technically it is a narrower meaning, because it applies to equality in real estate and goods."[4]

The definition of *mufāwaḍah*

When we seek a comprehensive definition for *mufāwaḍah,* one that would cover all its types, we do not find it in the works of the *fuqahā'.* The only definition we find is one that gives the meaning of *mufāwaḍah* based upon *māl* (wealth). We may, therefore, attempt a definition as follows:

> It is a contract of participation between two or more persons, with the stipulation of complete equality with respect to capital, profit and status, for working with their own wealth, or with their labour in another's wealth, or

---

[1] Al-Sarakhsī, *al-Mabsūṭ,* vol. 11, p. 152.

[2] Loc. cit.

[3] Loc. cit.

[4] Ibn'Ābidīn, *Ḥāshīyah,* vol. 4, p. 302.

on the basis of their credit-worthiness, so that each partner is a surety for the other.[5]

12.1.2 Legal justification

Al-Marghinānī, the author of *al-Hidāyah,* says:

> This type of partnership is permitted in our view on the basis of *istiḥsān.* It is not permitted on the basis of analogy, which is al-Shāfi'ī's opinion. Mālik said: "I do not know what is meant by *mufāwaḍah*."[6] The implication of analogy is that it incorporates within it *wakālah* for an unknown category, as well as *kafālah* for an unknown category, and each of these considered by itself is *fāsid.* The basis for *istiḥsān* is the saying of the Prophet (peace be upon him): "Engage in *mufāwaḍah* for it is full of blessings." Further, the people used to practice it without its denial (by the Prophet). For this reason (the rule of) analogy was given up. Moreover, the *jahālah* (uncertainty) involved in it is no different from that in *muḍārabah.*[7]

To this we may add that *wakālah* and *kafālah* are both used for carrying out trade, and the uncertainty involved is not present in *muḍārabah* alone, but also in *'inān.* Al-Sarakhsī says:

> Our proof (*ḥujjah*) in this is that this partnership incorporates *kafālah* and *wakālah,* and each one of these is valid in itself, for the realization of its objective, so also within a partnership. *Jahālah* in itself does not annul *kafālah,* but may lead to disputes, however, that is absent here as each one of them becomes a surety for the other for what is due from him by virtue of trade. In such a case, the subject-matter of trade, as well as the person for whom he is liable, are both known. This certainty is not known in *'inān,* because agency for purchasing things

[5]See also §1331 of the *Majallah.*

[6]We do find the Mālikī school talking about some kind of *mufāwaḍah* partnership, the details of which will be discussed later. Apparently, this statement means that the term *mufāwaḍah* has been employed by the Mālikīs in a different sense.

[7]See the text of *al-Hidāyah* in Ibn Humām, *Fatḥ al-Qadīr,* vol. 5, p. 6.

> of unknown specie is not permitted (that is, *'inān* for general trade), but despite this *'inān* is permitted when the things purchased by each are not mentioned in the contract; likewise, the *mufāwaḍah.*[8]

We may further elabourate that if *'inān* is permitted for purchases of unknown species when it is based upon *wakālah,* the permissibility of *mufāwaḍah* should be easier as it is strengthened by the contract of *kafālah.* This is exactly the response of the Ḥanafī jurists to al-Shāfi'ī: If you have approved *'inān,* you have to approve the *mufāwaḍah,* because it is based upon stronger contracts. We shall see, however, that instead of approving *mufāwaḍah,* al-Shāfi'ī restricts even the *'inān* partnership so that it is reduced to the status of a mere co-ownership (*sharikat al-milk*).

As for the tradition from the Prophet (peace be upon him), which has been recorded by the author of *al-Hidāyah,* it has also been relied upon by al-Sarakhsī. The other schools, who oppose the Ḥanafī concept of *mufāwaḍah,* say that this tradition is not to be found in the sound compilations of *ḥadīth.* Ibn al-Humām points out that Ibn Mājah has recorded a tradition about trade to the effect that the Prophet (peace be upon him) said that there is great blessing in three things: credit sale, *muqāraḍah,* and the mixing of wheat and *sha'īr* for use in the house. In some manuscripts by Ibn Mājah, the word *mufāwaḍah* is found in place of *muqāraḍah.*[9]

12.2 The Implication of the Absolute Term *Mufāwaḍah*

Al-Sarakhsī says: "If two persons conclude a contract of *mufāwaḍah* and they record an explicit deed between them that they have participated in each minor and major thing by way of *mufāwaḍah,* and that the capitals such and such are equal, and that each one of them will act according to his considered opinion, then, if they have participated in this way, they are partners in a *mufāwaḍah.*"[10] He further adds: "*Kafālah,* according to the requirements of *mufāwaḍah* means that each partner is a surety (*kafīl*) of his partner, just as he is an agent of his partner, in whatever becomes due from someone on the basis of *kafālah.*"[11]

[8] Al-Sarakhsī, *al-Mabsūṭ,* vol. 11, p. 153.

[9] Ibn al-Humām, *Fatḥ al-Qadīr,* vol. 5, p. 7.

[10] Al-Sarakhsī, *al-Mabsūṭ,* vol. 11, p. 177.

[11] Ibid., vol. 11, p. 196.

From these statements, we understand that the absolute term *mufāwaḍah* requires the following as a minimum:

1. Equality in wealth (capital), profit, and work. This equality is also required in contractual capacity and religion, as we shall see.

2. Each partner operates according to his opinion. This implies that the *mufāwaḍah* is general for all types of trade.

3. The contract of *wakālah* between the partners.

4. The contract of *kafālah*.

12.2.1 Does the *mufāwaḍah* have to be for trade in general?

In the preceding statement, as noted in point number three, al-Sarakhsī says: "And each one of them acts according to his opinion." Are we to conclude from this that *mufāwaḍah* is meant for general trade and cannot be concluded for a specific trade? Ibn Nujaym says in *al-Baḥr al-Rā'iq:* "In *Tātārkhānīyah* it is stated that among its conditions is that it be general for all types of trade. This has been indicated by Muḥammad in his book. The Shaykh al-Islām has mentioned at the end of the chapter on *mufāwaḍah* that it is permitted in specific trade as well."[12] Commenting on this, Ibn 'Ābidīn says: "This requires that *mufāwaḍah* may not be general, but it is as is expressly stated in *al-Baḥr*."[13]

This is a crucial point in understanding the nature and meaning of *mufāwaḍah.* It yields two forms: one that is general for all types of trade and another that is general for a specific type of trade. The contract that is general for all types of trade would require equality in all assets of the partners as well as participation in the work of the partnership to the exclusion of all types of personal business ventures. This, it is true, would be a highly cumbersome form of partnership to conclude as well as to maintain, because any inequality in the wealth of one would lead to the vitiation of the partnership or its conversion to the a general *'inān.*

The second form of *mufāwaḍah* that requires equality of capitals and other things in one particular trade would be a highly useful

[12] Ibn Nujaym, *al-Baḥr al-Rā'iq,* vol. 5, p. 168.

[13] Ibn 'Ābidīn, *Ḥāshīyah,* vol. 4, p. 311.

type of partnership. For example, there may be two persons, who are both traders in wheat and who wish to participate in a contract of *mufāwaḍah* in a specific type of trade, that is, trading in wheat alone. All they have to do, to form this partnership, is to make their stocks of wheat equal by buying if one has less or selling if the other has more. When equality of stocks is achieved they form the partnership. They can easily maintain the partnership too by converting anything one of them receives (by gift or inheritance) in the form of wheat to another asset. The main purpose would be not to hold business stocks in wheat that do not belong to the partnership. Now the question is that why should they form a *mufāwaḍah* and why not a general *'inān* instead? The reason is that this form of partnership preserves and applies a basic business practice; namely, that none of the partners is permitted to carry on a similar business outside the partnership on his own account. All his skills in that trade should be devoted to the benefit of the partnership. In our example above, one of the wheat traders cannot trade in wheat on his own account. Such provisions are found in modern law of partnership as well. On the other hand, the *'inān* partnership by its very nature cannot prevent one partner from undertaking the same business on his own account.

When this principle is highlighted, the conditions of similarity of religion and contractual capacity start making sense too. The reason is that one partner should not be less than the other in any way when both are not allowed to carry on the partnership business outside of it on their own account. Full commitment requires total equality as well, because such commitment cannot be demanded of people who are not equal in every way; it would lead to injustice. If one partner has some edge over the other he may feel that his superior status or other merits are being exploited in the name of the partnership. This leads us to the types of the *mufāwaḍah* partnership.

12.2.2 Expanded types of *mufāwaḍah*

We first have two broad categories:

1. *Mufāwaḍah* in all types of trade.

2. *Mufāwaḍah* in a single trade.

Each of these is further subdivided on the basis of the subject-matter: wealth, labour and credit-worthiness. This gives us six types of *mufāwaḍah*.

12.3 Contractual Capacity of Partners

The stipulations with regard to contractual capacity of a partner in a *mufāwaḍah* are the same as those for the *'inān*. In addition to this, the capacity required for the contract of *kafālah* is added. Thus, a person who does not have the capacity to conclude a *kafālah* contract cannot become a partner in *mufāwaḍah*. This makes his legal capacity the same as that required for the *'inān* based upon *kafālah*. Some of these conditions have been mentioned earlier, but they are described in a little more detail below:

1. The partner should have contractual capacity for *kafālah*. Therefore:

   (a) He must be a freeman. *Kafālah* by a slave is not permitted. Al-Sarakhsī says: "*Mufāwaḍah* is not allowed between a freeman and a slave, nor between two slaves, nor between a freeman and a *mukātab*, nor between two *mukātabs*."[14]

   (b) The partner must be a *bāligh*, that is, one who has attained puberty and is a major. The reason is that an authorized discriminating minor does not have the legal capacity for *kafālah*. It is stated in *al-Mabsūṭ*: "*Kafālah* is not permitted between two minors, even when they have been authorized by their fathers.[15] The author explains this by saying: "Because the *mufāwaḍah* is based upon *kafālah*..., and the *ṣabī* is not one who has contractual capacity for it."[16]

2. The partners must belong to the same religion. The reason for this is perfect equality. The author of *al-Mabsūṭ* says:

> The *mufāwaḍah* is not permitted between a Muslim and a *Dhimmī*, according to Abū Ḥanīfah and Muḥammad (God bless them), while Abū Yūsuf (God bless him) said that it is permitted though not commendable (it is *makrūh*). The basis of this statement (Abū Yūsuf's) is that each one of them

[14] Al-Sarakhsī, *al-Mabsūṭ*, vol. 11, p. 198. It is obvious that the *mudabbar* slave too is included in this restriction.

[15] Loc. cit.

[16] Loc. cit.

> has contractual capacity for *wakālah* and *kafālah*.... Do you not see that *mufāwaḍah* is valid between two *Dhimmīs* and two Muslims. Likewise, it is permitted between a Muslim and a *Dhimmī* and their differences with respect to transactions are not to be given consideration insofar as a Muslim does not deal in *khamr* and *khinzīr,* while the *Dhimmī* does.... So also the *mufāwaḍah* is valid between one belonging to the Ḥanafī school and the other to the Shāfi'ī school even though the Ḥanafī deals in *nabīdh,* declaring it something of value, while the Shāfi'ī deals in *matrūk al-tasmīyah 'amdan* for he considers it as having a value.... The other two jurists reason that *mufāwaḍah* is based upon absolute equality and there is no equality between a *Dhimmī* and a Muslim, neither in transactions nor in the subject-matter of transactions.[17]

12.4 The Conditions of *Mufāwadah* according to Subject-matter

We shall discuss the conditions for each category of subject-matter separately. The subject-matter of *mufāwaḍah* may be wealth, labour or credit-worthiness.

12.4.1 Stipulations When the Subject-matter is Wealth

1. **Eligibility of different types of wealth as subject-matter of *mufāwaḍah.*** All that we said about *'inān* under this heading is applicable to *mufāwaḍah* too. Thus:

   (a) The capital must be absolute currencies: *dīnārs* and *dirhams.*

   (b) When the capital is composed of fungibles of different specie or of goods from one side and currency from the other, then, the ways described earlier for *'inān,* including the *ḥiyal,* have to be followed for the *mufāwaḍah* too.

   (c) When the fungibles are of the same specie, the partnership is concluded only with the mingling (*khalṭ*) of the capital.

---

[17]Ibid., vol. 11, 197.

In addition to this, it is stipulated for *mufāwaḍah* that the partner should not be in possession of trading capital outside the partnership, that is, capital that is eligible to be the capital of *mufāwaḍah*. For this purpose, we have to distinguish between the two types of *mufāwaḍah* derived earlier. When the *mufāwaḍah* is general and is for all business activity, it is based on the rule that all business that the two partners do will be together and they will not engage in business outside their joint business. In this case, if the partner possesses trading capital in the form of currency, he should convert it to a personal account and not employ it in business. If he does that the *mufāwaḍah* stands vitiated and is converted to general *'inān,* that is, *'inān* for all types of business.

If, on the other hand, the *mufāwaḍah* was concluded for a single trade, possession of capital that does not pertain to that trade should not affect the partnership. If, for example, the *mufāwaḍah* was for trading in wheat, then, any partner coming to own wheat should not use it for business. He should either allocate it for personal consumption or convert it into another form of capital to do away with allegations of using it for personal business. This may happen when a partner inherits wheat or receives it as a gift. If he intentionally buys wheat, it should be considered a violation of the *mufāwaḍah* agreement thereby converting it to *'inān.*

2. **That the capital should be available for transaction.** This is the same stipulation as in *'inān.* Absent wealth is one that denies the possibility of transactions in it.[18]

3. **A partnership constituted with currencies is completed with transactions in the joint capital—as in *'inān.*** This creates joint liability.[19]

4. **The equality stipulated should be maintained for the *mufāwaḍah* to continue, otherwise the partnership will convert to *'inān.*** This has already been explained in the first point above. We may add here that this condition applies when

[18]Loc. cit.

[19]Loc. cit.

the partnership is constituted with wealth. The ruling will be altered for *mufāwaḍah* constituted with labour or with credit-worthiness. Despite all that we have said about the utility of *mufāwaḍah,* some modern scholars have upheld a different view. For example, 'Alī al-Khafīf talking about *mufāwaḍah* and its continuity says:

> The fact is that *sharikat al-mufāwaḍah* as approved by the Ḥanafīs and Zaydīs cannot be counted as a *sharikah* in practice. Its existence is temporary even if it is found to exist. The stipulation of equality of capital is value and the denial of trading capital to a partner outside the *sharikah* in all stages of its existence will not let it exist for long. The continued possession of cash that the partner had at the time of the contract is indeed a difficult task.[20]

With due respect to the learned 'Alī al-Khafīf, this appears to be a hasty conclusion. One that completely ignores the vital principles of the *mufāwaḍah* contract. All that the *mufāwaḍah* contract requires is that when the partnership is general, no partner should engage in other business on the side, and must devote his loyalties to his chosen partner to whom he has given full commitment. In this situation, all that it means is that the partner should not hold cash assets for some other business. There is no bar on holding cash for personal use. When the partnership is for a particular trade, the contract requires that a partner should not start a similar trade on his own and become a competitor, because this would shake his loyalty to the business started with his partner.

A view such as 'Alī al-Khafīf's confirms that even the most astute of scholars have not devoted the deep study to the Islamic law of partnership, an effort that it rightly deserves. Such views also create an unjust impression about earlier Muslim scholars. In this case, for example, believing 'Alī al-Khafīf would mean that the Ḥanafī *fuqahā'* had spent more than a thousand years studying and writing about a contract that was totally hypothetical and utterly useless. The truth as we have repeatedly stated was otherwise. The *mufāwaḍah* is a highly useful

[20] 'Alī al-Khafīf, *Fiqh al-Sharikāt,* p. 31.

contract. It not only provides a unique form of business organization, but also tries to circumvent the actions of certain partners who would like to set up competing businesses when they had given full commitment to one partnership. The work of the *fuqahā'* on this contract is, therefore, highly commendable considering the fact that it was designed almost 1400 years ago. The principle it is based on is still valid and useful, and is upheld by modern law.

A very simple reason for disagreeing with this learned scholar is that his arguments, if conceded, apply only to the *mufāwaḍah* based on *māl.* They do not apply to the other types based upon labour or on credit-worthiness. These are not affected by the possession of excess wealth. The reason why this was not noticed by 'Alī al-Khafīf is that he never analyzed the *mufāwaḍah* into its various types, but followed the classification of the majority schools and applied their methods to judge the Ḥanafī forms of business organization.

5. **Profit and loss in *mufāwaḍah*.** This contract requires that the partners meet on equal terms, when they are expected to devote themselves to the chosen business. Profit and loss are, therefore, shared equally just as the capitals are equal.

6. **Excess work is of no consequence for additional profits.** This stipulation helps avoid the construction of a second partnership over and above the existing one as was done in the *'inān* due to *istidānah.* In this it is supported by equality of profits and losses and the contract of *kafālah.*

7. **Transactions of partners.** The partners have all the rights that they have in *'inān.* In addition to this, each partner has a right to conclude *'inān* partnerships with third parties. This will be in all things when the *mufāwaḍah* is general and in the same trade when the *mufāwaḍah* is confined to a specific trade. Concluding further contracts of *mufāwaḍah,* however, is not permitted.[21]

8. **Types of transactions not allowed:**

[21] See al-Sarakhsī, *al-Mabsūṭ,* vol. 11, pp. 182, 221 for a detailed discussion of what further partnerships may be concluded and why.

(a) *Qarḍ* and *i'ārah:* Because both types are linked to charity and are philanthropic acts. It is obvious that this may be possible as a joint act of the partners.

(b) *Hibah* and *ṣadaqah* are not allowed for the same reason.

(c) Standing surety for a third party is allowed by Abū Ḥanīfah, but his two disciples disagree as they treat such an act as *tabarru'*.[22] Again, this would be possible jointly on behalf of the partnership.

(d) *Kafālah bi-al-nafs* is different from bail in modern times where a money bond is posted. For this reason *kafālah bi-al-nafs* is permitted to a partner and is considered something that is outside the scope of the *mufāwaḍah*.[23]

(e) The parties are not sureties for each other in torts and crimes that are related to the business.[24] Though standing surety for dower and *arsh* is permitted by Abū Yūsuf and Muḥammad, who do not hold the partner liable for this. Abū Ḥanīfah does, by treating the two cases of surety to be linked.[25]

(f) Misappropriation affecting third parties as well as torts and delicts in the course of business make the other partner liable. The aggrieved party can sue either partner.[26]

(g) All purchases made by a partner to a general *mufāwaḍah* will be presumed to be for the joint partnership and intended for trade, excepting those purchases that are for personal consumption and use. The general rule for analogy for loyalty governs here and is broken for personal consumption on the basis of *istiḥsān*.[27] In certain cases, a partner may be sued for goods purchased by his partner for personal use.[28] This apparently means that as long as a general *mufāwaḍah* continues, both partners should become insolvent together.

---

[22]Ibid. p. 182.

[23]Loc. cit.

[24]Ibid. p. 195.

[25]Ibid. pp. 204–205.

[26]Ibid. p. 204.

[27]Ibid. p. 208.

[28]Ibid: p. 209.

12.4.2 Stipulations when the subject-matter of *mufāwaḍah* is labour

Most of what has been said about the *'inān* partnership based upon labour is applicable to *mufāwaḍah* as well, except for stipulations pertaining to the sharing of profits and losses as well as participation in *ḍamān al-'amal.* There must be equality in *mufāwaḍah* in sharing profits and losses as well as in *ḍamān al-amal,* which is the liability for the performance of the work contracts accepted and all this is now based upon *wakālah* along with *kafālah.* Let us recall the conditions laid down for *'inān* and make suitable amendments where necessary.

1. This partnership cannot be based on the gathering or acquisition of free goods, the acquisition of which is dependent upon individual effort. Nor can it be made for beggary.
2. The partnership is valid with the *manfa'ah* of tools and implements as well as property.
3. Similarity of profession is not necessary.
4. As for acceptance of work and its completion or performance is concerned:
   (a) It is permitted to each partner to accept work and promise to perform it.
   (b) No partner can be forced to perform the work accepted by him, unless the customer insists that he do it personally, which does not affect the contract of partnership in any way.
   (c) The performance or completion of work accepted is the liability of each one of the partners. In *'inān,* this liability was created on the basis of *istiḥsān* whereas in this partnership it arises directly out of the contract of *kafālah.*

The Distinction between *'inān* and *mufāwaḍah* when the subject-matter is labour

The distinction between the two forms is visible in the following three ways:

1. Equality in profit, loss and *ḍamān al-'amal* is stipulated for *mufāwaḍah,* but not for *'inān.*

2. *Mufāwaḍah* may be formed only by those persons who have contractual capacity for *kafālah.* This distinction disappears when *kafālah* is inserted into *'inān* as well.

3. All compensation received for the work is shared equally by the partners of the *mufāwaḍah.* In case of *mufāwaḍah* for all kinds of business, this stipulation will apply even when the work is done outside the business. In the *'inān* partnership, wages for work done by a partner outside the business belong to the partner alone. Al-Sarakhsī says:

> If one of the *mufāwaḍah* partners offers his services on wages for the safe custody of something or for stitching a dress or some other work determined by wages, then, whatever he earns this way is shared between them...and the act of one partner in this is like the act of both. The position is different if he offers his personal bodily services, because the compensation here has become due by making his body available to another, and his body is not part of the *sharikah*.... As for the *'inān* partner, if he earns by accepting work that is not part of their *sharikah,* then, this earning is his exclusively. The reason is that he is only an agent in transactions in the wealth (business) of the *sharikah* and the acceptance of such work is not a transaction in the wealth of the *sharikah,* and his partner is like a stranger for him in this.[29]

We see from the above that al-Sarakhsī is making a distinction between skilled labour and pure manual labour. Pure manual labour is permitted outside the *sharikah.* Will the earning from such labour amount to a vitiation (*fasād*) of the *mufāwaḍah.* Obviously not. This confirms what we have said earlier that equality of wealth applies to trading capital and renting out labour is not part of that. This point also clarifies that partnership based upon pure manual labour is not valid and is of the same status as *mufāwaḍah* for begging jointly.

The above distinction applies when a *mufāwaḍah* is general for all types. If, however, the *mufāwaḍah* is confined to a particular

[29] Al-Sarakhsī, *al-Mabsūṭ,* vol. 11, p. 202.

trade, the work of a partner outside this trade should entitle him to those wages, just like *'inān*. For example, if two motor mechanics have formed a *mufāwaḍah,* then any car fixed by either would be considered as part of the *sharikah,* but if one of them were to repair a television set, he should be entitled to the wages exclusively.

12.4.3 Stipulations when the subject-matter of *mufāwaḍah* is credit-worthiness

The conditions of *mufāwaḍah* based upon credit-worthiness differ from those of *'inān* in the following respects:[30]

1. It is not necessary in this partnership to specify the share of a partner in the goods purchased on credit, because the contract of *mufāwaḍah* requires equality, and all the shares are equal. This makes equality of shares in goods purchased a condition for this partnership. In *'inān,* the shares have to be specified.

2. Any partner may be sued for payment of the goods purchased because he is an agent as well as a surety for his partner(s). In *'inān,* the *ḥuqūq* revert to the dealing partner, and the other partner cannot be sued.

3. Each thing purchased on credit by a partner for business purposes is bought for the joint business. Does this stipulation apply to goods purchased on *cash* for his personal business too? We could not find an answer to to this in the works of the *fuqahā'.* The logical answer should be that business transactions that are entirely on a cash basis should not be a part of the credit *sharikah,* because business on credit-worthiness is based upon credit purchases alone. The employment of cash payments would convert it to a *mufāwaḍah* based on *māl.*

   This also raises the question whether possession of wealth outside the partnership would annul a *mufāwaḍah* based upon credit-worthiness, or even one based on labour? The answer is no. The condition of owning wealth eligible as capital is applicable to *mufāwaḍah* based on wealth. It does not apply to the other two types.

---

[30]These points have been derived through the application of the general rules discussed in the previous sections.

Again, what we have said above applies to a *mufāwaḍah* based on general trade. In a *mufāwaḍah* based upon credit-worthiness for a particular trade, like trading in wheat, any purchases made of rice, for instance, credit or cash, have nothing to do with the partnership.

12.5 The Termination of the *Mufāwaḍah* Partnership

There are two major ways in which a *mufāwaḍah* may be terminated:

1. It is terminated in all those ways that are mentioned for *'inān*. When one of these methods or events comes into operation, the *mufāwaḍah* is dissolved and no new partnership is born out of this termination.

2. The *mufāwaḍah* partnership may be vitiated and converted into an *'inān* partnership in ways that we have discussed in detail under the topic of formation of *'inān* through the conversion of *mufāwaḍah*.[31]

In the first case, the rules of *sharikat al-milk* take over upon termination and the rights of creditors and the partners are settled accordingly. In the second case, the partnership continues with altered conditions based upon changes of capital contribution and other things.

12.6 The Importance of *Mufāwaḍah* and its Utility

We have shown earlier that modern scholars have been quick to conclude that the *mufāwaḍah* has a temporary existence and is of no practical use. In the preceding pages, we have repeatedly pointed out that the *mufāwaḍah* is based upon an important business principle. This principle requires loyalty to the business and non-engagement in competing business. There are other cases in which *mufāwaḍah* may be formed by default. The *mufāwaḍah*, therefore, fulfils the following two needs:

1. Non-engagement in a competing business.

2. Formation of *mufāwaḍah* by default.

---

[31] See the detailed discussion about the formation of *'inān* through the conversion of the *mufāwaḍah* in section 10.3.

The principle of non-engagement in competing businesses is laid down in §16 of the Pakistan Partnership Act, 1932. The section states that if a partner acquires profit from the transactions of the partnership or by the employment of its assets, then, the profit gained belongs to the partnership. Further, if he engages in a type of business that competes with the business of the firm, then, he is under an obligation to make over the profits to the partnership. This is called competing business. As compared to this, *fiqh* does not force all partners in all types of partnerships to abide by this rule or even to make over the profits to the partnership; it merely converts the partnership into an *'inān*. This eliminates the requirement of the competing business rule and provides the opportunity to the partners to continue in another form of participation where the principle they had agreed to follow, and which they violated, is no longer applicable.

The cases of *mufāwaḍah* by default are mentioned by Ibn 'Ābidīn and they are also mentioned in the *Majallah*[32] These are cases where a man dies and leaves his running business to his children. There are other instances like something resembling the Hindu undivided family that may be cited, but this should suffice.

[32] Ibn 'Ābidīn, *Ḥāshīyah,* vol. 4, p. 307; *Majallah,* §1331.

Part III

The First Category of Partnerships in *Fiqh*: Majority Schools

During our study of the method of the Ḥanafī school applied to partnerships, we saw that there are a large number of partnerships in the first category that are approved by this school. Each type of partnership has some rules that are common with the other types and some that are specific to each type. The variation in the rules depends upon several things: the type of the underlying contract; the subject-matter of the partnership; the scope of trade, whether of all types or a specific trade; and the type of *wakālah*—general or specific; and whether authority for *istidānah* is available to the partners. Even when we consider a few of these factors, the following partnerships emerge:

1. *'Inān* with *wakālah* for general trade:

   (a). when the subject-matter is wealth (*māl*);
   (b) when the subject-matter is (*'amal*);
   (c) when the subject-matter is credit-worthiness (*wujūh*).

2. *'Inān* with *wakālah* for a specific trade:

   (a) when the subject-matter is wealth (*māl*);
   (b) when the subject-matter is (*'amal*);
   (c) when the subject-matter is credit-worthiness (*wujūh*).

3. *'Inān* with *wakālah* and *kafālah* for general trade:

   (a) when the subject-matter is wealth (*māl*);
   (b) when the subject-matter is (*'amal*);
   (c) when the subject-matter is credit-worthiness (*wujūh*).

4. *'Inān* with *wakālah* and *kafālah* for a specific trade:

   (a) when the subject-matter is wealth (*māl*);
   (b) when the subject-matter is (*'amal*);
   (c) when the subject-matter is credit-worthiness (*wujūh*).

5. *Mufāwaḍah* for general trade.

   (a) when the subject-matter is wealth (*māl*);
   (b) when the subject-matter is (*'amal*);
   (c) when the subject-matter is credit-worthiness (*wujūh*).

6. *Mufāwaḍah* for a specific trade.

(a) when the subject-matter is wealth (*māl*);

(b) when the subject-matter is (*'amal*);

(c) when the subject-matter is credit-worthiness (*wujūh*).

In the *'inān* with *wakālah* as well as *kafālah,* we can derive further types depending upon the agency granted, that is, whether the agency is general or special. When the *fuqahā',* like al-Sarakhsī, use the term *sharikah 'āmmah,* they usually mean for all types of trade. Even is such a partnership it is possible that the agency be special, which would mean that the partners are permitted to perform certain specific acts and not others. For additional acts, they will have to seek special permission from the other partners. For example, through a special agency sale and purchase may be permitted, but for cash only and not for credit. For selling on credit, the partners may have to seek further permission. As partnership needs a general agency with respect to its business, and this is what the Ḥanafīs feel too, we have not further subdivided the types on this ground. The possibility, however, is present.

The purpose of listing these types once again is to raise the question: Do the majority schools permit all these types? If not, what types do they permit, and on what grounds do they deny permission to others?

In addition to this—and this is most important—are the terms *'inān* and *mufāwaḍah* used by the majority schools in the same meaning as they are used by the Ḥanafīs? In other words, does the absolute and unqualified use of the term *'inān* in the Mālikī school mean the same partnership that is available in the Ḥanafī school? If not, then, what type of partnership is implied by the term? The same applies to the term *mufāwaḍah.* These are the main questions that we will keep in mind, while examining the law of partnership in the Mālikī, Shāfi'ī and Ḥanbalī schools.

Chapter 13

Mālikī School: First Category of Partnerships

In the first category of partnership, the Mālikī school approves three types. These are *sharikat al-'inān, sharikat al-mufāwaḍah* and *sharikat al-a'māl.* As for *sharikat al-wujūh* and *sharikat al-dhimam,* and they make a distinction between the two, they are void in their view. *Al-Mudawwanah al-Kubrā* says: "Partnership is not valid, except in wealth or in an *'ayn* (ascertained commodity), or in labour. *Sharikat al-dhimam* is not valid, unless their purchase is of a commodity present, or one that is absent, when all of them (that is, the partners) are present, and one partner acts as a surety (*ḥamīl*) for the other."[1]

Before we go into the detailed implications of this statement, it is important to notice that the division into types adopted by the Mālikīs is different from the one adopted by the Ḥanafīs. Thus, *sharikat al-a'māl* is not a type of *'inān* or of *mufāwaḍah,* but an independent type, and so are *sharikat al-wujūh* and *dhimam,* even though they are void. This means that during our study, we shall have to analyze each type of partnership and to associate it with the corresponding type in the Ḥanafī school.

We shall take up such a study in the following three sections:

1. *Sharikat al-'inān* in the Mālikī school.

2. *Mufāwaḍah* in the Mālikī school.

3. *Sharikat al-a'māl* and *sharikat al-wujūh* in this school.

[1] Saḥnūn, *al-Mudawwanah al-Kubrā,* vol. 5, p. 41.

13.1 *Sharikat al-'Inān* in the Mālikī School

Ibn Rushd says: "*Sharikah,* on the whole, according to the jurists of the provinces is of four types: *sharikat al-'inān, sharikat al-abdān,* and *sharikat al-wujūh.* One of these is agreed upon, and this is *sharikat al-'inān,* though some of them did not know this term, and even though they differed on some of its conditions."[2] The reader will notice at once that this statement does not apply to the Ḥanafī school. In fact, it attempts to ignore the whole nature of partnership law as conceived by the Ḥanafīs. This is the primary reason why we have separated the study of each school. A comparison will be more meaningful once the separate study of each school is completed. The reader may notice further that the author of *al-Hidāyah* said that Mālik said: "I do not know what is meant by *mufāwaḍah.*"[3] Here, Ibn Rushd appears to imply that this was intended for the term *'inān.* We will solve this riddle soon. Let us first try to understand the meaning of the term *'inān* as used by the Mālikīs.

13.1.1 The meaning of *'inān* according to the Mālikīs

Al-Mudawwanah al-Kubrā states: "I said: 'Did Mālik recognize the *sharikat al-'inān?*' He replied: 'I did not hear about it from Mālik, nor do I think any of the jurists of Ḥijāz acknowledged it.... As for *'inān,* he did not recognize it, nor have we heard of it from Mālik, except what I have described for you.'"[4] Al-Khirashī, commenting on the *Mukhtaṣar* of Sīdī Khalī, states:

> *Sharikat al-'inān*... it means *sharikat al-'inān* is valid and is derived from the reins of an animal, that is, each one of the partners has stipulated for the other that he should act on his own in any matter pertaining to the *sharikah,* except with the permission of his partner and with his knowledge. It is as if he has taken hold of his rein, that is, by his fore-lock, so that he does not do anything without his permission."[5]

---

[2] Ibn Rushd, *Bidāyat al-Mujtahid,* vol. 2, p. 251.

[3] Al-Marghinānī, *al-Hidāyah,* vol. 3, p. 4.

[4] Saḥnūn, *al-Mudawwanah al-Kubrā,* vol. 5, p. 68.

[5] Al-Khirashī, *Sharḥ al-Mukhtaṣar,* vol. 6, p. 49. See also Muḥammad 'Ulaysh, *Taqrīrāt 'alā al-Sharḥ al-Kabīr,* on the margin of al-Dasūqī, *Hāshiyah,* vol. 3, p. 359.

The meaning of *'inān* appearing in this statement is completely different from the meaning of *'inān* elabourated upon by the Ḥanafī school. The Mālikīs understand by it, the taking "hold of his rein, that is, by his fore-lock so that he does not do anything without his (partner's) permission." This is not even a special agency (*wakālah khāṣṣah*) in which a partner is given prior permission to do certain things without consulting his partner every time. The meaning emerging here is that of co-ownership (*sharikat al-milk*) where a co-owner may undertake an act with the permission of the other co-owner and with his knowledge. In the Ḥanafī *'inān,* the minimum authority given to a partner is to undertake sale and purchase and to perform related acts according to his own considered opinion. The partner in *'inān,* according to them, can even sell and purchase on credit. The meaning of *'inān* so far, according to the Mālikīs, is not better than co-ownership. Let us see the full implication of the word when used in the formation of the contract.

13.1.2 The implication of the absolute term *'inān*

We have seen earlier that the *'inān* partnership according to the Ḥanafī school is based on the contract of *wakālah* and it may even include the contract of *kafālah* if it is mentioned specifically in the contract. According to the Mālikīs too, the contract of *wakālah* is included when the *'inān* is concluded. There is a big difference though in the form of agency granted. The Ḥanafī form of *wakālah* within an *'inān* provides a broad range of powers to the partner—powers through which he can act independently for the partnership. The Mālikī form of *wakālah,* on which the *'inān* is based, places severe restrictions on the partner making him virtually ineffective; he can only act jointly with his partner as in a co-ownership. Al-Khirashī states:

> This means that if a person says to his companion, 'Buy such and such goods for me and for yourself, then, this amounts to a *sharikah* between them, and he becomes his agent for half of the goods, but it is a restricted agency (*wakālah qāṣirah*) that does not extend beyond purchase, that is, the agent does not have the right to sell the half belonging to his partner, except by his permission.... And the term, "*wakālah,*" means *sharikah* between them. He did not mention the word *sharikah,* because that is understood. The aspect of *wakālah* in it was concealed so

> he mentioned it specifically. This issue, mentioned after *shairkat al-'inān,* makes it obvious that it is part of it. It is correct, therefore, that he is not permitted to transact further."[6]

This statement is explicit about the Mālikī *'inān* being a mere mode of acquiring joint ownership. The words, "Buy for me and for yourself," are indicative of this. This is further emphasized and elabourated by the *wakālah qāṣirah* (restricted agency) granted, which curtails the right of further transaction, that is, sale of the acquired property.

There are two major defects with this concept of *'inān,* which restrict it to a mere form of co-ownership and do not permit it to become a regular form of partnership. First, this partnership is for acquiring joint ownership alone and the purpose is not the sharing of profits, whereas the goal of any business partnership is the sharing of profits. Profits, however, do not arise through purchase alone. The goods bought have to be sold for the realization of profit. This right to sell is not available to either partner as part of the partnership contract, and has to be sought later. It may be observed here that the partner does give the right to the other partner for the sale of the goods bought. The answer to this would be that this is possible in any ordinary co-ownership (*sharikat al-milk*) and a contract of partnership is not needed to achieve all that the Mālikī *'inān* achieves. Second, this partnership is a one-time arrangement. It is restricted to a single transaction. A business partnership requires continuity, if not perpetuity like a corporation.

The conclusion, then, is that the Mālikī *sharikat al-'inān* is merely a mode for the creation of co-ownership and it has all the characteristics of a co-ownership. It, therefore, cannot be classified as a partnership. We may support this conclusion with the words of 'Ulaysh: "It is derived from the reins (*'inān*) of a riding animal, as if each one of them has taken hold of the reins of his companion not releasing him to transact as he likes."[7]

---

[6]Al-Khirashī, *Sharḥ al-Mukhtaṣar,* vol. 6, p. 49. See also al-Dasūqī, *Ḥāshīyah,* vol. 3, p. 359 where it is explained further that the *wakālah* is restricted to purchase alone.

[7]Muḥammad 'Ulaysh, *Taqrīrāt 'alā al-Sharḥ al-Kabīr* on the margin of *Ḥāshiyat al-Dasūqī,* vol. 6, p. 359.

13.1.3 Profits are Proportional to Capital

The principle of proportionality between the capital contributed and share of profits is visible in all categories of partnership according to the Mālikīs, except the *muḍārabah.* This is stated in the *Mudawwanah:* "Partnership (sharing of profits) is not permitted, except in proportion to the *amwāl* (capital contributed)."[8]

We, therefore, conclude from all that has been said that there is no difference between the concept of *sharikat al-'inān* as conceived by the Mālikīs and the concept of *sharikat al-milk* as elaborated by the Ḥanafīs. The two basic reasons for this are:

1. A co-owner (partner) in *'inān,* according to the Mālikīs, is not permitted to undertake transactions in the share of his partner without his special permission. This is called *nafy istibdād* in their terminology, which means a complete denial of independent transactions, that is, sale and purchase. The same meaning is found in a *sharikat al-milk* when this is in an *'ayn.*

2. The profit in this type of partnership always corresponds with the share of the partner. This is true also in a co-ownership, when profits are generated.

We will not insist on the third reason, which is that like co-ownership, the purpose of this partnership as evidenced from the mechanism provided, is not to make profits—and that is the basic goal of every partnership. If one were to insist that this goal is there and that is why it is called *sharikat al-'inān,* the response would be that such a goal is implicit even in a co-ownership, as all owners want their property to yield some revenue. Further, the only distinction between this *'inān* and co-ownership is that co-ownership in general may be acquired or it may occur by default (inheritance for instance), while this *'inān* is an active mode of acquiring co-ownership.

It is for this reason that we tend to disagree with Abraham L. Udovitch when he says that the Mālikī *'inān* is like the Ḥanafī special *'inān.*[9] The Ḥanafī special *'inān* may be of two types: 1) Partnership in a single type of trade, but the partner has full powers of sale and purchase f·· cash or for credit. 2) A special *'inān* where the *wakālah* is for a limited number of acts. For example, the partner may not be

[8]Saḥnūn, *al-Mudawwanah al-Kubrā,* vol. 5, p. 41.

[9]Abraham L. Udovitch, *Partnership and Profit in Medieval Islam,* p. 146.

given the right to buy or sell on credit, but he has the right to buy and sell as he likes. Yes, if someone is determined enough, to restrict the Ḥanafī *'inān* partnership further, it is possible, but he still cannot take it to the stage where making of profits is no longer the goal. Any arrangement that drops this feature automatically becomes a co-ownership according to the Ḥanafī school. On the other hand, 'Alī al-Khafīf has drawn the correct conclusion. He says: " And based on the above, it is to be seen that it is a type of *sharikat al-milk* according to the Ḥanafīs. This issue will become clearer when we examine the Mālikī *mufāwaḍah.*"[10]

13.2 The Mālikī *Mufāwaḍah*

13.2.1 The meaning of *mufāwaḍah* according to the Mālikīs

The Ḥanafī jurists say: "Mālik said: 'I do not know what is meant by *mufāwaḍah.*'"[11] When we examine the *Mudawwanah,* however, we see that the truth is just the opposite:

> I said: "Did Mālik recognize the *sharikat al-'inān?*" He replied: "I did not hear about it from Mālik, nor do I think any of the jurists of Ḥijāz knew about it...." (Ibn al-Qāsim said:) "If the things in which they participate cover all things (types of trade), then, they have concluded a *mufāwaḍah,* and if they participate in the buying for a single type of trade, then, they have concluded a *mufāwaḍah* in that type. As for *'inān,* he did not recognize it, nor have we heard of it from Mālik, except what I have described for you."[12]

This is a clear statement and closer to the legal reality in the school. It tells us several things. First, that *'inān* is not a form of partnership according to Mālik, and he never recognized it. We arrived at this conclusion when we studied it in the previous section; it is merely a co-ownership or a mode of acquiring it to which some later Mālikīs gave the name *'inān.* Second, when the partner, unlike the Ḥanafī *'inān,* grants the general right of transaction to a partner in all

[10] 'Alī al-Khafīf, *al-Sharikāt fī al-Fiqh al-Islāmī,* p. 34.

[11] Al-Sarakhsī, *al-Mabsūṭ,* vol. 11, p. 152; al-Kāsānī, *Badā'i' al-Ṣanā'i',* vol. 7, p. 3534; al-Marghinānī, *al-Hidāyah,* vol. 3, p. 4.

[12] Saḥnūn, *al-Mudawwanah al-Kubrā,* vol. 5, p. 68.

types of trade, or a single type of trade, the partnership concluded is *mufāwaḍah*. By general right here, we mean that the partner is free to act according to his opinion and is not required to have recourse to his partner each time he acts. This permission is continuous. Third, this statement does not indicate that Mālik denied the term *mufāwaḍah*. On the contrary, he did not recognize the term *'inān*. Perhaps, the Ḥanafī jurists were trying to say that the Mālikī *mufāwaḍah* is not *mufāwaḍah* as they understand it. The elabouration of this implication will be taken up in the next section.

The meaning of *mufāwaḍah,* as the Mālikīs use it, appears to be as follows:

1. The term *mufāwaḍah* is derived from *tafwīḍ* (delegation) and it is sometimes a delegation for all types of trade and sometimes in one type of trade. In other words, *mufāwaḍah* is general with respect to trade or is special being confined to a single type of trade.

2. The meaning of *tafwīḍ* is realized in this form when it is compared to the Mālikī *'inān,* because the partner is not in need of seeking authorization from his companion each time he wishes to enter into a transaction for the partnership. The permission granted at the time of the contract is sufficient.

Having said this, we may look at the full implication of the term *mufāwaḍah* used while forming the partnership contract.

13.2.2 The implication of the *mufāwaḍah* contract

Is *kafālah* required by the Mālikī *mufāwaḍah*?

The first question we raise is: Does the Mālikī concept of *mufāwaḍah* include the contract of *kafālah?* There is no dispute among the Mālikīs that the contract of partnership incorporates the contract of *wakālah* within it. This *wakālah* is granted from both sides.[13] In *'inān* we said that this *wakālah* is highly restricted. In *mufāwaḍah* it is unrestricted and does not require renewal. But does this *mufāwaḍah* require *kafālah* as it does in the Ḥanafī form of the contract. We return to the text of the *Mudawwanah* for responding to this question:

[13]Al-Dasūqī, *Ḥāshīyah*, vol. 3, p. 348.

> What do you think when one of them brings forth wealth (of a certain amount) and the other comes up with a like sum, and they then participate by way of *mufāwaḍah* (on the condition) that they will purchase with this wealth (on cash) and on credit as well, and whatever sustenance Allah gives of this will be shared (equally) by them. He said: "I am not persuaded that they should participate on the condition that they will make purchases that go beyond the contributed capitals. The reason is that *sharikah* is not permitted except with wealth. Thus, if they do this and purchase on credit, then, what they have purchased is between them too. I have already informed you of the ruling for the partners who do not mix their capitals and this falls under that too."[14]

We find two major points in this statement:

1. He said that he was not persuaded that they exceed the capital for credit purchases. This is similar to the Ḥanafī view for the simple *'inān* that does not include *kafālah* where a partner is not permitted to exceed the partnership capital for credit purchases, unless the other partner has authorized *istidānah.* The Ḥanafīs in that case construct a second partnership of *wujūh* over and above the original partnership.
2. He said: "If they do this and purchase on credit then what they have purchased is between them too." This is what happens after *istidānah* in the Ḥanafī simple *'inān.* Is that what is happening here? Is the authority of *istidānah* implied? This appears to be the implication of the words quoted, but the truth is different.

This problem needs to be analyzed in detail. When we read on in the *Mudawwanah,* for doing so, it has the following to say:

> I said: "If he independently purchases goods on credit in excess of their contributed capital, and his partner does this too, will their purchases be for their own account, because the *sharikah* in credit beyond the contributed capitals is not approved by you." He replied: "No, in fact,

[14]Saḥnūn, *al-Mudawwanah al-Kubrā,* vol. 5, p. 71.

> I hold that whatever they have purchased is to be shared between them, because his partner has asked him to purchase for him too. I, therefore, hold that whatever each one of them has purchased is to be shared between them with one-half going to one partner and one-half to the other."[15]

This makes it quite clear that the partner has been authorized by his partner to buy on credit. He, thus, possesses the authority of *istidānah.* We have elabourated earlier that the authority for *istidānah,* according to the Ḥanafī school, arises from a special permission in the ordinary *'inān* with *wakālah,* and in *mufāwaḍah,* it arises from the underlying contract of *kafālah* and is, thus, implicit in the partnership contract; no special permission is required. What, then, is the nature of the *istidānah,* according to the Mālikī school, in this contract of *mufāwaḍah?*

There is a difficulty we need to deal with here before this question can be answered. This pertains to the relationship that exists between the partners with respect to the excess credit purchases, after the authority for *istidānah* is granted. According to the Ḥanafīs this relationship is based upon *sharikat al-wujūh.* In the ordinary *'inān,* as well as in *muḍārabah,* this relationship has to exist expressly. In *'inān* with *kafālah* and in *mufāwaḍah,* it is implicit in the main contract. The problem is that *sharikat al-wujūh* is illegal according to the Mālikīs, as we shall soon study, because of *jahālah* in the object of the partnership—the purchased commodity. How, then, can we maintain the permission of *istidānah* here, that is, on what legal grounds or principles? Let us have recourse to the explanation given by the Mālikī jurists about this issue or an issue related to it. The following is stated in *Ḥāshīyat al-Dasūqī:*

> The meaning conveyed by what the commentator has stated is that a partner buying on credit is doing so either on permission of his partner or without such permission. In each case, the goods are either ascertained or they are not. If the purchase is without permission, then, it is not allowed whether or not the goods are ascertained. If it is with authority, it is permitted if the goods are ascertained, otherwise it is not allowed.[16]

---

[15] Ibid. p. 7.

[16] Al-Dasūqī, *Ḥāshīyah,* vol. 3, p. 352.

Muḥammad 'Ulaysh is even clearer on the issue:

> He has the right to sell on credit without the permission of his partner, but not make a purchase, that is, on credit without such permission. If he does this, the other partner is given an option to accept or reject this, and in the latter case the liability will be that of the buyer. If he permits him to buy an ascertained commodity, it is permitted otherwise not, because in such a case it will amount to a *sharikat al-dhimam,* which is void.[17]

It appears from these two passages that these jurists are not talking about the authority of *istidānah,* but about the credit purchase in general, and the same stipulation should apply to *istidānah* as well. The conclusion is that credit purchases are not permitted by the Mālikīs, except in a situation where the goods have been ascertained. This is not a *sharikat al-wujūh* in their view as well as in that of the Ḥanafīs. The Mālikī jurists attempt to evade the objection raised by them against *sharikat al-wujūh* and to prevent it from acting against them in credit purchase, by stipulating that the goods be ascertained. This, however, is not all that they do. The stipulations laid down for the credit purchase by them present a somewhat strange and and highly restricted manner of doing business and determines the nature of their *sharikah.* The credit purchase is called *sharikat al-dhimam* by these jurists. This is evident from statements in *al-Mudawwanah:*

> He said: '*Sharikat bi-al-dhimam* is disapproved.' Ibn al-Qāsim said: '*Sharikah* is not valid except in *māl* (currency) and in ascertained commodities

Let us understand this by listing the stipulations and pointing out the defects. A credit purchase for the Mālikī partnership requires the following:

1. The goods must have been ascertained whether or not they are present at the time of the contract.

2. All the partners must be present at the time of the contract, even when one of them has been authorized to buy on credit. It appears that this authorized partner will negotiate the terms and then all of them will come and say a collective "Yes." Otherwise, their being present has no meaning.

3. When a credit purchase is made by all these partners they will be considered sureties (*kafīls*) for each other.

Now, the Ḥanafīs use *istidānah* for making the absent partner liable for the payment of the goods purchased to the extent of his own share in such goods. They use the contract of *kafālah* to make the *kafīl* liable not only for his own share, but also for his partner's share. They require this, because in *wakālah* the *ḥuqūq* belong to the agent, that is, the partner making the transaction. In the first case of *istidānah,* it is the agent who will go back to his partner who granted him *istidānah* for payment of his share. When *kafālah* is introduced, the distinction between *ḥuqūq* and *hukm* is avoided. The creditor can sue any or all partners for the recovery of this payment. The use of *istidānah* and of *kafālah* is, therefore, justified.

The Mālikīs, on the other hand, do not make a distinction between the *ḥuqūq* and the *ḥukm.* Thus, if an agent buys for the partnership, both agent and principal can be sued, as in modern law. If, however, the agent does not have authority for making credit purchases, a special permission will be required. This permission is not *istidānah,* but a widening of *wakālah. Istidānah* will be needed when the credit purchase exceeds the capital employed. In each case of such permission both agent and principal, that is, all partners can be sued by the creditor, by virtue of the Mālikī *wakālah.* In other words, the partners do not have to be present at the time of the sale for this to happen. The Mālikīs, therefore, make an unnecessary stipulation of making all the partners present. The joint liability of the partners exists even if these partners are not present. It appears that the Mālikīs are not satisfied with joint liability even for a normal credit purchase. By making all the partners present, the liability is not joint alone, it is also several. As each partner has acted for himself as well as for the other partners, each one can be sued for the entire price and they can all be sued for it as well; it is up to the creditor. The Mālikīs, however, make a further stipulation that is not required, because it will not bring any additional benefit in terms of creation of liability: they go ahead and make each partner a *kafīl* for the other. Why? The logic of the Mālikī jurists fails us here.

In any case, one thing is obvious: that the contract of *kafālah* is not part of the Mālikī *mufāwaḍah,* as it is in the Ḥanafī *mufāwaḍah.* When it is inserted for an ordinary credit purchase, the purchase is more like a special transaction that does not a require a partnership relationship to exist and can be undertaken jointly by any group of people who are not partners. Yet, in a way it is a new partnership within the existing partnership. The Ḥanafīs called it *sharikat al-wujūh,* but the Mālikīs cannot do so.

We may now turn to the other aspect of the Ḥanafī *mufāwaḍah,* that is, the requirement of equality in capital and other things.

Does the Mālikī *mufāwaḍah* require equality?

We have seen in the earlier sections that the Ḥanafī *mufāwaḍah,* as distinct from *'inān,* requires equality of capital, equality in contractual capacity, and even equality in religion according to some jurists. Does the Mālikī *mufāwaḍah* require equality in such things too. Let us take up the points of comparison one at a time.

Equality in contractual capacity. The Mālikī concept of *mufāwaḍah* unlike the Ḥanafī *'inān,* does not require equality among partners with respect to contractual capacity. This is quite clear from the text of the *Mudawwanah:*

> I said: "Is the *mufāwaḍah* between a freeman and a slave valid in Mālik's opinion?" He replied: "I do not see any harm in this. Mālik said that there is no harm in a partnership between a slave and a freeman, if the slave is one who has been authorized (by his master) to do business. There is no harm if he contributes the wealth of his master to a *mufāwaḍah.*"[19]

It is stated further in the same source:

[19] Saḥnūn, *al-Mudawwanah al-Kubrā,* vol. 5, p. 70.

> I said: "Is the partnership of a Christian and a Muslim or a Jew and a Muslim valid in Mālik's opinion? He replied: "No! Only if the Christian or the Jew are present at the time of purchase. Further, there can be no sale, possession or demand for debt, unless the Muslim is present with him. If the case is what I have described to you, it is valid, otherwise not."[20]

The Mālikī *mufāwaḍah* is, therefore, valid between people of different contractual capacities and religions with the stated restrictions. The Ḥanafīs do not permit this, except what has been transmitted from Abū Yūsuf.

The conclusion we have drawn from these views is that equality in legal capacity is not a required condition for the *mufāwaḍah*. It is also obvious that similarity of religion is also not required. The permissibility of this partnership between a slave and a freeman also tells us that the contract of *kafālah* is not required for this partnership, because a slave does not have the contractual capacity for *kafālah* anyway. This confirms what we concluded earlier about the Mālikī view of not stipulating *kafālah* for the *mufāwaḍah* contract.

Equality of Contributed Capital. We have seen that the Ḥanafīs stipulate equality among partners in the capital of the *mufāwaḍah,* that is, in wealth that is eligible for being the capital of the partnership. If this equality is disturbed, the *mufāwaḍah* is converted into an *'inān*. Alongwith capital, they also stipulate an equality in the shared profits.

The Mālikīs do not stipulate such equality at the time of the contract nor during a continuing partnership. We may quote the *Mudawwanah* again to show this:

> "What do you think if he (a partner) establishes evidence that it is a *mufāwaḍah* on the basis of one-third capital and two-thirds. Is this permitted according to Mālik so that they may be considered partners to the *mufāwaḍah*." He said: "Yes, because it is permitted in Mālik's view to participate in this way."[21]

He then said about the entire capital of the partnership:

---

[20]Loc. cit.

[21]Ibid. p. 68.

> I said: "Will they continue to be partners to *mufāwaḍah* if one of the partners has wealth not given to the partner, whether this is in the form of property of cash?" He said: "Yes." I said: "And the *mufāwaḍah* between them does not become valid when one of them has *dirhams* or *dīnārs* or property that excludes the partner?" He said: "Yes, this does not render the *mufāwaḍah* between them void." I said: "Is this Mālik's opinion?" He said: "This is my opinion."[22]

This is also the opinion of all the Mālikī jurists after Ibn al-Qāsim, and it is not a condition for the partner to participate in a *mufāwaḍah* with his entire eligible capital, whatever the form of these assets. Likewise, equality in wealth and profit is also not a condition.

With respect to acquiring wealth through *hibah* (gift), or inheritance, the *Mudawwanah* states:

> "What do you think when one of them has excess wealth in the shape of *dīnārs* and *dirhams* that he has inherited or that has been gifted to him or that he has been given as charity; does the *mufāwaḍah* between them come to an end in Mālik's view?" He said: "The *mufāwaḍah* is not terminated because of this, and what he has acquired by way of inheritance or gift or charity belongs to him exclusively and not to his partner."[23]

Equality of work. Equality of work is not a condition according to the Mālikīs. The principle is that work is to be done in proportion to the contributed capital. It is stated in the *Mudawwanah:* "The principle for this is that partnership is not valid, unless both participate in work and they do this in proportion to their contributed capitals."[24]

Equality of Profits. We see the same principle operating in the division of profits, and profits are always shared in proportion to the contributed capitals.

[22]Ibid. p. 69.

[23]Loc. cit.

[24]Ibid. p. 61.

13.3 Comparison Between the Mālikī *Mufāwaḍah* and the Ḥanafī *'Inān*

After an explanation of all the above distinctions we find that the Mālikī *mufāwaḍah* differs from the Ḥanafī *mufāwaḍah* in each and every condition. The Mālikī *mufāwaḍah* has nothing to do with the Ḥanafī form of *mufāwaḍah;* they are completely different forms of partnership. At the same time we find that the Mālikī *mufāwaḍah* is almost identical to the simplest form of the Ḥanafī *'inān* partnership, an *'inān* based upon wealth with *wakālah* alone and not the contract of *kafālah.* The Mālikī *mufāwaḍah* is a little more restricted than the Ḥanafī *'inān* insofar as the Ḥanafīs permit credit purchases to a partner, while the Mālikīs require not only special permission for this, but also the presence of the partners at the time of the credit purchase for a collective "yes." The following similarities exist between the Mālikī *mufāwaḍah* and the Ḥanafī basic *'inān* contract.

1. The partners should have the contractual capacity for accepting and granting agencies.
2. The contract of *kafālah* is not part of either partnership.
3. Both forms permit differences in religion of the partners.
4. Both permit the partners to hold excess capital in any form outside the partnership.
5. Both permit the partners to contribute unequal amounts of capital.
6. Both permit the formation of the partnership in all types of trade or in a special trade.
7. The receipt by one partner of wealth through gift, inheritance or charity, does not negate the partnership, and there is no need to convert the partnership to another form as is the case in the Ḥanafī *mufāwaḍah.*
8. Both partnerships place a restriction on making credit purchases beyond the capital amount of the *sharikah.* Both stipulate *istidānah* beyond this limit though in different forms.

The two forms differ in the following respects:

1. The Ḥanafī *'inān* permits the sharing of profits in ratios different from the ratio of the capital contributed. The Mālikī *mufāwaḍah* requires that profits always follow capital contribution.

2. The Ḥanafīs permit the stipulation of excess work by one partner, but do not insist upon actual work. The Mālikī *'inān* requires work in proportion to the capital contributed and insists on actual work.

3. The Ḥanafī *'inān* permits, by virtue of the contract alone, a partner to buy on credit within the capital limit. The Mālikī *mufāwaḍah* stipulates special permission for this and requires further that all partners be present at the time of a credit purchase.

WE, THEREFORE, CONCLUDE that the Mālikī *mufāwaḍah* is altogether different from the Ḥanafī *mufāwaḍah,* and the two forms of partnership are totally different. On the other hand, the Mālikī *mufāwaḍah,* with its separate restrictions, is almost similar to the Ḥanafī *'inān* based upon the contract of *wakālah* alone, when its subject-matter is wealth (*māl*).

The above study and analysis renders the following statement of the learned Ibn Rushd absolutely more or less irrelevant:

> They (all the jurists) differed with respect to *sharikat al-mufāwaḍah.* Mālik and Abū Ḥanīfah agreed as a whole about its permissibility, though they differed about some of its conditions."[25]

If Ibn Rushd could face this danger, while comparing opinions, the modern scholars who choose opinions across different schools are definitely engaged in a hazardous activity. The truth is that Mālik and the Mālikīs, while fully aware of the Ḥanafī *mufāwaḍah,* designed their own *mufāwaḍah* in the form of a rudimentary *'inān.* The view of the Ḥanafī jurists now appears to make some sense, when they quote Mālik as saying: "I do not know what is meant by *mufāwaḍah.*"[26]

---

[25] Ibn Rushd, *Bidāyat al-Mujtahid,* vol. 2, p. 254.

[26] The text is: لاأعرف ماالمفاوضة

13.4 Mālikī School: *Sharikat al-A'māl* and *Sharikat al-Wujūh*

In this section, we shall first take up the discussion of *sharikat a'māl* and *sharikat al-wujūh.*

13.4.1 *Sharikat al-a'māl* (or *abdān*) according to the Mālikīs

Sharikat al-a'māl, also called *sharikat al-abdān,* is the participation of two (or more) artisans in joint work and the division of wages in the ratio of work done by each. It is of two types according to the Mālikīs. These are explained as follows:

When the trade does not depend on the use of tools

This type of partnership is one in which the trade does not depend upon the use of tools and implements or the implement is so insignificant that it is ignored. For example, in tailoring a needle will not be considered an implement. In such a partnership, the following stipulations are made.

Similar or interdependent work. This is like the work of two tailors, whose work is almost similar or is divided up in a manner that their tasks are interdependent, like one cutting cloth according to a pattern and the other stitching it into dresses. Another example is that of two persons diving for pearls where one of them dives and the other holds on to him with a rope.[27] In such work cooperation of some sort is necessary, otherwise the partnership will be unnecessary and not permitted.

Division of profits is according to work. It is stipulated that they work equally so that they can share the receipts equally as well. If one of them does two-thirds of the work and the other does one-third, then, the revenue has to be shared in this ratio. For determining the ratios of work, commercial practice (*'urf*) will be taken into account.

---

[27] Al-Dasūqī, *Ḥāshīyah,* vol. 3, p. 361.

Presence in one location is not required. It is possible for the partners to be located in different places, like the tailors occupying separate shops when each has access to both shops.[28] If they are located independently, but both of them do not have access to both loacations, the partnership is not valid.[29] Al-Khirashī, however, records two opinions in this: "*Al-'Utaybīyah* says that they can be in two locations, while the *Mudawwanah* says that the location must be the same."[30] With respect to prospecting for minerals and water or undertaking construction work, it is stipulated that the location be one, and it is not permitted that one of them work in one mine and the other in a separate mine.[31]

When the trade involves the use of implements

Al-Khirashī states: "What the writer has presented pertains to the situation where the trade does not need implements, or if he does then these are insignificant, as in tailoring. He then discusses the situation where implements are involved, dyeing as a trade and hunting. Here he further stipulates that their equality of implements (contributed) is either through ownership or through renting."[32] For this additional stipulation, ownership is achieved by buying half of each implement for equal ownership or renting it by paying equal amounts of rent.[33] The reason why ownership of implements is stipulated is that a joint liability is created in accordance with the principle of liability.[34]

Stipulations for labour and liability in both forms

Al-Khirashī says that "if one of the parties accepts something for working on it, his partner is equally liable for performing work on it, however, there is no requirement for joint acceptance of work. If the thing accepted is destroyed, the liability is shared by the parties

---

[28]Muḥammad 'Ulasyh, *Taqrīrāt 'alā Sharḥ al-Dardīr* on the margin of al-Dasūqī, *Ḥāshiyah,* vol. 3, p. 361.

[29]Abū 'Abd Allāh Muḥammad al-Khirashī, *Sharḥ al-Mukhtaṣar,* vol. 6 (Cairo, 1318) p. 52.

[30]Loc. cit.

[31]Ibid., vol. 6, p. 53

[32]Ibid. p. 52.

[33]Loc. cit.

[34]Loc. cit.

prior to separation (termination of partnership) and even after it."[35] He then goes into details of liability if the partner has been ill for some time, whether it would amount to termination in fact. He also explains issues of *muṭālabah* from either partner.[36]

From the statements of the Mālikī jurists, we understand the following:

1. Acceptance of work may be by one partner or by both (jointly).

2. Each partner is liable for performance of work to the extent of his part in the work.

3. *Muṭālabah* of suing for performance may be directed toward wither partner. The details of this condition are to follow.

4. These three stipulations do not apply to a partner who has been absent for a long time, whether this was due to an excuse without it. Al-Khirashī explains that being absent for a day or two at repeated intervals does not affect the partnership or the liability of the partners. When the absence of one partner is for more than five days, however, the other partner is entitled to reasonable wages, but the liability still remains joint.[37] It should be clear here that wages paid to the partnership will be shared by both. It is only in the case of prolonged absence that the wages received will belong to the partner who is working and present.[38]

   From al-Khirashī's statements we understand that either partner can be sued for the performance or work. This is what the Ḥanafī's call *ḍamān al-'amal,* and they use *istiḥsān* to make both partners liable to *muṭālabah.* Do the Mālikīs have some similar reasoning? Does one partner become a surety for the other? Here we must distinguish between *ḍamān al-'amal* and *ḍamān al-talaf.* With respect to *ḍamān al-'amal,* it is stated in the *Mudawwanah* that both are liable for the performance of the work.[39] While the Mālikī's assign no clear reason for making both liable, it is obvious that they do not distinguish between

[35]Ibid. p. 54.

[36]Loc. cit.

[37]Loc. cit.

[38]Al-Dasūqī, *Ḥüshiyah,* vol. 3, p. 363.

[39]Saḥnūn, *al-Mudawwanah al-Kubrā,* vol. 5, p. 47.

the *ḥuqūq* of a contract and its *ḥukm,* a distinction that the Ḥanafīs make. What stands in the way of *muṭālabah* from both is this distinction made by the Ḥanafīs. As the Mālikīs do not acknowledge this, *muṭālabah* is valid from both on the basis of their concept of *wakālah.* It is explained further in *Ḥāshiyat al-Dasūqī* that the liability for destroyed goods also lies with both.[40]

From the above discussion, we conclude that the Mālikī *sharikat al-a'māl* is almost similar to the Ḥanafī *'inān* when its subject-matter is labour. As the Mālikīs have a different concept of *wakālah,* they do not have to resort to *istiḥsān* to make both partners liable for *muṭālabah* and for the performance of work. The distinction between the two forms is that the Mālikīs stipulate similarity or interdependence of profession. The Ḥanafīs do not impose this restriction. In addition to this, the Mālikīs require that wages earned be shared in proportion to the work done, while the Ḥanafīs link it to *ḍamān al-'amal.*

13.5 *Sharikat al-Wujūh* and *Sharikat al-Dhimam*

Some Mālikīs, as indicated earlier, differentiate between *sharikat al-wujūh* and *sharikat al-dhimam. Sharikat al-dhimam* is further divided into two types, and both are void according to the Mālikīs. *Sharikat al-dhimam* is the contract between two or more persons that they will buy an unascertained commodity on credit so as to create a joint liability for both. The liability is created by each one accepting the purchased goods on behalf of the other partners and then after selling this jointly the profit is shared between them. This partnership is not permitted by the Mālikīs. As this partnership is the same as *sharikat al-wujūh* according to the Ḥanafīs, we may conclude that the *sharikat al-wujūh* permitted by them is void according to the Mālikīs.[41]

The second type of *sharikat al-dhimam* is where one person has credit worthiness in the market and another does not. The person who does not enjoy credit worthiness operates through the person

[40] Al-Dasūqī, *Ḥāshiyah,* vol. 3, p. 362.

[41] Saḥnūn, *al-Mudawwanah al-Kubrā,* vol. 5, p. 41.

who does. The profit is shared between them. This type is not permitted by the Mālikīs on the basis of *gharar* and *jahālah.*[42]

As for the purchase of an ascertained (*mu'ayyan*) commodity, whether present or absent, it has been discussed earlier within the discussion of the Mālikī *mufāwaḍah* with respect to credit purchases beyond the capital limit. This is permitted by the Mālikīs and requires the presence of all the partners on the spot and the all the partners accept the transaction themselves.

This shows that there are three types of such partnerships according to the Mālikīs:

1. *Sharikat al dhimam* in which all the partners have credit worthiness. This partnership is called *sharikat al-wujūh* by the Ḥanafīs.

2. *Sharikat al-dhimam* where one partner has credit worthiness, but the other partner does not. It is the other partner who does business on the basis of the credit worthiness of the first.

3. Credit purchase through a joint contract in which each partner is required to be present and to participate personally in the purchase contract.

The first two are void according to the Mālikīs and the third is not a partnership at all, as discussed earlier.

---

[42]Muḥammad 'Ulaysh, *Taqrīrāt 'alā Sharḥ al-Dardīr* on the margin of al-Dusūqī, *Ḥāshiyah,* vol. 3, p. 364.

Chapter 14

Shāfi'ī School: First Category of Partnerships

The Shāfi'ī law of partnership, as indicated earlier, seems to be a somewhat restricted version of Islamic law on the issue. We will present this version in two sections.

1. The concept of *'inān* according to the Shāfi'īs.
2. The views of the Shāfi'īs about the illegality of other forms of partnership.

14.1 The Concept of *'Inān* According to the Shāfi'īs

14.1.1 The meaning of *'inān*

Al-Ramlī says: "It is valid, that is, *'inān*, by *ijmā'* (consensus), because it is free from all kinds of *gharar*. The meaning is derived from the reins of an animal due to this equality in transactions and other things, like the equality of the two reins or in **each one preventing the other in whatever he likes, and this too is like pulling the reins of the animal.**"[1]

According to the Ḥanafīs, *'inān* meant handing over one of the reins to the other partner so that he had freedom to transact in some part of the other partner's wealth. The Mālikīs, on the other hand, meant by *'inān* "the taking hold by one partner of the *'inān* of the other partner, that is, by his forelock so that he could not act without

[1] Al-Ramlī, *Nihāyat al-Muḥtāj*, vol. 5, p. 4. The sentence shown in bold letters represents the attitude of the Shāfi'īs with respect to the Islamic law of partnership.

his permission."[2] The meaning given by al-Ramlī is quite close to the meaning fixed by the Mālikīs. The Mālikī *'inān,* we concluded, is a type of co-ownership and not a partnership. Is the Shāf'ī *'inān* similar to the Mālikī *'inān?* Let us examine some of the details to find out.

Al-Ramlī says:

> It has five elements: the two parties, the subject-matter of the contract, work and the form (*ṣīghah*). The writer has begun with the last of these treating it as a requisite condition in accordance with what has preceded in sale. He, therefore, said: An express pronouncement of this word is stipulated for each partner in response to the other so as to indicate permission for either person making the transaction or for one of them making a transaction, that is, for trade involving buying and selling.[3]

This indicates that partnership is valid if one person permits a transaction to another, even if the other person has not granted such permission. In other words, transactions may be permitted to one partner and not the other. We have understood from the study of partnerships, according to the Ḥanafīs and Mālikīs, that permission for transactions must be granted by both parties to each other and both of them should have the right to deal in the wealth of the partnership. If permission is granted by one partner alone, the wealth in the hands of the transacting partner is to be trated as capital of *muḍārabah.* The Shāfi'īs, thus, go against this and call such a relationship *'inān* in one of its forms. What, then, is the difference between such an arrangement, which they call *'inān,* and between *muḍārabah?* Al-Ramlī says: "If only one of them is granted permission, such authorized partner has the right of transaction in the entire wealth, while the authorizing partner has the right of transaction in his own share alone. If it is stipulated that he cannot transact in his own share, then, the partnership is not valid."[4] What al-Ramlī appears to be saying here is that the *rabb al-māl* in a *muḍārabah* has no right of transaction in the capital of the *muḍārabah,* which is handed over to the *muḍārib,* but the partner in an *'inān* who has authorized

[2] Al-Khirashī, *Sharḥ al-Mukhtaṣar,* vol. 6, p. 49. See also Muḥammad 'Ulaysh, *Taqrīrāt 'alā al-Sharḥ al-Kabīr,* on the margin of al-Dasūqī, *Ḥāshiyah,* vol. 3, p. 359.

[3] Al-Ramlī, *Nihāyat al-Muḥtāj,* vol. 5, p. 4.

[4] Loc. cit.

his other partner to be responsible for all the transactions still has the right of disposal in his own share.

Unfortunately, al-Ramlī's statement does not conform with the legal logic established for the issue, nor is it analytically consistent with the other principles. The reason is that the wealth of the partnership exists in the form of a co-ownership, and each partner owns every particle of this wealth through an undivided share by way of *mushā'*. A partner, if authorized, can enter into transactions on behalf of all the other partners along with his own share, or not at all; it is not possible for one partner to act in his own share out of this mingled wealth even to the extent of his share. We are sorry to say that this statement made by al-Ramlī is purely theoretical and cannot be put into practice.[5] The result of authorizing one partner alone would be what the Ḥanafīs have concluded: the relationship established would be that of *muḍārabah* and not *sharikat al-'inān.* In fact, when the remaining Shāfi'ī conditions are associated with this point, like the sharing of profits in proportion to the the capital contributed, that is, no additional share for the single working partner, the relationship will be converted to one of *biḍā'ah.* This type of relationship is usually found in *sharikat al-milk* (co-ownership) according to the Ḥanafīs.

The next point to note here is that the Shāfi'īs stipulate complete mingling of the capitals, so that one contribution cannot be distinguished from the other. This creates the problem with respect to the the unauthorized partner, discussed above: how can he make a transaction in his own share if it is completely mingled with the share of the other partner?

The discussion so far leaves us with a single type of *'inān* that is approved by the Shāfi'īs, and in which all partners have been authorized transactions. The other form in which a single partner has been authorized is not possible, and can only exist as an arrangement within co-ownership. The Shāfi'īs, however, permit the conversion of the first type in which both partners are authorized to a form in which only one is authorized. This they attempt to achieve by merely restricting the powers of one partner, as we shall see.

---

[5] A similar theoretical assumption has been made by modern scholars and, following them, the Islamic Fiqh Academy of the OIC when they try to permit the sale of shares of a corporation on the basis of co-ownership.

14.1.2 The contract of *sharikat al-'inān*

The contract of *sharikah,* according to the Shāfi'īs is based upon *wakālah* and not on *kafālah.* Al-Ramlī says: "The objective of *sharikah* is achieved by volition, by the intention to make transactions and profit; it is, in fact, not an independent contract, but agency and the delegation of powers."[6]

Is legal capacity for agency stipulated for the parties in such a contract? Al-Ramlī points out the following:

> If both of them are entering into transactions, the capacity of accepting and granting agency is stipulated for them with respect to wealth as each one of them is an agent for the other as well as his principal. If only one will undertake transactions, the capacity for being an agent is stipulated for him and the capacity for being a principal for the other. Thus, it will be valid if the other is dumb.[7]

The partnership in which permission has been granted from both sides is converted into the other form if permission granted for transactions is withdrawn by the other partner. Al-Ramlī says:

> The contract of *sharikah* is valid from both sides, as he has stated, and each partner has the right to terminate it when he likes, as in *wakālah,* leading to the suspension of transactions from both sides. But if one of them were to say, "I have terminated your agency," or he were to say, "Do not undertake transactions in my share," then, the agency of the addressee is terminated, while that of the speaker continues. The reason is that the other has not stopped him, and he can still transact in the share of the agent removed."[8]

We have already pointed out that suspending or taking away the powers of one partner renders this arrangement a co-ownership rather than a partnership.

The Shāfi'īs do not permit temporary *wakālah,* which also means that a temporary partnership is not permitted.

---

[6]Loc. cit.

[7]Ibid., vol. 5, p. 5.

[8]Ibid., vol. 5, p. 10 See also al-Shīrāzī, *al-Muhadhdhab,* vol. 1, p. 384.

14.1.3 Formation of the partnership and stipulation for sharing profits

Formation of the partnership

A partnership, according to the Shāfi'īs, is formed in two stages. In the first stage actual physical mingling of the capitals takes place in a manner that distinction, or separation, of one from the other is not possible. This creates a co-ownership (*sharikat al-milk*). In the second stage the contract of partnership is created through permissions from both sides or from one side, as stated earlier.

We do not find a convincing reason in the Shāfi'ī texts for the actual physical mingling of capitals. Al-Shāfi'ī says in *al-Umm:* "The *mufāwaḍah* partnership is void, and I do not know of anything else in the world that deserves more to be void than the *sharikat al-mufāwaḍah,* unless the partners construct the *mufāwaḍah* by mingling of capitals and by working with them and sharing the profits, because there is nothing wrong with this."[9] Here al-Shāfi'ī emphasises the mingling of capitals, but does not elaborate upon the underlying reason for it. Al-Muzanī too, in his *al-Mukhtaṣar,* does not give us a reason: "A valid partnership is one in which each partner contributes *dīnārs* in the same amount as his partner and they mix them up, and they become partners in it (the wealth). If they purchase with these, **it is not permitted to one partner to sell the goods, unless the other is present.**"[10]

Now, al-Muzanī does not give a reason for the *khalṭ,* but it appears that partnership itself is formed by it and is complete without any further formalities. This is evident from his words: "and they become partners in it." The permissions granted after this are not an independent contract, but merely *wakālah* as has been explicitly stated by al-Ramlī: "It (partnership) is not an independent contract, but is, in fact, *wakālah* and the granting of agency, as is understood from what follows."[11]

All this means that the Shāfi'ī *'inān* based upon wealth, which is the only form permitted by them, is nothing more than co-ownership with agency for one or for both partners being turned on or off at will and according to need. The reason why we hold it similar to co-ownership is that all that the Shāfi'ī *'inān* does can be achieved

---

[9] Al-Shāfi'ī, *al-Umm,* vol. 3, p. 206.

[10] Al-Muzanī, *Mukhtaṣar,* p, 109 al-Shāfi'ī, *al-Umm,* vol. 6.

[11] Al-Ramlī, *Nihāyat al-Muḥtāj,* vol. 5, p. 3.

through a co-ownership and occasional agency. As compared to this, the Ḥanafīs have the following to say:

> The mixing of capitals is not a condition for the validity of this partnership, in our view, while al-Shāfiʿī (God bless him) said it is a condition. It is also the opinion of Zufar. The principle according to him is that *sharikat al-milk* (co-ownership) is the sole basis and the contract of partnership is a term depicting *ikhtilāṭ* (mingling by the partners) and this is realized through (joint) *milk*. The matter to be considered in each contract is the requirement of the (name of the) contract, like *ḥawālah, wakālah, kafālah,* and *ṣarf*. Thus, if the two capitals are mixed in a manner that makes it impossible to distinguish one from the other, then, *sharikat al-milk* is established, and the contract of partnership is built upon it.[12]

This is an excellent analysis of the Shāfiʿite position by al-Sarakhsī. The problem is that what follows the creation of *sharikat al-milk* is not an independent contract of partnership, but mere permissions of a limited type of *wakālah,* which may be revoked for one of the partners. This has been stated clearly by al-Ramlī, as explained above.

An additional stipulation made by the Shāfiʿīs is that the currency offered must be of the same specie from both sides. The reason is that without this similarity *khalṭ* would not be possible.

Division of profits

The Shāfiʿīs stipulate that profit and loss must strictly follow the ratio of ownership with reference to value, and not on the basis of parts or on the basis of work. It does not matter, as far as the sharing of profits is concerned, whether or not the partners contribute equal amounts of work. If this condition is violated, the partnership is void.[13] All this is required in a co-ownership, which is the rule according to the Shāfiʿīs.

14.1.4 The powers of a partner

A partner, who has been authorized to undertake transactions, operates under severe restrictions in Shāfiʿite law. He cannot sell at the

[12] Al-Sarakhsī, *al-Mabsūṭ*, vol. 11, p. 152.

[13] Ibid., vol. 5, pp. 11–12.

market rate (i.e., without specifying the exact rate); he cannot sell on credit, because of *gharar;* he cannot sell for other than the local prevailing currency, like an agent. If he does violate any of these conditions, the transaction will take effect only against his own share. Further, he cannot give the wealth of the *sharikah* by way of *biḍā'ah* nor can he travel with it. For each of the above acts, the partner has to take special permission from his partner(s), but the basis of the contract of *sharikah,* or the *wakālah* included in it, does not authorize him to undertake such transactions.

Is the partner permitted to trade in all commodities or is he restricted to a specific trade? We have not found a clear text on this issue in the Shāfi'ī texts, however, the contract of *wakālah* in their view can be general. Al-Nawawī says in *al-Minhāj:* "If he says, 'I have appointed you an agent in all things big or small or for all my affairs and have delegated these to you,' it is not valid. If, however, he says, 'For the sale of my property or for the selling of my slaves,' it is valid."[14] This permission is for the sale of goods and not their purchase. With respect to purchase, he says, "If he appoints him an agent for buying a slave, it is necessary that the type be specified. If it is for a house, the locality must be specified."[15] Al-Ramlī, commenting upon this says: "'Buy the goods you like,' or those in which there is profit as in *qirāḍ*. This is what the text of *al-Rawḍah* implies, and Ibn Raf'ah has transmitted it from al-Māwardī and others and has acknowledged it, which is evident."[16]

We understand from this that *wakālah* accepts the general form according to the Shāfi'īs for trade in general, but is in need of special authorization each time a transaction is made. In other words, the unqualified contract of partnership does not grant this right to the partner; it has to be stated explicitly in the contract. Al-Shīrāzī says in *al-Muhadhdhab:*

> It is not permitted to one of the partners to undertake transactions in the share of his partner, except by his permission.... And it is not permitted to either to trade with the share of his partner, except in the in the commodity that has been permitted by the partner.... Unless the partner authorizes him, because each one of them is an

---

[14] Al-Nawawī, *Matn al-Minhāj* on the margin of al-Ramlī, *Nihāyat al-Muḥtāj,* vol. 5, p. 26.

[15] Loc. cit.

[16] Loc. cit.

agent for the other for his half, and possesses only what an agent possesses.[17]

In conclusion, we may say that the *'inān* partnership based upon wealth is quite similar to co-ownership (*sharikat al-milk*) found with the Ḥanafīs. It is not an independent contract, and is merely *wakālah.* By special authorization, the powers granted to a partner may be expanded, but even then the form of partnership created does not reach the simplest form of the Ḥanafī *'inān.* This is reflected in the powers available to a partner in the Ḥanafī school and the possibility of sharing profits in varying ratios. Further, the Ḥanafī co-ownership may be expanded like the Shāfi'ī *'inān* and yet not become the Ḥanafī *'inān.*

14.2 Views of the Shāfi'īs about the Illegality of Other Forms of Partnerhsip

The Shāfi'īs consider the *mufāwaḍah,* the *sharikat al-abdān,* as well as the *sharikat al-wujūh* to be void *bāṭil* (void). This means that the only form of partnership apporoved by them is the *sharikat al-'inān* incorporating the contract of *wakālah* and having its subject-matter as wealth. We have also shown that the manner in which this sole form is approved or is allowed to operate does not even bring it up to the level of the simplest form of partnership approved by the Ḥanafīs. In fact, the severe restrictions placed upon the approved form of partnership make it no better than *sharikat al-milk* or co-ownership with some permissions to make transactions based on *wakālah.* It would, therefore, not be an exaggeration if we said that the law of *sharikah* (partnership) is non-existent within the Shāfi'ī school. From this conclusion, it follows logically that the Shāfi'ī law on partnerships has never been applied in practice. The reason is that there is no law to practice in this area within this school.[18]

We will first examine the views of the Shāfi'ī school with respect to *mufāwaḍah* and then for the other two types considered and rejected by the school. The benefit of this examination is to see how the Shāfi'īs have applied the legal principles to reject these forms.

---

[17] Abū Isḥāq Ibrāhīm ibn 'Alī ibn Yūsuf al-Fīrūzabādī al-Shīrāzī, *al-Muhadhdhab fī Fiqh Madhhab al-Imām al-Shāfi'ī,* vol. 2 (Cairo, n.d.) p. 346.

[18] The purely theoretical nature of this law was obvious from al-Ramlī's statement about giving the right of transaction to one person in property that is undivided in each particle (*mushā'*). See section 14.1.3.

14.2.1 The Rejection of the *mufāwaḍah*

Al-Shāfiʿī says in *al-Umm*:

> *Sharikat al-mufāwaḍah* is *bāṭil* and I do not know of anything else in this world that can be declared void if it is not the *mufāwaḍah* partnership.... If they think that the *mufāwaḍah* according to them is that they are partners in all that is found in their ownership for some reason, whether wealth or something else, then, the partnership between them is *fāsid.* I do not know of gambling except in this or less than this that two persons participate with two hundred *dirhams* and then one of them finds a treasure and this is to be shared among them. What do you think if they stipulate this and do not mingle their capitals, is it not permitted, and what do you think of the person who has been given a gift or has hired out his services? If he earns something out of this, does the other become his partners in this? They have rejected lesser things than this.[19]

If the reader will review what we have said about the *mufāwaḍah,* after the analysis of the Ḥanafī views, he will find that this is not the *mufāwaḍah* the Ḥanafīs are talking about. Further, the extreme cases mentioned in the above statement do not force the richer partner to hand over his new found wealth to his other partner; the *mufāwaḍah* is converted automatically into *ʿinān.* Let us examine the views of al-Shīrāzī to understand the true concept of the *mufāwaḍah* according to the Shāfiʿīs. He says in *al-Muhadhdhab:*

> As for *sharikat al-mufāwaḍah,* it is a partnership between two person who participate in what they earn with their wealth and labour and each one of them is liable for what the other is liable through misappropriation, sale, or compensation. This partnership is not valid because of:
>
> 1. The tradition of 'Ā'ishah, may Allah be pleased with her, and the tradition was stated with reference to *sharikat al-abdān:* Each condition that is not in the Book of Allah is *bāṭil.* And this condition is not in the Book of Allah.

[19]Al-Shāfiʿī, *al-Umm,* vol. 3, p. 206.

2. It is a partnership formed on the basis that each one will be a surety for his companion for what is personal to him. It is, therefore, not valid as it amounts to a partnership on what they have come to own through inheritance and gift.
3. Further, it is a partnership formed on the condition that each will stand surety for what is due from the other as a result of torts. It is, therefore, not valid, because it amounts to forming a partnership for making one liable for the crimes committed by the other .[20]

All these points have already been explained in our discussion of the *mufāwaḍah* according to the Ḥanafīs, and each of these has been successfully refuted by the Ḥanafīs. Repeating the earlier discussion here will thus serve no useful purpose. Further, there is an element of exaggeration in the Shāfiʿī view on the *mufāwaḍah*. We will, therefore, let al-Sarakhsī respond to this and see what he has to say about the Shāfiʿī view. He responds as follows:

> As for al-Shāfiʿī (God bless him), he builds his views upon the fact that the basis is *sharikat al-milk,* but this is not the foundation of the *mufāwaḍah* at all, and as it is not established on the basis of *sharikat al-milk,* he declared it void. He said that it incorporates the *kafālah* contract with an uncertain basis for an uncertain object. Each one becomes the surety of the other for what he is liable for due to trade, and as *kafālah* for an unknown thing through a known thing is void, therefore, one through an unknown thing has a higher priority for voidability. What he says about its being a type of gambling pertains to the opinion of al-Thawrī, who said that if one of them inherits wealth, it belongs to both of them. We do not maintain this opinion and it, therefore, does not pertain to us. Our proof (*ḥujjah*) in this is that this partnership incorporates *kafālah* and *wakālah,* and each one of these is valid in itself, for the realization of its objective, so also within a partnership. *Jahālah* in itself does not annul *kafālah,* but may lead to disputes, however, that is absent

[20]Al-Shīrāzī, *al-Muhadhdhab,* vol. 1, p 346.

> here as each one of them becomes a surety for the other for what is due from him by virtue of trade. In such a case, the subject-matter of trade, as well as the person for whom he is liable, are both known. This certainty is not known in *'inān,* because agency for purchasing things of an unknown species is not permitted (that is, *'inān* for general trade), but despite this *'inān* is permitted when the things purchased by each are not mentioned in the contract; likewise, the *mufāwaḍah.*[21]

What al-Sarakshsī means by this is that some uncertainty (*jahālah*) is present even in the *'inān* when it is based upon general trade, "because what each one of them buys is not mentioned in the contract." Thus, if we were to base our view upon this type of uncertainty and declare the *mufāwaḍah* void, it would not be possible to permit the *sharikat al-'inān* for general trade either. Perhaps, this is what al-Shāfi'ī has done, as discussed in the previous section; there is no law of partnership left to deal with in his school. The matter is quite evident and does not need further elaboration.

14.2.2 Al-Shāfi'ī's views about the illegality of the *sharikat al-abdān*

Sharikat al-abdān, according to al-Shāfi'ī, is the participation of two persons with their physical labour. It is void, as is stated by the author of *al-Muhadhdhab:*

> Because of what is recorded from 'Ā'ishah, may Allah be pleased with her, that the Prophet (peace be upon him) said that each stipulation that is not in the Book of Allah is *bāṭil,* and this is a condition that is not in the Book of Allah. Further, because the labour of each person is exclusively his own; it is, therefore, not permitted to another to participate in this with him. If they form such a partnership and earn, then, each one will take what he has worked for because it is a compensation for his body (physical labour) and belongs exclusively to him.[22]"

[21] Al-Sarakhsī, *al-Mabsūṭ,* vol. 11, p. 153.

[22] Al-Shīrāzī, *al-Muhadhdhab,* vol. 1, p. 346. See also al-Ramlī, *Nihāyat al-Muḥtāj,* vol. 5, p. 3. Al-Ramlī says: "It is *bāṭilah,* because of *gharar* and the uncertainty involved in it."

These views lead us to conclude that a partnership according to the Shāfi'ī school is not possible without *khalṭ,* and *khalṭ* is the basis for *sharikat al-milk* on which alone this school builds the law of partnerhsip. As *khalṭ* or mingling of physical labour is not possible, this partnership is declared void. We may also note here that even the Ḥanafīs permit a partner to keep for himself the wages derived from pure physical labour. The Ḥanafīs focus more on similarity of labour or on interdependent labour based upon professional skills, like the work of artisans. The Shāfi'īs apparently did not make a distinction between pure physical labour and one based on some sort of skill.

14.2.3 The illegality of *sharikat al-wujūh*

As for *sharikat al-wujūh,* it is participation in the profits of what each partner purchases (and their skills) on the basis of credit-worthiness. It is a partnership that is void[23] "because what each partner purchases goes into his ownership and belongs exclusively to him. It is, therefore, not permitted to him to share this with another."[24] This is what is stated by the author of *al-Muhadhdhab.* As for al-Ramlī, he says that the basis for all the void partnerships is *gharar.*[25]

In our view, the reason here as well can be traced back to the lack of *khalṭ* and co-ownership.

[23] Al-Shīrāzī, *al-Muhadhdhab,* vol. 1, p. 347.

[24] Loc. cit.

[25] Al-Ramlī, *Nihāyat al-Muḥtāj,* vol. 5, p. 3.

Chapter 15

Ḥanbalī School: First Category of Partnerhsips

The Ḥanbalīs divide *sharikah* into *sharikah fī al-māl* and *sharikah fī al-'aqd.*[1] The first is defined as "participation in a right to entitlement," by which they mean *sharikat al-milk* or co-ownership. The second is defined as "participation in the right of disposal," which is of five types: *sharikat al-'inān, sharikat al-wujūh, sharikat al-abdān, sharikat al-mufāwaḍah* and *sharikat al-muḍārabah.* Each of these is an independent partnership. Thus, when we say *sharikat al-wujūh,* we do not mean that it is either formed as *'inān* or as *mufāwaḍah,* as it is in the Ḥanafite system. Here it is independent of *'inān* or *mufāwaḍah,* which are themselves independent partnerships unrelated to others.

This chapter is devoted to the study of the first four types according to the Ḥanbalī system. *Muḍārabah,* as stated earlier, will be studied in the next part. Before we begin the study of the first category of partnerships according to the Ḥanbalīs, it is important to say a few words about their approach to this subject in general.

The Ḥanbalī school was developed much later as compared to the other schools by the students of Aḥmad ibn Ḥanbal. Leaving aside the *'ibādāt,* this school has had very litte exposure as far as practice is concerned. It is only in the modern times that it is receiving greater attention. When one studies the law of partnership as expounded by this school, the results are somewhat surprising. The opinions in this school are more advanced than those of the Shāfi'ī or Mālikī schools. In fact, the forms of partnership accepted are quite similar to those approved by the Ḥanafī school.

---

[1] Manṣūr ibn Yūnus ibn Ṣalāḥ al-Dīn al-Bahūtī, *Kashshāf al-Qinā' 'an Matn al-Iqnā'*, vol. 3 (Cairo, 1968) p. 496 (hereinafter referred to as al-Bahūtī, *Kashshāf al-Qinā*).

There is one problem, however. The opinions in the Ḥanafī school are easily linked with the operation of general principles. One understands why a certain opinion is being upheld in the Ḥanafī school when recourse is had to the basic principles approved by them. This type of clarity and systematic elaboration is not found in the Ḥanbalī school. In short, when we wish to grasp the principles that underlie an opinion, it becomes somewhat difficult to do so. The emphasis is on the derived opinion rather than the underlying principle. One gets this impression from most of the *fiqh* material developed by the Ḥanbalīs. Even when an opinion is being based directly on a tradition, there is no explanation as to what principles of *fiqh* have been affected or amended. Take the case of *'urbūn* (earnest money). The Ḥanbalīs permit this, while the other schools do not. Though the Ḥanbalī opinion is based upon a tradition, it is not clear what kind of legal principle is laid down. The acceptance of the *'urbūn* establishes a very important principle; namely, that rights and options can be sold and are thus a category of *māl* in Islamic law. This principle, if accepted, can have far-reaching consequences for the entire Islamic law of contract. The Ḥanbalīs, however, do not identify the principle and give no legal analysis as to how this new principle will be reconciled with the remaining principles of traditional Islamic law of contract. Even the modern scholars who approve *'urbūn*, and that includes the Islamic Fiqh Academy of the OIC, have not attemped to lay down the principle. This is typical of the Ḥanbalī school: **focus on the opinion without elaborating the underlying principle and checking it for analytical consistency.**

Further, in the law of partnership, we find the Ḥanbalīs adopting quite a liberal approach, but here and there an opinion is inserted that appears to wreck the whole structure erected, and in fact works against the principles underlying the approved opinions. Take the case of the *'inān* partnership. Most of the rules devised for the partnership are similar to those of *'inān* based on *wakālah* approved by the Ḥanafīs. In the middle of this structure an opinion is arbitrarily inserted that attempts to deny one of the partners transactions for the partnership and yet permits him to undertake transactions in his own share. This point, and its purely theoretical nature, have been discussed in detail under the Shāfi'ite law of partnership in the previous chapter. The opinion clashes totally with the rest of the rules approved for this partnership by the Ḥanbalīs. The general impression one gets on studying Ḥanbalite law on partnerships is that opinions have been selected from other senior schools, but very little attention has been paid to the principles underlying such opinions, and no apparent attempt has been made to ensure analytical consistency in the opinions selected.

15.1 The *'Inān* Partnership according to the Ḥanbalīs

The *'inān* partnership approved by the Ḥanbalī school is exactly similar to the ordinary *'inān* based on *wakālah* with *māl* as its subject-matter, as approved by the Ḥanafīs. The only difference is where the Ḥanbalī scholars attempt to insert a Shāfi'ī opinion that is inoperable within the Ḥanafī system. All this will be evident from what follows.

15.1.1 The meaning of *'inān* according to the Ḥanbalīs

The meaning of this partnership is that two persons should participate with their wealth and work on the condition that the generated profits will be shared by them. The meaning is derived from the example of a man driving two horses when he gives equal rein to both. It is also said to be derived, according to al-Farrā', from matching each other equally in all things.[2]

Do the Ḥanbalīs, then, mean that the partners should participate with equal capital? The answer is no! The author of *al-Mughnī* says: "Equality in the amount of wealth is not stipulated."[3] The author of *Kashshāf* states that similarity/equality of wealth, either in species or in quality, may not be stipulated.[4]

Further, the Ḥanbalīs, like the Ḥanafīs and unlike the Shāfi'īs, do not stipulate the mingling of capitals (*khalṭ*). All that they require is that it be ascertained and be present.[5] Now the Ḥanafī rule for *dīnārs* and *dirhams* is that *khalṭ* does not stand in the way of the formation of partnership. This partnership is not treated as complete and effective, however, unless transactions are made in the contributed currencies. For the other things, the Ḥanafīs use different *ḥīlah*s to contribute the capitals. All this is done to create joint liability, to give operation to the rules of *sharikat al-milk* in case of *fasād*, and

[2] Ibid., vol. 3, p. 496; Ibn Qudāmah, *al-Mughnī,* vol. 5, p. 16.

[3] Ibn Qudāmah, *al-Mughnī,* vol. 5, p. 20.

[4] Al-Bahūtī, *Kashshāf,* vol. 3, p. 499.

[5] Ibn Qudāmah, *al-Mughnī,* vol. 5, p. 20.

to enable the partners to share the profits, because joint entitlement to profits is based upon the creation of joint *ḍamān,* which is completed with transactions in the case of currencies and through purchase *ḥīlahs* in the case of other things. Most of these issues have been discussed in the fundamental concepts. How do the Ḥanbalīs deal with these questions? It is only in the *Kashshāf* that one finds a half-hearted attempt to identify a principle.

The author of *Kashshāf* says: "The wealth stands mingled by the contract itself."[6] He further adds: "If one of the contributed capitals, or part of it, is destroyed even when this is before the *khalṭ,* then, the partners are equally liable for the destroyed wealth."[7] The first point to notice here is that if the *khalṭ* is achieved by the contract itself, then, the question of before or after the *khalṭ* is irrelevant. The second point is that this is an important principle, like the principle of *'urbūn,* but only if it is established. We have stated earlier that mingling of capitals should be treated as an accounting problem, and things should be mingled with value rather than through physical mingling. The problem here is that the analytical consistency of this principle should be checked with all the principles upheld by the Ḥanafīs, especially when some of the principles have been developed out of traditions like *al-kharāju bi al-ḍamān.* This analytical justification is not provided by the Ḥanbalī scholars.

Partnership with *'urūḍ*

There is no disagreement among the Ḥanbalīs that a partnership may be formed with absolute currencies, but with respect to property in general (*'urūḍ*),[8] there are two opinions:

1. Partnership is not permitted with *'urūḍ* for the same reasons stated by the Ḥanafīs. The Ḥanafīs achieve this through *ḥīlahs*, but the Ḥanbalīs do not.

2. *Sharikah* including *muḍārabah* is possible with *'urūḍ* and their value at the time of the contract is to be considered as the

[6] Al-Bahūtī, *Kashshāf al-Qinā'*, vol. 3, p. 499.

[7] Loc. cit.

[8] Abraham L. Udovitch has translated the word *'urūḍ* as goods. See Abraham L. Udovitch, *Partnership and Profit in Medieval Islam,* passim. The word, however, has a wider meaning insofar as it includes real estate and landed property as well.

capital.[9] The Ḥanafīs avoid this due to the *gharar* involved as it can lead to disputes. For example, if a house is contributed as capital, and before any transactions are made, if the price of the house falls steeply, or rises for that matter, it may lead to disputes. Further, before any transactions in the property, it is not justified to pass on the profit or loss, as the case may be, to the other partner when he has not done anything to deserve this. The Ḥanbalīs ignore this issue.

The Ḥanbalīs also stipulate that the capital contributed should be present and available for transactions.[10] This too is identical with the condition stipulated by the Ḥanafīs.

The Ḥanbalīs stipulate that profit should be specified as an undivided percentage of the whole (*mushā'*) profits, like half or a third. The sharing of profits does not have to follow the ratio of capitals contributed, and one partner may be given more on the basis of his skill and profession. Forming a partnership with an unknown share is not permitted.[11] This condition is also similar to that laid down by the Ḥanafīs.

15.1.2 The implication of the absolute term *'inān* and powers of partners

As most of the implications of the term *'inān* used in the contract of partnership, without qualification, are the same as those for the Ḥanafī *'inān* based upon *wakālah,* we shall summarize its implications as they are stated in *al-Mughnī.*[12]

The Ḥanbalī *'inān* is based upon *wakālah* and *amānah* and does not include the contract of *kafālah.* The partnership is general for all trades or special for one type of trade, if that is specified. A partner in this *'inān* has all the powers that we have mentioned for the Ḥanafī *'inān* constituted with wealth (*māl*). Thus, he can engage in *musāwamah, murābaḥah, tawliyah* and *muwāḍa'ah* in accordance with what he sees to be the interest of the partnership and as is the practice of the traders.[13] Further, a partner has the right to take delivery of goods or the price and to make claims for receivables of

[9]Ibn Qudāmah, *al-Mughnī,* vol. 5, pp. 16–17.

[10]Al-Bahūtī, *Kashshāf al-Qinā',* vol. 3, p. 479.

[11]Ibid. p. 498.

[12]Ibn Qudāmah, *al-Mughnī,* vol. 5, pp. 21–22.

[13]Loc. cit.

the partnership and to accept assignments, as well as to return goods on the basis of defects.

In the Ḥanbalī *'inān,* as against its Ḥanafī counterpart, each partner may sue and be sued for the debts of the partnership or those due to it. The reason is that here the distinction between the *ḥuqūq* and *ḥukm* of a contract has not been drawn. In the Ḥanafī system, it is the dealing partner alone who can be sued.

The partner does not have the right to form another partnerhip or to invest the money by way of *muḍārabah.* This is something that is permitted by the Ḥanafīs, but the Ḥanbalīs have restricted it. They argue that this establishes some rights in the wealth of the partnership, and makes another person eligible for sharing the profits.[14] Apparently, they are not making a distinction here between admitting another person into part of the wealth of the firm.

Further, the partner cannot mix up his own wealth with that of the partnership. Finally, he does not have the right or authority of *istidānah.* If he raises credit beyond the limit of the capital of the partnership, he is personally liable.[15]

15.1.3 Sale and purchase on credit and liability of partners

The stipulations for sale and purchase on credit for the *'inān* partnership are also no different from those stipulated by the Ḥanafīs for the ordinary *'inān* based on wealth. The author of *al-Mughnī* states:

> If he buys on credit with the type of currency that he has or for a currency that is different, or buys on the basis of fungibles, and he possesses these, it is permitted. The reason is that when he buys for a species that he has, he will be paying with these and it will not lead to an excess payment (over the capital) for the partnership. If he does not have this currency, nor a fungible of the species with which he has purchased, or he has other property (*'arḍ*) and he buys property on credit through *istidānah,* then, the purchase is his own, as is its profit; he is liable for it himself, as this amounts to *istidānah* against the wealth of the *sharikah.*[16]

[14] Loc. cit.

[15] Loc. cit.

[16] Ibid. p. 23.

This is the case when he does not possess the authority to raise credit beyond the capital employed (*istidānah*). However, when his partner has granted him such authority, the author of *Kashshāf al-Qinā'* has the following to say:

> *Istidānah* is purchase by a partner in excess of the capital of the partnership, or with a currency whose species he does not possess besides the two currencies (*dīnārs* and *dirhams*) that it is customary to accept as a substitute for one another. If he does this, that is, indulges in *istidānah* against the partnership, then, the *ḍamān* (liability) for this *istidānah* is upon him in case a loss is made and the profit is for him if a profit is made, because their partnership has not taken place in this. Unless, his partner permits him to do so, in which case the permitted acts of trade will be undertaken in the ususal way.[17]

It is important to mention here that when a partner grants the authority for *istidānah* to the other partner in the Ḥanafite system, a new partnership is created on top of the first, and this is by way of *sharikat al-wujūh* for whatever credit is raised beyond the existing capital. It is a new venture on different terms between the partners. This situation has been acknowledged by the Mālikīs as well. Now, we have not been able to discover an explicit text about this in the Ḥanbalite texts, except what the author of *Kashshāf al-Qinā'* has said above: "Because their partnership has not been created in this."

We have stated earlier that the Ḥanbalite scholars are simply expressing opinions and they do not elaborate their principles. Let us apply their principles for them, or at least the Ḥanafite principles that appear to have been imported. When we apply these principles, we find that the statement of the author of *Kashshāf al-Qinā'*, "Because their partnership has not been created in this," becomes difficult to apply in practice.

The reason why the Ḥanafīs need to construct a separate, though related *sharikat al-wujūh* in this situation is that profits in a *sharikat al-wujūh* are shared in proportion to the *ḍamān*. If a share in excess of this is stipulated for one partner, it is simply ignored; the stipulation is not valid. In the ordinary *'inān* based upon wealth, however, an excess profit may be stipulated for one partner for whatever reason this is done. The rules of the two partnerships clash and they cannot

---

[17] Al-Bahūtī, *Kashshāf al-Qinā'*, vol. 3, p. 5.

be combined into a single partnership. The Ḥanafīs, therefore, need two separate partnerships combined into one.

When we examine the Ḥanbalī *sharikat al-wujūh,* as we will soon, we find that excess profits, different from proportional *ḍamān,* may be stipulated for one of the partners. This would mean that the principles of excess profits for one partner in the two types of partnership do not clash. Thus, there is no need to construct a separate partnership for the sake of *istidānah;* the same partnership can accept the further permission. The *sharikat al-wujūh* will merge into the *'inān* without clash.

The problem, however, is not that simple. The Ḥanbalīs cannot introduce *istidānah* in their concept of *'inān.* The reason is that the *sharikat al-wujūh* formed as an ordinary *'inān* in the Ḥanafī system is not based upon *kafālah.* In other words, a partner provides *ḍamān* for his own liability alone, and not that of his partner. He will be responsible for all debts in proportion to his own *ḍamān.* The share of his partner is not his liability. As compared to this, the Ḥanbalī *sharikat al-wujūh* is based upon the contract of *kafālah.* Introducing *istidānah* into their *'inān* partnership necessarily means intorducing *sharikat al-wujūh* into it, and doing this means introducing the contract of *kafālah* into the concept of *'inān.* The moment they do this, their *'inān* will no longer remain *'inān,* but will be converted into the Ḥanbalī *mufāwaḍah,* which is based upon *kafālah* and is somewhat similar to the Ḥanafī *'inān* based on *kafālah.*

The conclusion we draw from this is that while the Ḥanbalīs have adopted the ordinary *'inān* of the Ḥanafī school, they have not maintained the complete logic of the Ḥanafī principles. They should either accept the whole concept or create their own concept in the light of whatever principles they adopt.

Let us now turn to another problem pertaining to the powers of the partners. The author of *al-Mughnī* states: "If one of the partners terminates the agency of the other partner, the authority of this partner is terminated, and he cannot make any transaction, **except to the extent of his own share,** while the partner who has terminated his authority may transact in the entire wealth."[18]

This stipulation appears to have been taken directly from the Shāfi'ī concept of *'inān,* and we have discussed this problem at great length in the previous chapter. Restricting the rights of one partner

[18]Ibn Qudāmah, *Al-Mughnī,* vol. 5, p. 25; see also al-Bahūtī, *Kashshāf al-Qinā',* vol. 3, p. 506.

negates completely the concept of contract partnership and reduces it to a co-ownership where one of the co-owners has the right of disposal over property. This may be verified through their own statements. Thus, the meaning of *'inān* according to the Ḥanbalīs is: "It has been called *'inān* as the partners are equal in wealth as well as *taṣarruf* (right of disposal)." It also negates the statement: "On the condition that they participate with their wealth and work in it with their *abdān*."[19]

In fact, even in a co-ownership, one of the co-owners cannot undertake transactions in his own share, unless he is permitted by the other co-owners to do so. The reason is the concept of *mushā'*, which is an undivided or mingled share in every particle of the property.[20] The stipulation of this, more or less theoretical, condition makes the Ḥanbalī concept of *'inān* very shaky, because it lacks analytical consistency.

The main differences that we find between the Ḥanafī *'inān* and the Ḥanbalī form are as follows:

1. The distinction made by the Ḥanafīs with respect to the *ḥukm* and *ḥuqūq* of the contract are not to be found in the Ḥanbalī *'inān,* because of the different concept of agency. This creates a difference in who can be sued.

2. The authority of *istidānah* operates in the Ḥanafī concept by the construction of *sharikat al-wujūh* on top of *'inān.* There is no such provision in the Ḥanbalī system, and a closer examination shows that the introduction of *istidānah* is not possible in the Ḥanbalī *'inān,* because doing so converts it into a different partnership. This new form may be similar to the Ḥanbalī *mufāwaḍah* or the Ḥanafī *'inān* that includes *kafālah.*

3. The stipulation made with respect to the termination of the authority of one partner is incompatible with the concept of partnership. The permission for this partner with restricted

---

[19] Ibn Qudāmah, *al-Mughnī,* vol. 5, p. 16; al-Bahūtī, *Kashshāf al-Qinā',* vol. 3, p. 496.

[20] See section 1088 of the *Majallat al-Aḥkām al-'Adlīyah* for this point, as well as Ibn Nujaym, *al-Baḥr al-Rā'iq,* vol. 5, p. 167. We have already stated that there is some confusion on this issue in Islamic law. The confusion does not pertain to the sale by one co-owner of his share to a stranger, but whether he needs permission of the other co-owners. The law of pre-emption (*shuf'ah*) supports the assertion about taking permission, at least for some types of property.

authority to undertake transactions in the amount of his own share is not possible in a partnership.

15.2 The Ḥanbalī *Sharikat al-Wujūh*

The *sharikat al-wujūh* is defined as "the purchase on credit by two persons of something whose profits they share on the condition of half or third or the like, as agreed."[21] This is an independent partnership, and is not formed as *'inān* or *mufāwaḍah,* as is the case in the Ḥanafite system.

This partnership has the following features:

1. Each partner is the agent of the other in sale and purchase.

2. The partnership is supported by *kafālah bi al-thaman,* which means that for the liability of their payments, each partner stands surety for the other while being liable for his own share as well. Thus, each partner will be severally liable for the entire price.

3. The ownership of each partner is established in the thing purchased in accordance with the ratio agreed upon, whether or not the type of commodity to be purchased is determined. This pertains to the issue of *jahālah* on the basis of which al-Shāfi'ī rejected this partnership. The Ḥanbalīs maintain that this *jahālah* applies to independent *wakālah,* but when it is employed within a *sharikah* the *jahālah* is eliminated. The reasoning appears to be the same as that employed by al-Sarakhsī.[22] The Ḥanbalīs state that this is also present in *muḍārabah* and *'inān.*[23]

4. The profit is shared by the partners in accordance with ratios agreed upon, while the loss follows the ratio of ownership in what is purchased.[24] The Ḥanafīs, as pointed out earlier, maintain that profit is linked to *ḍamān* here and the stipulation of excess profit for one partner amounts to a violation of the principle of *al-kharāj bi al-ḍamān.*

---

[21] Al-Bahūtī, *Kashshāf al-Qinā',* vol. 3, p. 526.

[22] Al-Sarakhsī, *al-Mabsūṭ,* vol. 11, p. 153.

[23] Loc. cit.

[24] Loc. cit.

In other words, the basis for entitlement to profit is *ḍamān* and *ḍamān* requires that profits be shared in accordance with the liability to bear loss. The reason why profits are linked to *ḍamān* is that there is no capital in the possession of the partners and they will use their credit worthiness, which is the capacity to bear loss, that is, *ḍamān*. What reasoning do the Ḥanbalīs employ, then, to justify excess profits for one partner. Ibn Qudāmah says in *al-Mughnī:*

> As for *sharikat al-wujūh,* the general implication of the text of al-Khiraqī is that it is permissible to share according to what they have agreed upon, whether there is equality or disparity. This is analogy based on the opinion of the school, because all other forms of partnership provide for profit being shared in accordance with what is agreed upon; so also in this case. Further, because *sharikah* is formed on the basis of work and other things. What they have agreed upon is, therefore, permitted. Al-Qāḍī, however, said that profit is to be shared by them in accordance with the extent of their ownership in the purchased commodity, because entitlement to profit is on the basis of *ḍamān* and the partnership here has been constituted on this basis alone for they do not have capital and they share their work, and *ḍamān* does not accept profits. Excess in profits is, therefore, not permitted. Our argument is that it is a partnership in which there is work. It is, therefore, permitted according to the shares of profit they have agreed upon, as in all other partnerships. As for the opinion of al-Qāḍī that they do not have wealth on which they can work, we would say that they participate on the **condition that they will work in the future** on what they will acquire through their credit-worthiness. In all other partnerships work is done on things that are received in the future, so also here.[25]

Ibn Qudāmah appears to be saying the following in the above passage:

---

[25]Ibn Qudāmah, *al-Mughnī,* vol. 5, p. 32.

(a) That this partnership is not based on *ḍamān,* but on work. Work, therefore, is the reason for entitlement to profit, however, work here is not done on existing wealth as in *'inān,* but on future wealth that will be acquired through credit-worthiness.

(b) The Ḥanbalīs have formed a broad principle that entitlement to profit is based upon the agreement of the parties. As all other Ḥanbalī partnerships are enforcing this principle, and analogy constructed upon that principle implies that the same rule be applied here.

The reasoning adopted by the author of *al-Mughnī,* Ibn Qudāmah, does not appear to be very convincing in the light of the principles of Islamic law as well as in the light of their own methods of interpretation. The reasons are as follows:

(a) The first point is about the formation of the partnership. A partnership cannot be formed on the basis of wealth that will be acquired in the future. This involves *jahālah* and the Ḥanbalīs themselves require the wealth to be present and available for transactions. The other schools also stipulate *khalṭ* (mingling) of the wealth for the same reason.

(b) If buying and selling are treated as a form of work, and the partnership is based on that, then, why include *kafālah.* A partnership for work involves *ḍamān al-'amal,* which means liability for performance of work by either partner. Without the *ḍamān al-'amal* a partnership based upon work is not possible. *Ḍamān al-'amal,* however, is useless in a situation where the liability is for payment of a price and not the performance of work. Payment cannot be made with *ḍamān al-'amal.* The Ḥanbalīs are, therefore, forced to introduce *ḍamān al-thaman* or liability for making payment. This is called *kafālah bi al-thaman.* Claiming that this partnership is based on work would amount to saying that it is *ḍamān al-'amal* and not *ḍamān al-thaman* that is the real reason for sharing profits. This is not possible.

(c) Making a principle that entitlement to profit is based upon agreement of the parties and then performing analogy on this for *sharikat al-wujūh* comes into direct conflict with the principle of *al-kharāj bi al-ḍamān*. As the latter principle is based upon a tradition from the Prophet, while the former is a derived principle justified on the basis of analogy, it amounts to preferring analogy over a tradition and this is against the principles of interpretation ascertained by the Ḥanbalī school in *uṣūl al-fiqh*.

The opinon of al-Qāḍī, quoted by Ibn Qudāmah in the above passage, appears to be more in line with the principles of this school and also in conformity with the general principles of Islamic law.

5. The rest of the powers of a partner are almost the same as those for the partner in *'inān*.

In conclusion, therefore, we would say that except for some of the apparent defects, the Ḥanbalī *sharikat al-wujūh* is almost similar to the Ḥanafī form when it is based upon *kafālah* and *wakālah*.

15.3 *Sharikat al-Abdān* according to the Ḥanbalīs

15.3.1 Types of *sharikat al-abdān*

There are two types of partnership under this category in the Ḥanbalī school.

1. The participation of two or more persons in what they accept for their physical labour and are liable for through their work. This is a valid partnership even if the professions are different.

   (a) Similarity of prfessions is not stipulated in it.

   (b) Whatever work they accept, or what one of them accepts, becomes their joint liability, and they are both liable for it, and both have to perform it. This is *ḍamān al-'amal*. It should be remembered here that in the absence of *kafālah* in this contract, the Hanafīs use *istiḥsān* to make both liable. It is not clear what principle is employed by the Ḥanbalīs for the creation of joint liability. Perhaps, it is the different concept of *wakālah* employed by them.[26]

[26] That is, a concept of agency closer to the modern concept and different from agency employed by the Ḥanafīs that makes a distinction between the *ḥukm* of a contract and its *ḥuqūq*.

   i. If one of them says that he will accept the work and his partner should perform the work, it is valid.
   ii. Each one of them has the right to claim wages from the client irrespective of who accepted the work. The client is absolved of the liability if he pays to one of them.
   iii. The liability for loss of property is joint, unless one of them will be made personally liable. The reason is that the partners are not sureties for each other.

2. The second type of partnership is in the acquisition of free goods like grass and firewood, and even in making raids for goods on the Dār al-Ḥarb. This partnership is permitted by the Ḥanbalīs, but has not been allowed by the other schools on the principle that there can be no partnership in personal physical labour. The Ḥanbalīs apparently ignore this rule. At the same time they do not permit a partnership between two brokers, because brokerage does not accept *wakālah,* as it pertains to another's wealth for which there is no *ḍamān*.

15.3.2 The use of implements and property

A partner is not entitled to excess profit for the employment of his tools and implements. The author of *Kashshāf al-Qinā'* states: "A partner is not entitled to any compensation for the employment of tools or houses, because these are being used in joint work. They are to be treated in the same way as beasts of burden on which they load what they are jointly liable for, and their liablity is also joint.[27]

15.3.3 Vitiation of *sharikat al-abdān*

The author of *Kashshāf al-Qinā'* states:

> If the partnership is vitiated for some reason, like *jahālah* about profit sharing, the receipts are divided among them in accordance with the work done, and in accordance with the wages of a house or a beast of burden. The reason is that compensation has been taken in lieu of profits. It is,

[27] Al-Bahūtī, *Kashshāf al-Qinā',* vol. 3, p. 529.

therefore, necessary to divide it among them proportionately. It is as if they had rented out something for one wage.[28]

15.4 The Contract of *Mufāwaḍah* according to the Ḥanbalīs

The author of *Kashshāf* says: "In its literal meaning, *mufāwaḍah* is participation in each thing."[29] It is of two types according to the Ḥanbalīs.

1. That they form a partnership for sharing what each one of them receives through inheritance, or through finding a treasure or found property, and each one is liable for whatever is due from the other by way of *arsh* for offences or usurpation and all kinds of *kafālah*. This partnership is void according to the Ḥanbalīs.[30] The implication here is that the Ḥanafīs approve this partnership, as was stated by al-Shāfi'ī, but this is not true as has been discussed in considerable detail under the topic of the Ḥanafī *mufāwaḍah*.

2. The second type of *mufāwaḍah* is valid according to the Ḥanbalīs. This *mufāwaḍah* is formed by combining all the other types of partnership, that is, *'inān, abdān* and *wujūh*. The partnership is considered valid, because all the other types are valid individually.[31]

What kind of partnership is formed in this round about way, as compared to the Ḥanafite *mufāwaḍah?* First, it is a partnership that is formed on the basis of *māl* (wealth). Second, it is a partnership that is based upon the contract of *wakālah*. Third, this partnership can include the contract of *kafālah* either initially in the contract or as part of *istidānah*. Fourth, each partner becomes a surety for the other partner, besides being his agent and principal. Fifth, each partner can be sued for the debts of the partnership, and on the

---

[28] Ibid., vol. 3, p. 529.

[29] Loc. cit.

[30] Ibn Qudāmah, *al-Mughnī*, vol. 5, p. 30; al-Bahūtī, *Kashshāf al-Qinā'*, vol. 3, p. 531.

[31] Ibn Qudāmah, *al-Mughnī*, vol. 5, p. 30; al-Bahūtī, *Kashshāf al-Qinā'*, vol. 3, p. 531.

basis of the Ḥanbalī contract of *wakālah* he can sue for the recovery of debts owed by third parties.

This partnership is identical to the Ḥanafī *'inān* formed on the basis of wealth, when it includes the contract of *kafālah.* Thus, while trying to form a *mufāwaḍah,* the Ḥanbalī jurists have accidentally formed an *'inān* that includes *kafālah.* The reason is that this partnership does not stipulate equality and proportionality like the Ḥanafī *mufāwaḍah.*

Having said that, we may note that this partnership may be closer to the modern forms of partnership, especially the general partnership. The reason is that it permits a partner to sue for the partnership debts. The Ḥanafī form does not due to the different concept of agency.

Chapter 16

Comparison Between the Schools

In the previous chapters we have had the opportunity to study the basic principles of Islamic law of business organization. We have also studied the first category of partnerships in the light of these principles. During this study, we have seen that the Ḥanafī law on partnerships is more developed and elaborate as compared to the other three schools. The distinctive feature of the Ḥanafī system is that all the principles established for this branch of the law have been applied with precision keeping in view the demands of analytical consistency. As compared to this school, the Mālikī and Shāfi'ī schools have considerably restricted forms of partnership law. In fact, we were forced to conclude that the Shāfi'ī law of partnership is almost non-existent and barely extends beyond co-ownership. The basic reason for this is the importance given to *jahālah* (uncertainty) and a reluctance to extend the meanings found in the texts, especially the traditions. Wherever al-Shāfi'ī felt that agency involves *jahālah,* he has denied validity to a legal form. Another reason is that most of the Shāfi'ī law of partnership has been built around co-ownership. His concept of *'inān* consists of simple additions to the concept of co-ownership. Further, in both Mālikī and Shāfi'ī laws, the credit sale becomes extremely difficult to undertake, and it is well known that modern transactions would become highly cumbersome without this facility. Mālikī and Shāfi'ī laws can, therefore, be practiced in very small local markets.

The Ḥanbalī law, surpisingly, is much more developed than the Shāfi'ī and Mālikī schools. In fact, it comes quite close to the Ḥanafī law. A major difference between the Ḥanafī and Ḥanbalī schools lies in the identification and application of general principles. The Ḥanbalī law is more opinion oriented, and sometimes it is not clear what principles are being relied upon for their legal opinions and how these are applied. In addition to this, the flexibility provided by the Ḥanbalī jurists in some of their opinions is taken away when they follow two opinions from the Mālikī and the Shāfi'ī schools for no apparent reason. The first concerns the Shāfi'ī view that the agency granted to one of the partners can be taken away by the other partner, but he can continue to transact to the extent of his own share. This negates the concept of contract partnership, and is possible in co-ownership alone. The other opinion is about the restrictions placed on the credit sale.

The Ḥanafī law is not only much more elaborate and developed, the principles applied are also identified with clarity and are applied with great precision. This helps the reader to understand the rationale behind the law and even to judge what the law ought to be in a new situation. In our study, the importance of the Ḥanafī school has been clearly visible. The major reason for this may be that the Ḥanafī school has had a greater opportunity and exposure where practice is concerned, and this may have forced it to develop its law. The relationship of this law to practice is clearly visible in the statements of the Ḥanafī jurists.

One major distinction between the Ḥanafī school and the other three schools is in the concept of agency. In this respect, the Ḥanafī concept differs from modern law as well. Abraham L. Udovitch has tried to compare the Ḥanafī concept with the Roman concept of the sociius. The distinction is that the Ḥanafī school had a developed theory of agency, whereas the Roman law did not. What is surprising is that the Ḥanafite distinction between the *ḥukm* and *ḥuqūq* of a contract can provide great flexibility to modern scholars in the designing of new forms of business organization as well as financial instruments. This concept has been explained in this study as well as in the study on corporations to propose new forms of business organization that take into account the principles of Islamic law.

16.1 The Forms of Partnership Approved by the Schools

Our study shows that out of the 12 or more forms of partnership approved by the Ḥanafī school in the first category, the Shāfi'ī school approves only one, and that too does not go beyond co-ownership. The *sharikat al-'inān* approved by the Shāfi'īs is actually a somewhat extended form of co-ownership. The Mālikī school approves only two of the partnerships approved by the Ḥanafīs. What they call *'inān*, however, is again an extended form of co-ownership, while their *mufāwaḍah* is nothing but the simplest form of *'inān* approved by the Ḥanafīs and that too with some restrictions about the sale on credit by the partners. The Ḥanbalī school approves 4 out of the 12 forms permitted by the Ḥanafīs. Their *'inān* is similar to the ordinary *'inān* based upon *wakālah* and wealth approved by the Ḥanafī school. Their *sharikat al-a'māl* is the same as the simple Ḥanafī *'inān* based upon *wakālah* and work. Their *mufāwaḍah* is the Ḥanafī *'inān* with *kafālah* having wealth as its subject-matter. Their *sharikat al-wujūh* involves *kafālah* and is, therefore, like the Ḥanafī *'inān* with *kafālah* based on credit-worthiness. All these comparisons were made in the preceding chapters of this study at some length, however, the results have been summarized as follows for easy reference.

16.1.1 Classification according to the Ḥanafī school

There are primarily two categories of partnerships in Islamic law. In the first category all partners participate in work and management, while in the second category management or labour is undertaken by one partner alone. The second category, according to most jurists, includes *muzāra'ah* and *musāqāh* as well besides *muḍārabah*. The second category will be discussed in the next part; here we are concerned with the first category of partnerships.

The first category of partnerships according to the Ḥanafīs is classified as follows:
The First Category of Partnerships

1. *'Inān* with *wakālah* for general trade:
    (a) when the subject-matter is wealth (*māl*);
    (b) when the subject-matter is (*'amal*);
    (c) when the subject-matter is credit-worthiness (*wujūh*).
2. *'Inān* with *wakālah* for a specific trade:
    (a) when the subject-matter is wealth (*māl*);
    (b) when the subject-matter is (*'amal*);
    (c) when the subject-matter is credit-worthiness (*wujūh*).
3. *'Inān* with *wakālah* and *kafālah* for general trade:
    (a) when the subject-matter is wealth (*māl*);

(b) when the subject-matter is (*'amal*);

(c) when the subject-matter is credit-worthiness (*wujūh*).

4. *'Inān* with *wakālah* and *kafālah* for a specific trade:

(a) when the subject-matter is wealth (*māl*);

(b) when the subject-matter is (*'amal*);

(c) when the subject-matter is credit-worthiness (*wujūh*).

5. *Mufāwaḍah* for general trade (based on *wakālah* and *kafālah*).

(a) when the subject-matter is wealth (*māl*);

(b) when the subject-matter is (*'amal*);

(c) when the subject-matter is credit-worthiness (*wujūh*).

6. *Mufāwaḍah* for a specific trade (based on *wakālah* and *kafālah*).

(a) when the subject-matter is wealth (*māl*);

(b) when the subject-matter is (*'amal*);

(c) when the subject-matter is credit-worthiness (*wujūh*).

In the *'inān* with *wakālah* as well as *kafālah,* we can derive further types depending upon the agency granted, that is, whether the agency is general or special. The same is true of *muḍārabah.* When the *fuqahā',* like al-Sarakhsī, use the term *sharikah 'āmmah,* they usually mean a partnership dealing with all types of trade. Even in such a partnership it is possible that the agency be special, which would mean that the partners are permitted to perform certain specific acts and not others. For additional acts, they will have to seek special permission from the other partners. For example, through a special agency sale and purchase may be permitted, but for cash only and not for credit. For selling on credit, the partners may have to seek further permission. When the agency is general, permission is not needed for the credit sale, according to the Ḥanafī school. As partnership needs a general agency with respect to its business, and this what the Ḥanafīs feel too, we have not further subdivided the types of this ground. The possibility, however, is present.

16.1.2 Classification according to the Shāfi'ī school

The Shāfi'ī school permits only one of the above forms and that too with severe restrictions. The classification according to this school is as follows:

The First Category of Partnerships

1. *'Inān* with *wakālah* for a specific trade:

   (a) when the subject-matter is wealth (*māl*);

In reality, the *'inān* partnership permitted by the Shāfi'ī school is loaded with such restrictions that it is no better than a co-ownership. For example, a credit purchase is possible only when both partners are present for concluding the contract. This can be achieved in a co-ownership (*sharikat al-milk*) as well. Further, according to the Shāfi'īs, one partner can terminate the agency of the other partner. This is contrary to the principles of partnership and is only possible in a co-ownership. There are many other restrictions, and these have been explained in the preceding chapters on various occasions.

16.1.3 Classification according to the Mālikī school

The Mālikī school does a little better than the Shāfi'ī school insofar as it permits the *'inān* with *wakālah* for general trade as well, but calls it by the name of *mufāwaḍah.*
The First Category of Partnerships

1. *'Inān* with *wakālah* for general trade:

   (a) when the subject-matter is wealth (*māl*). This partnership is called by the name of *mufāwaḍah* by the Mālikīs.

2. *'Inān* with *wakālah* for a specific trade:

   (a) when the subject-matter is wealth (*māl*). This is the prototype for the Shāfi'ī *'inān,* and in reality is a co-ownership.

   (b) when the subject-matter is (*'amal*). This partnership is approved independently and is not considered a type of *'inān* or of *mufāwaḍah.* We have shown it here for the sake of comparison.

This shows that the only real partnership approved by the Mālikī school is what they call *mufāwaḍah,* which when analyzed turns out to be the Ḥanafī *'inān* for general trade, but with a special agency. The reason is that for a credit purchase, the Mālikīs also insist that the partners be present. If they are not present, and the transaction is undertaken by one partner on his own, it becomes a *sharikat al-dhimam,* which is prohibited in their view.

Classification according to the Ḥanbalī school

The Ḥanbalī school is the most interesting. Surprisingly, the partnerships it permits appear to be quite flexible, considering the fact that they do not make a distinction between the *ḥukm* of a transaction and its *ḥuqūq*. They permit the following types:[1]

The First Category of Partnerships

1. *'Inān* with *wakālah* for general trade:
   (a) when the subject-matter is wealth (*māl*);
   (b) when the subject-matter is (*'amal*);
2. *'Inān* with *wakālah* and *kafālah* for general trade:
   (a) when the subject-matter is wealth (*māl*). This is called *mufāwaḍah* by the Ḥanbalī school.
   (b) when the subject-matter is credit-worthiness (*wujūh*).

With the introduction of *kafālah* into two partnerships, the Ḥanbalī partnerships become quite flexible. Yet, it is somewhat shocking to find that *wilāyat al-istidānah* cannot be introduced into the regular *'inān* partnership. This is shocking, because the rest of the partnership is quite similar to the Ḥanafī *'inān.* A closer examination reveals that the Ḥanbalīs do not apply their principles consistently. In fact, the reader gets the feeling that they have borrowed the forms mainly from the Ḥanafīs and have changed the Ḥanafī stipulations that were objected to by al-Shāfi'ī. The situation is further aggravated when the Ḥanbalī jurists for some odd reason suddenly import a provision of Shāfi'ī law that one partner can terminate the agency of the other and the partnership may still continue. In reality, this knocks out the concept of contract partnership and participation from their law.

IN CONCLUSION, we would like to state two major points with reference to further research on the subject as well as modern applications.

1. The general trend of research in Islamic law is to undertake comparative studies of the major schools of law without

[1] We have not shown *'inān* for specific trade here, but this may be possible for the Ḥanbalī school. The Ḥanbalī texts, however, do not spell it out.

first understanding each school separately. In our view, a better method would be to study each school separately and then bring the results together in a comparative study. This method has been exhibited in our study so far. The advantages have been obvious. This method has made us realize that it would be impossible to make a statement such as this: "The *mufāwaḍah* partnership was approved by the Ḥanafīs, Mālikīs and Ḥanbalīs." A statement such as this, often found in modern books, is totally meaningless and without foundation when examined in the light of our conclusions.

In the next part of our study, we shall not adopt the method we have followed so far. Thus, *muḍārabah* will be studied following the usual methods of comparison, that is, all the schools together. Why? There are two reasons for this. First, *muḍārabah* is a very simple contract and does not involve the complexity found in the other forms. Second, the contract of *muḍārabah,* in our view, is not a very useful contract as far as modern applications are concerned. We say this despite its adoption by modern scholars and by some of the legal systems. In our view, the whole law of business organization should have been studied more deeply before jumping into the *muḍārabah* arrangements. This has not been done. Perhaps, the experts were wary of the lack of limited liability for the investor in the regular forms. It appears that the forms adopted are going to be shortlived or will carry the name of *muḍārabah* without its legal form.

2. The detail, complexity and precision of the Ḥanafī school in the area of business law makes it the obvious candidate for leading us to modern applications. This is the school that we are going to lean on most in the last part of the study in which we will attempt to present new forms of partnership for Islamic law. The same approach has been adopted in a separate study of the corporations in which a new Islamic model of the corporation has been suggested that can be implemented with minor amendments to the existing structure. Some of the opinions of the Ḥanbalī school will also be employed, whereever they are found to be compatible and the use of the underlying principles is clear and analytically consistent.

Comparison of Basic Types

Ḥanafī Partnership Forms	Mālikīs	Shāfi'īs	Ḥanbalīs
Sharikat al-milk	*'inān*	*'inān*	*milk*
'Inān with *wakālah* plus *māl*	*mufāwaḍah*	none	*'inān*
'Inān with *wakālah* plus *'amal*	*abdān*	none	*abdān*
'Inān with *wakālah* plus *wujūh*	none	none	none
'Inān with *kafālah* and *wakālah* plus *māl*	none	none	*mufāwaḍah*
'Inān with *kafālah* and *wakālah* plus *'amal*	none	none	none
'Inān with *kafālah* and *wakālah* plus *wujūh*	none	none	*wujūh*
mufāwaḍah with *kafālah* and *wakālah* plus *māl*	none	none	none
mufāwaḍah with *kafālah* and *wakālah* plus *'amal*	none	none	none
mufāwaḍah with *kafālah* and *wakālah* plus *wujūh*	none	none	none

Part IV

The Second Category of Partnerships in *Fiqh*

The traditional law of business organization has been divided, for purposes of this study, into two categories. Both are categories of the contract partnership (*sharikat al-'aqd*). *Sharikah* that is not the result of a contract is called *sharikat al-milk* (co-ownership) by the jurists.

In the first category of partnerships, management and participation is stipulated for all partners, whether or not all partners actually participate in the management. In the second category, management of the firm is stipulated for one of the partners and the other partners are simply investors who share the profits in return for the capital they have provided. The investors have full and unlimited liability for the debts of the partnership, but the worker has no liability. This is the exact opposite of the limited partnership found in the law whose early prototype was called the *commenda.*

The first category of partnerships have been discussed in the previous part. This part is devoted to the second category. It has been divided into two chapters. The first chapter in this part will deal with *muḍārabah* according to all the schools. The second chapter will deal with *musāqah* and *muzāra'ah.*

The contract of *muḍārabah* has gained importance in modern applications, because it provides limited or no liability for the worker or the managing partner. This makes it attractive for banks and financial institutions that hope to fill the role of the worker. During the discussion of this contract, the shortcomings of the contract will be pointed out, and it will be shown that it may not be as useful as it is thought to be.

Chapter 17

Muḍārabah or *Qirāḍ*

The discussion of *muḍārabah* has been divided into the following four sections:

1. Definition of *muḍārabah,* its validity and elements.
2. Types of *muḍārabah* and the implications of its unqualified contract.
3. Conditions of *muḍārabah.*
4. Liability of the partners and the termination or dissolution of *muḍārabah.*

17.1 Definition of *Muḍārabah* and its Legal Validity

17.1.1 Definition of *muḍārabah*

The term *muḍārabah* been derived from *ḍarb fī al-arḍ,* which means journeying though the land seeking the bounty of Allah.[1] As a result of his work and travel, the *muḍārib* becomes entitled to part of the profits of the venture. According to the terminology used by the jurists of Medina, *muḍārabah* is also called *muqāraḍah* or *qirāḍ.* Al-Kāsānī says: "Likewise the term *muqāraḍah,* in the terminology of the jurists of Medina. is explicit in expressing this meaning. They used to call *muḍārabah* by the name *muqāraḍah,* just as they used to call *ijārah* by the name of *bay'* (sale)."[2] The term *muqāraḍah,* in turn. is derived from the word *qarḍ,* which means refraining or abstaining from something. The venture was, therefore, called *muqāraḍah* as the

[1] Al-Kāsānī, *Badā'i' al-Ṣanā'i',* vol. 8, p. 3588.

[2] Ibid., vol. 8, p. 3589.

rabb al-māl refrained from the right of disposal in his own wealth and delivered it to the *muḍārib* (worker).

It is also called *mu'āmalah* by some insofar as it comprises sale (*bay'*) transactions. *Mu'āmalah* is a word that includes both sale and purchase. Al-Kāsānī says: "*Mu'āmalah* is a term that includes both sale and purchase, and this is exactly the purpose of this contract."[3]

Al-Sarakhsī choosing between these terms says: "We selected the first term (that is, *muḍārabah*) as it corresponds with what is in the Qur'ān, 'And others who journey through the land (*yaḍribūna fi'l-arḍ*) seeking the bounty of Allah,'[4] that is, journeying for trade."[5] Abraham L. Udovitch, trying to find an equivalent in Western law for *muḍārabah,* has used the word *commenda* to convey the meaning.[6] In our view, this is not an appropriate term for *muḍārabah* insofar as it is used for exactly the opposite concept. In a *commenda,* it is usually the investor who has limited liability, and losses in excess of the investment are to be borne by the worker. In this meaning the term *commenda* may be considered the prototype for a limited liability partnership found in modern law.

In the early sections of this study, it was pointed out that the word *sharikah* is applied in two meanings. The first is the mingling of assets (*khalṭ*) that does not result from a contract, and leads to co-ownership. The second type of *sharikah* arises from a contract. Thus, when we use the term *sharikah* in the second meaning, we mean thereby the contract of partnership and there is no need for the actual physical mingling of capitals.

While defining a *muḍārabah,* those jurists who focused on the first meaning defined it as "a participation in profits." They chose this because they found the idea of mingling (*khalṭ*) in profits alone, as wealth cannot mingle with work. This definition is popular among modern writers, but it defines a very broad category and could be a definition for all types of partnership that we have studied in the previous part. Thus, *sharikat al-a'māl* is also a participation in profits, and these are the profits arising out of labor, and there is no other type of mingling in it as may be required for a *sharikah.* Likewise, the *sharikat al-wujūh,* but in that there is participation in transactions.

---

[3] Loc. cit.

[4] Qur'ān, 73 : 20.

[5] Al-Sarakhsī, *al-Mabsūṭ,* vol. 22, p. 18.

[6] See generally Abraham L. Udovitch, *Partnership and Profit in Medieval Islam,* and especially the chapter on *Qirāḍ*.

Those who wanted to distinguish *muḍārabah* from the other types, within this broad definition, added the words: "with wealth from one side and work from the other." Al-Qudūrī said: "*Muḍārabah* is a contract for participation in profits with wealth from one partner and work by the other."[7] The same definition is found in *al-Hidāyah:* "*Muḍārabah* is a contract for partnership with wealth from one side—and he means thereby participation in profits, for which the entitlement is through wealth from one side—and work from the other side—and there is no *muḍārabah* without it."[8]
There are two objections to such definitions:

1. The purpose of the contracts of partnership is not participation (mingling) in profits, rather the purpose is the acquisition of profit through joint work with or without wealth and, then, it is the division of these profits after acquisition. The author of *Fatḥ al-Qadīr,* commenting on the text of the *Hidāyah,* says: "His statement—he (a partner) may make an investment by way of *muḍārabah*—means that loss in partnership is the liability of the partner and not that of the *muḍārib,* thus, the *sharikah* includes the *muḍārabah.* From Abū Ḥanīfah there is a narration that he does not have this right (of investing in a *muḍārabah*) as it is in itself a type of *sharikah* in profits. The correct view, however, is the first, and it is the original narration, because participation (mingling) in profits is not its purpose rather it is the acquisition of profit."[9]

2. Contract partnerships of the first category also involve participation in profits, as stated, but the meaning of participation is found in them whether or not actual profit is realized. As for a *muḍārabah,* the definition cannot be applied to it, except after the realization of profit. What should we call it when there is no profit?

This difficulty of defining *muḍārabah* is not visible in the works of the Ḥanbalī jurists. Ibn Qudāmah, commenting on a definition by al-Khiraqī, says: "Our companions have mentioned four cases of permissible partnership. We have mentioned one of these and this the *sharikat al-abdān.* Three of these types are left that have been

[7]See the chapter on *muḍārabah* in al-Qudūrī, *Mukhtaṣar.*

[8]Al-Marghinānī, *al-Hidāyah,* vol. 3, p. 202.

[9]Ibn al-Humām, *Fatḥ al-Qadīr,* vol. 5, p. 26.

mentioned by al-Khiraqī in five types, three of which are types of *muḍārabah,* which is participation by two persons with the wealth of one, or two persons with their wealth, or the wealth of both and the body of one person."[10] He says again: "The participation of a body and wealth, and this is *muḍārabah.*"[11] It is obvious here that the purpose of such participation is the acquisition of this profit and its sharing.

A similar definition is found in the *Majallat al-Aḥkām al-'Adlīyah:* "*Muḍārabah* is a type of *sharikah* in which wealth is contributed from one side and labour from the other side."[12]

The Shāfi'īs define it as follows: "*Qirāḍ* and *muḍārabah* have as their legal subject-matter a contract comprising agency by the owner to another by giving him wealth so that he may trade with it and share its profits."[13]

As for the Mālikīs, it is stated by al-Khirashī in his comments on the *Mukhtaṣar* by Sīdī Khalīl as follows: "The author has defined it as: '*qirāḍ* is agency for trading in delivered cash for a part of the profits if their extent is known.'"[14]

The main idea in the discussion of these definitions is that the concept of *sharikah* as mingling (*khalṭ*) of things is not verified or visible in the *muḍārabah.* It is the contract itself that is important. The contract provides for capital from one side and labor from the other, but the purpose of the contract is acquisition of profit and its sharing.

17.1.2 Legal justification of *muḍārabah*

The legal evidences employed by the jurists from the sources are as follows:

1. **The Book:** The verse used by al-Sarakhsī, as indicated earlier, is: "And others who journey through the earth (*yaḍribūna fi al-arḍ*) seeking the bounty of Allah."[15]

---

[10] Ibn Qudāmah, *al-Mughnī,* vol. 5, p. 14.

[11] Loc. cit.

[12] *Majallah,* §1404.

[13] Al-Ramlī, *Nihāyat al-Muḥtāj,* vol. 5, p. 218.

[14] Al-Khirashī, *Mukhtasar Sīdī Khalīl,* vol. 6, p. 203.

[15] Qur'ān: 73 : 20

2. **The Sunnah:** The jurists rely on the contract of *muḍārabah* concluded by the Prophet (peace be upon him) with Khadījah prior to his marriage as a result of which he travelled to Syria. The Prophet is also reported (by Ibn Mājah)[16] to have said: "There is great blessing in three things: "The credit sale, *muqāraḍah,* and mixing wheat and barley for domestic consumption not sale."

   There are reports about *muḍārabah* transactions by the Companions as well, but some of these reports are considered weak by the traditionists.[17]

3. **Consensus (Ijmā'):** Some of the Ḥanafī jurists have reported the *ijmā'* of the Companions about *mudārabah,* although these are cases of *ijmā' sukūtī.*[18]

4. **Analogy (Qiyās):** Al-Kāsānī says: "As far as analogy is concerned, it is not permissible, because it is hiring for unknown wages, in fact for non-existent wages. The work too is unknown. We have, however, given up this analogy in favor of the evidences in the Book, the *Sunnah* and *ijmā'.*"[19] This means they had recourse to *istiḥsān.* As for the Shāfi'īs, they permit it through analogy on the contract of *musāqāh* for which there is a tradition.[20]

5. **Economic necessity:** Al-Sarakhsī says: "[It is permitted,] because the people have a need for this contract. The owner of wealth may not have the opportunity for a profitable investment, while the person who has such an opportunity may not have wealth, and profit is acquired through both, that is, wealth and the ability to transact. In permitting this contract, the goals of both are achieved."[21]

---

[16] Al-Shawkānī states that in the *isnād* of this tradition there are two unknown persons. Al-Shawkānī, *Nayl al-Awṭār,* vol. 5, p. 301.

[17] See al-Zayla'ī, *Tabyīn al-Ḥaqā'iq,* vol. 5, pp. 52–53; Ibn Hajar, *Talkhīṣ al-Ḥabīr,* vol. 3, p. 85.

[18] See al-Kāsānī, *Badā'i' al-Ṣanā'i',* vol. 8, p. 3587; *al-'Ināyah* on the margin of Ibn al-Humām, *Fath al-Qadīr,* vol. 7, p. 59.

[19] Al-Kāsānī, *Badā'i' al-Ṣanā'i',* vol. 8, p. 3589.

[20] Al-Ramlī, *Nihāyat al-Muḥtāj,* vol. 5, p. 218.

[21] Al-Sarkhsī, *al-Mabsūṭ,* vol. 22, p. 19.

17.1.3 The *rukn* (element) of the contract of *muḍārabah*

Its single element (*rukn*), according to the Ḥanafīs, is offer and acceptance. As for the majority schools, the contract has several elements. This difference goes back to their different views on the theory of contracts. Thus, according to the Shāfi'īs, "the contract has six elements: the two parties to the contract, work, profit, wealth, and the form (offer and acceptance)."[22]

Offer and acceptance are permitted with words that indicate its meaning, whether or not the words *muḍārabah*, or *muqāraḍah*, or *mu'āmalah*, or their derivatives, are used. The express form takes place when the *rabb al-māl* (investor) says to the *muḍārib* (worker): "Take this wealth by way of *muḍārabah* (or *muqāraḍah* or *mu'āmalah*) on the condition that the profits will be shared by us equally," or that "you will have a third of the profits and I will take two thirds," and so on. The worker then says, "I have accepted," or whatever conveys the same meaning, like "I will take it" or "I agree." A form that is not express occurs when the *rabb al-māl* says, for example, "Take this wealth and trade with it so that the profit is shared by us." The worker then accepts it. The reason for acceptance of such forms is that the consideration is for the meaning of the statements rather than the words used.[23] It may, however, be remembered that Islamic law favours the objective theory of contracts and the outward meanings of words are adhered to.

Explaining such forms, al-Sarakhsī says:

> If he says, "Take this and trade with it and whatever sustenance Allah grants from it will be shared equally by us," but he does not mention the word *muḍārabah,* then, it is a valid *muḍārabah,* because the meaning of *muḍārabah* is expressed clearly, even though the word has not been used nor has the purpose been identified. Likewise, the contract is concluded with an express meaning. For this contract there is no specific implication that the word *muḍārabah* may indicate with respect to its *ḥukm* as against the term *mufāwaḍah* is the *sharikat al-mufāwaḍah,* as we have elaborated in the book on *sharikah.* Similarly, if he says, "Take this 1000 and work with it on the condition that you will get one-half of the

[22] Al-Ramlī, *Nihāyat al-Muḥtāj,* vol. 5, p. 219.

[23] Al-Kāsānī, *Badā'i' al-Ṣanā'i',* vol. 8, p. 3588.

> profits," or a part of ten parts, it is permitted. The reason is that the *muḍārib* becomes entitled to his share on the basis of a condition and this condition of his share has been expressed here.
>
> If he says, "Take this 1000 and work for one-half," or he says, "for a third," it is permissible *muḍārabah* by way of *istiḥsān*.[24] It is not permitted by way of analogy due to the absence of a specification as to the person who is entitled to one-half or a third.[25]

As for the Shāfiʿīs, they agree with the Ḥanafīs on most of the issues in this, but they permit these things by way of analogy and not *istiḥsān*.[26] The Mālikīs maintain that there is no need for an express form for this contract, and this is also obvious from their definition of *qirāḍ*.[27] The Ḥanbalī opinion is expressed by Ibn Qudāmah as follows: "It is concluded with the words *muḍārabah* and *qirāḍ,* because these are words that are specified for it. It is also concluded with words that express their meaning, because the purpose of the figurative use will be seen as in the case of the word *tamlīk* in sale."[28]

17.2 Types of *Muḍārabah* and the Implications of its Unqualified Contract

17.2.1 The implications of the contract of *muḍārabah*

As in the case of *ʿinān* and *mufāwaḍah,* what is meant by the implications of the contract of *muḍārabah* is the meaning and accompanying conditions that are established by the mere use of the word *muḍārabah,* without the stipulation of additional conditions. Al-Sarakhsī says: "This contract has no *ḥukm* that is indicated by the word *muḍārabah* as against the word *mufāwaḍah* in (the conclusion of) *sharikat al-mufāwaḍah*."[29] On another occasion he says:

---

[24]Here the usage of the people (*ʿurf*) will be taken into account.

[25]Al-Sarakhsī, *al-Mabsūṭ,* vol. 22, p. 24. See also al-Kāsānī, *Badāʾiʿ al-Ṣanāʾiʿ*, vol. 8, p. 3589.

[26]Al-Ramlī, *Nihāyat al-Muḥtāj,* vol. 5, p. 226.

[27]Al-Dusūqī, *Ḥāshiyah,* vol. 3, p. 517.

[28]Ibn Qudāmah, *al-Mughnī,* vol. 5, p. 27; al-Bahūtī, *Kashshāf al-Qināʿ*, vol. 3, p. 508.

[29]Al-Sarakhsī, *al-Mabsūṭ,* vol. 22, p. 24.

> This contract has several *aḥkām* with respect to various contracts. If the investor delivers the capital to the *muḍārib*, then, he is an *amīn* like the custodian of a deposit. If he enters into transactions with it, then, he is an agent (*wakīl*) with a right of recourse to the *rabb al-māl* like and agent. If there is profit (from these transactions) he becomes his partner in the profits. If the contract is vitiated, it is converted into a vitiated *ijārah* so that the *muḍārib* will be entitled to reasonable wages for his work. If the *muḍārib* violates the stipulations, he becomes a usurper and is liable for compensating the investment. The purpose, however, of this contract is participation in profits, and each condition that tends to terminate this partnership in profits between them when such profit has appeared, then, such condition annuls the contract, because it destroys the obligatory purpose of the contract.[30]

We will use this statement to elaborate the *aḥkām* of *muḍārabah* so as to show how the underlying contracts govern it during its various stages.

The *muḍārib* as *amīn*

The *muḍārib* becomes a trustee (*amīn*) for the capital entrusted to him by way of *muḍārabah*. This means that he should have taken possession of the capital with the permission of the owner and not as compensation in some kind of exchange (*bay'*) nor as a security arrangement like mortgage. Thus, if this capital is destroyed in his possession without there being any negligence on his part, there is no liability for him.[31]

---

[30]Ibid., vol. 22, p. 19. A similar statement was made by Ṣadr al-Sharī'ah in *Sharḥ al-Wiqāyah* on the margin of *Kashf al-Ḥaqā'iq Sharḥ Kanz al-Daqā'iq*, vol. 2, p. 134. This statement has also been recorded by al-Jurjānī in his *Ta'rīfāt*: "*Muḍārabah* is derived from *ḍarb*, which is traveling in the land. Technically, it is a contract for partnership in profits with wealth contributed by one person and labor by another. Primarily, it amounts to a deposit, becomes agency on the commencement of work, a partnership on the emergence of profit, *ghaṣb* when the stipulations are violated, *biḍā'ah* if all the profit is stipulated for the investor, and it is *qarḍ* if it is stipulated for the *muḍārib*." It may be stated here that in the last case, it will become a contract of compassion, because the *qarḍ* can only be a gracious loan (*qarḍ ḥasan*) that does not have a fixed period of repayment.

[31]Ibn 'Ābidīn, *Ḥāshiyah*, vol. 5, p. 647.

Accordingly, if he purchases something with capital that is similar to what is he has accepted by way of *muḍārabah,* and he does not mention whether this is for the *muḍārabah* or it is on his personal account, then, the his statement will be accepted.[32] As for the Shāfiʿīs as well as the Ḥanbalīs, they maintain that what he purchases with the capital of the *muḍārabah* belongs to the *muḍārabah* without regard for any counter-claim that there may be.[33] In practice, however, when the capital stands mixed up with the personal business capital of the *muḍārib,* it is difficult to see how this will be implemented. The acceptance of the statement of the *muḍārib* as an *amīn* is, therefore, of greater practical significance.

The Ḥanafīs have also mentioned some *ḥiyal* in this respect that may be pointed out here. To do so we may quote a passage from al-Shaybānī's book:

> "What do you think about the person who wishes to give his capital to another by way of *muḍārabah,* but he also wishes that the *muḍārib* should be made liable for it—what is the *ḥīlah* for this and the security?" He said: "The *rabb al-māl* gives all the wealth less one *dirham* to the *muḍārib* by way of *qarḍ.* He should then form a partnership with this *muḍārib* with this *dirham* along with all that he has lent to the *muḍārib* on the condition that they will both work with the entire wealth and whatever Allah grants them will be shared by them equally or in whatever ratio he wants. This is permitted." I said: "If one of them works with the wealth and not the other with the permission of his partner?" He said: "This is permitted and the profit will be shared by them in accordance with what has been stipulated."
>
> I said: "What do you think if he wishes to give his wealth by way of *muḍārabah,* but he wishes that in case of loss the *muḍārib* should be held liable for the entire loss—what is the *ḥīlah?*" He said: "The *rabb al-māl* should give as *qarḍ* the entire capital. The *muḍārib* should then give this to the *rabb al-māl* on half the profits or whatever he wishes. The *rabb al-māl* should then return this to

---

[32]See *Fatāwah ʿĀlamgīrīyah,* section on *muḍārabah.*

[33]Al-Ramlī, *Nihāyat al-Muḥtāj,* vol. 5, p. 240; Ibn Qudāmah, *al-Mughnī,* vol. 5, p. 192.

the *muḍārib* by way *biḍā'ah.*[34] This would be valid in the opinion of Abū Ḥanīfah and Abū Yūsuf, while Zufar has stated that the entire profit[35] is for the person who performs the work."[36]

The *muḍārib* as *wakīl*

The *muḍārib* is the agent of the *rabb al-māl* in whatever transactions he undertakes in the wealth of the *muḍārabah.* Consequently, the *ḥuqūq* (performance of the contract) revert to him as he is the person who is undertaking the transactions, and he is the person toward whom the *muṭālabah* will be directed by the sellers for the payment and the buyers for the delivery of goods. He is the person who will be able to return the goods bought on the basis of defects. He will be the defendant or the plaintiff in all suits pertaining to the business of the partnership.

The *ḥukm* of the contract will revert to the *rabb al-māl.* This is the case when there is no profit in the *muḍārabah,* however, when there is a profit and the *muḍārib* makes a purchase after this, the *ḥukm* will revert to him as well in proportion to his share in the profits. This has been discussed in the earlier part of this study.

This is the position according to the Ḥanafīs. As for the majority schools, they agree with the Ḥanafīs on some of these issues, but they do not make a distinction between the *ḥukm* and *ḥuqūq* of the contract. They also make distinction in the case of return of goods due to defects depending on whether or not the price consists of the entirety of the wealth of the *muḍārabah.*

Further, it is permitted by way of *istiḥsān,* according to the Ḥanafīs, for the *rabb al-māl* to enter into transactions with the *muḍārib,* who may use the wealth of the *muḍārabah.* Thus, he can buy from him and sell to him. The reason is that the *rabb al-māl* is like a stranger with respect to the wealth of the *muḍārabah* after having delivered its possession. According to strict analogy (*qiyās*), this is not permitted, because the wealth is that of the principal, that

[34] *Biḍā'ah* is trading on behalf of another without sharing the profits. The entire profit is for the owner of wealth.

[35] In other words, Zufar is saying that the *muḍārib* has just taken a *qarḍ* and is working with it for himself.

[36] Al-Shaybānī, *al-Makharij fī al-Ḥiyal,* pp. 76–77; al-Kāsānī, *Badā'i' al-Ṣanā'i',* vol. 8, p. 3205.

is, the *rabb al-māl,* and a person is not allowed to sell his own wealth to himself.[37]

The Shāfi'īs adopt this analogy,[38] and so do the majority of the Ḥanbalīs.[39] As for the Mālikīs, they adopted *istiḥsān,* but with two conditions:[40]

1. That this trading should not be stipulated in the contract of *mufāwaḍah.*
2. That the partner does not intend thereby the acquisition of part of the profit in a concealed manner.

The *muḍārib* is a partner when profit emerges

The *muḍārib* becomes a partner of the *rabb al-māl* when profit emerges, because *muḍārabah* is a partnership in profit, and an agent is not entitled to profit on the basis of his work after the emergence of profit, but he becomes a partner here due to the contract, that is, the contract of partnership. The wealth of the *muḍārabah,* then, becomes a joint ownership between the *muḍārib* and the *rabb al-māl,* and the share of the *muḍārib* is now on the basis of his undivided share in the co-ownership.[41] This is a devastating provision and renders the contract of *muḍārabah* quite temporary. It is valid or it exists during the period when profits have not emerged. What happens when there is a loss after the emergence of profits? Does it revert back to a *muḍārabah?* A clear answer is not provided by the jurists. In accordance with this statement, the appearance of profits would mean that the *muḍārabah* stands converted to a *sharikah.* What type of *sharikah* is this? On the face of it, it should be the basic *sharikat al-'inān* based on *wakālah?* This requires further research, and we have not been able to find a clear answer.

The answer may be available if we examine another provision that pertains to *muḍārabah.* In the fundamental concepts, as well as within the discussions on *'inān,* we saw that if the *muḍārib* is granted *wilāyat al-istidānah* by the *rabb al-māl* (that is, permission

[37] Al-Kāsānī, *Badā'i' al-Ṣanā'i',* vol. 8, p. 3600.

[38] Al-Ramlī, *Nihāyat al-Muḥtāj,* vol. 5, p. 231.

[39] Ibn Qudāmah, *al-Mughnī,* vol. 5, p. 172.

[40] Al-Khirashī, *Sharḥ al-Mukhtaṣar,* vol. 6, p. 213.

[41] Ibn 'Ābidīn, *Ḥāshiyah,* vol. 5, p. 650.

to purchase on credit beyond the limit of the capital invested), another partnership between the two is constituted. This partnership is called *sharikat al-wujūh,* and is a second partnership over and above the *muḍārabah.* It is of the basic category of *'inān,* that is, *'inān* based on *wakālah* having its subject-matter as the credit-worthiness of the partners. Apparently, this arrangement is also viable till the emergence of profits.

Once the profits have emerged, we can combine the two situations. This will give us a simple *'inān* partnership in which one partner, originally the *rabb al-māl,* has granted *istidānah* to the other. What about work by the *rabb al-māl* in the new arrangement. We saw earlier in the discussion of *'inān* that it cannot be stipulated in the contract that only one partner will work, however, in practice some partners may not actually work with the permission of the other partners.

Even if it is assumed that the co-ownership and the partnership is constituted to the extent of the profit earned, the difficulty is still there. Can separate accounts be kept for transactions with the profit during a financial year? Will these transactions and the profit be kept separate from the rest of the *muḍārabah?* If the transactions can be kept separate, the *muḍārib* will have unlimited liability for all these transactions and he will not have the protection he enjoys as a mere worker. If the profit cannot be kept separate, and apparently it cannot, then the situation is aggravated further and the whole arrangement will be converted into an unlimited liability partnership.

This shows that the contract of *muḍārabah* will be difficult to implement in the modern times, or at least its utility will be quite limited. Yet, modern Islamic banking is relying heavily on this contract. One wonders how, and why? Apparently, this has been done in ignorance of these provisions and without understanding the complete contract, or it is only the name that has been borrowed. The analysis of the *muḍārabah* contract as applied in modern banking will be undertaken in a later study.

The vitiated *muḍārabah* becomes a vitiated *ijārah*

The term vitiated *ijārah* is being used here as the wages in this arrangement are ambiguous, and the *muḍārib* is entitled to reasonable wages for his work, while the profit is entirely for the *rabb al-māl.* The consideration of a vitiated *muḍārabah* as a vitiated *ijārah* is agreed upon between the Shāfi'īs and Ḥanbalīs, even when there is no profit.[42] As for the Mālikīs, some of them maintain that the *muḍārib* is entitled to reasonable profit, while others have said that he is entitled to reasonable wages. The details are to be found in *Bidāyat al-Mujtahid*.[43]

The problem here, however, is not so simple as may appear from the texts of the jurists. We have stated in the previous section that *muḍārabah* may start out as a simple contract, but this may change once profit is earned and if *istidānah* is granted. After these events, the *muḍārabah* turns into a cluster of contracts that incorporate not one, but several partnerships. For example, the Ḥanafīs say that after profits have emerged a co-ownership is established and profits are shared between the *muḍārib* and the *rabb al-māl* in accordance with the shares in this co-ownership. Supposing the contract of *muḍārabah* is vitiated after this has happened. A relationship based upon co-ownership cannot be converted into one of a vitiated *ijārah*.

The only way we can reconcile the two situations is to say that a *muḍārabah* will turn into a *fāsid ijārah* only when there is a defect in the formation of the original contract or because of the non-fulfillment of an original condition. Once layers of other partnerships have been superimposed on the original contract, this provision cannot apply.

Incidentally, the majority of the schools do not construct other partnerships that are linked to the *muḍārabah*. The reason is that their thinking on the contract is not fully developed, as is the Ḥanafite reasoning. Once they start dealing with the details and develop the contract to its logical conclusion in the light of the actual realities, they may have the same opinion as that of the Ḥanafī school.

The *muḍārib* becomes a usurper if he violates the conditions of the contract

If the *muḍārib* violates the conditions stipulated for his work by the *rabb al-māl*, the *muḍārabah* is annulled and the *muḍārib* becomes liable for compensating whatever he was delivered by way of capital. In this case, if there was some profit, it belongs to the *muḍārib*.

In practice, especially today, this provision will provide a loophole for unscrupulous people to violate a condition when substantial profit has been made. All they will have to do is to retain the profit from

---

[42] Ibn Qudāmah, *al-Mughnī*, vol. 5, p. 188.

[43] Ibn Rushd, *Bidāyat al-Mujtahid*, vol. 2, p. 242.

the investment and return the principal to the investor. There are some difficulties in imposing damages in this case in the traditional Islamic law. This will be discussed in a future study on the law of contract. It is proposed here that the modern applications should provide for additional damages besides compensation in this case, and these damages may be in excess of the profit earned where the *muḍārib* is in breach of the stipulations.

The *muḍārabah* is annulled if a stipulation negating sharing of profits is made

If the entire profit is stipulated for the *muḍārib*, the *muḍārabah* is annulled, and the capital in the hands of the *muḍārib* is considered a *qarḍ*. If it is stipulated for the *rabb al-māl,* the relationship is considered one of *biḍā'ah*.

17.2.2 Types of *muḍārabah*

Muḍārabah is divided into several types. Some of these classifications have been adopted by modern scholars, while others are to be found in the traditional texts. For example, the first classification into simple and complex has been adopted by 'Alī al-Khafīf. Unfortunately it is a useless classification. The classifications are as follows:

1. **Simle and complex:** The simple *muḍārabah* is *muḍārabah* by itself, while the complex *muḍārabah* arises in combination with *'inān*.
   (a) Simple *muḍārabah* may have two parties to the contract, an investor and a worker, or it may have more than one party on either side, that is, a number of investors and a number of workers, and the arrangements may vary.
   (b) Complex *muḍārabah* in combination with the *'inān* partnership may take several forms.
      i. The investor may be a partnership.
      ii. The worker may be a partnership.
      iii. To add to 'Alī al-Khafīf's classification, we may say that the *muḍārabah* itself may give rise to an *'inān* based on wealth after profits have emerged and to a *sharikat al-wujūh* based on a simple *'inān* after *istidānah* has been granted.

2. **Restricted and unrestricted *muḍārabah:*** This classification is based upon the type of restrictions placed on the work of the *muḍārib*. Al-Kāsānī says: "*Muḍārabah* is of two types: absolute and restricted. The absolute type is one in which the capital is handed over without determination of the type of work that is to be done, nor the location, nor the time, nor the quality of work, or with whom he is to trade. The restricted type is one in which some or all of these things are determined."[44] Al-Kāsānī adds to the above "that the *ḥukm* of the restricted *muḍārabah* is the same as that of the absolute *muḍārabah* in all that has been described by us, and is not different from it except in the restriction placed on it. The basic rule in this is that if the restriction is beneficial it is implemented, because the principle for conditions is that they are applied as far as is possible. Thus, when the condition is beneficial it can be taken into account and this is done because of the words of the Prophet (peace be upon him): 'Muslims abide by their stipulations.'"[45]

3. **Permitted and *makrūh muḍārabah:*** This classification can be gleaned from the words of al-Sarakhsī. He says: "There is no harm if a Muslim accepts money from a Christian by way of *muḍārabah,* because it is a type of trade and *mu'āmalah.* It is, therefore, an agency granted by the *rabb al-māl* for transactions in the wealth. Further, there is no harm if a Muslim undertakes sale and purchase for the Christian by virtue of the agency."[46] To this he adds: "It is considered *makrūh* for the Muslim to give wealth to a Christian by way of *muḍārabah,* though it is legally valid, just as it is considered *makrūh* to appoint a Christian as agent for transactions in wealth. The reason is that the person undertaking the transactions here is a Christian and he would not refrain from dealing in interest, nor would he avoid factors leading to *fasād* and he would not refrain from them due to his belief. Likewise, he would deal in wine and pork....

[44]Al-Kāsānī, *Badā'i' al-Ṣanā'i',* vol. 8, p. 3605–06. See also *Majallah,* §§1406–1407; Ibn Rajab, *Qawā'id,* §123.

[45]Al-Kāsānī, *Badā'i' al-Ṣanā'i',* vol. 8, p. 3631. The tradition quoted by him is recorded by Abū Dāwūd and is narrated by Abū Hurayrah. It has been declared weak by Ibn Ḥazm, while it has been called *ḥasan* by al-Tirmidhī. See Ibn Ḥajar, *Talkhīṣ al-Ḥabīr,* vol. 3, p. 230.

[46]Al-Sarakhsī, *al-Mabsūṭ,* vol. 22, p. 173.

This disapproval, however, does not pertain to the contract of *muḍārabah* itself nor to the underlying agency. It is, therefore, valid in law. It is not considered *makrūh* for a Muslim to give his wealth to a Christian and a Muslim (jointly)."[47]

17.3 The Conditions of *Muḍārabah*

The conditions of *muḍārabah* are summarized under: parties to the contract, capital, sharing of profit, and transactions or powers.

17.3.1 Parties to the contract

The *rabb al-māl* must have the legal capacity for becoming a principal in a contract of agency, while the *muḍārib* must have the capacity for being an agent. Thus, a *muḍārabah* concluded when the investor is suffering from temporary insanity or is a minor is not valid, however, the *muḍārabah* of an authorized minor is valid. For the *muḍārib* it is sufficient that he understand the terms of the contract.[48] The conditions of Islam and unity of religion are not stipulated, except for what has been stated above about the *makrūh muḍārabah.* According to the Shāfi'īs, it is permitted that the *muḍārib* be under interdiction due to insolvency and that the investor be blind.[49]

17.3.2 The capital invested

All such capital with which other partnerships are valid is acceptable for the *muḍārabah.* It is, however, preferred that the capital be offered in absolute currencies and not in *'urūḍ* (tangible property) or debts. If the capital is to be derived from the sale of property and then employed as capital the formation of the partnership is valid.[50] *Muḍārabah* cannot be formed with the *tijārīyah dirhams.* Al-Kāsānī says: "Ibn Samā'ah has related from Abū Yūsuf about the *tijārīyah dirhams* that *muḍārabah* is not permitted in them, because they have been demonetized and have become more like goods. He said that if it had been permitted in them, it would also have been permitted

---

[47] Loc. cit.

[48] Ibn Qudāmah, *al-Mughnī,* vol. 5, p. 17.

[49] Al-Ramlī, *Nihāyat al-Muḥtāj,* vol. 5, p. 217.

[50] Ibn Qudāmah, *al-Mughnī,* vol. 5, p. 17; al-Ramlī, *Nihāyat al-Muḥtāj,* vol. 5, p. 217.

in Mecca with wheat, because they used to buy with wheat just like others used to do so with copper coins."[51]

Another condition pertaining to capital is that it must be delivered to the *muḍārib,* who cannot commence his work prior to this. The management or work is done entirely by the *muḍārib*. Thus, if it is stipulated that the entire wealth or part of it should always remain in the hands of the *rabb al-māl,* then, the condition is detrimental to the contract. If, however, the *muḍārib* takes possession of the entire capital and then decides to leave part of it in the investor's hand, it is permitted if there is no condition attached to it.[52]

The amount of capital should be known to the parties at the time of the contract. If the amount is uncertain or unknown, the *muḍārabah* is not valid, as this will also lead to an uncertainty in the profit, and the certainty of profit is a necessary condition of *muḍārabah.*[53]

17.3.3 The conditions of profit

The profit must be expressed as a ratio or as a part of the total profit. The profit cannot be expressed as a percentage of the capital invested. Any condition that leads to uncertainty in this or does not correspond with this will render the contract unenforceable.[54]

Al-Mudawwanah al-Kubrā has the following to say on the issue: "I said to 'Abd al-Raḥmān ibn al-Qāsim: What do you think if I take a palm grove on the condition that the entire produce that Allah may grant will belong to me. He replied: Mālik said that there is no harm in this. I said: Did Mālik permit this? He said: The reason is that it is the same as a *biḍā'ah* given to you on the condition that the entire profit is for you. Further, as it is permitted that he leave half the produce for your labor, he can also leave the entire produce to you."[55] Ibn Rushd said: "Mālik permitted that the entire profit may be assigned to the worker, as he did in *qirāḍ*. This is *qarḍ* (loan) as has preceded while discussing the Ḥanafī opinion, and the liability is

---

[51] Al-Kāsānī, *Badā'i' al-Ṣanā'i',* vol. 8, p. 3595.

[52] Ibid. p. 3599.

[53] Ibid. p. 3595. This is true when it is not expressed in ratios.

[54] Ibid. p. 3601.

[55] Saḥnūn, *al-Mudawwanah al-Kubrā,* vol. 5, p. 6.

that of the worker in this case. But here (according to the Mālikīs), we do not know what it means."[56]

The general rule in the sharing of profits is equality;[57] thus, if the ratio of sharing is not mentioned the profit will be shared equally. A percentage expressed by one party is deemed sufficient. If any part of the profit is stipulated for a third party from either side, the *muḍārabah* is not valid. This is permitted for the slave of the *rabb al-māl.* Ibn Rushd says: "Mālik, al-Shāfi'ī, and Abū Ḥanīfah permitted this, while Ashhab, from among the disciples of Mālik, said that it is not."[58]

17.3.4 The authority of the *muḍārib* or the conditions of *taṣarruf*

The powers of the *muḍārib* vary according to the contract of *muḍārabah* concluded between the parties, that is, whether the *muḍārabah* is absolute or restricted. Some of these powers are implied in each contract of an unrestricted *muḍārabah,* while others must be specifically spelled out. It is also possible to give full powers to the *muḍārib* provided that this is mentioned in the contract. Accordingly, the *muḍārib* may exercise his powers in the following ways.

Powers implied in the contract of an unrestricted *muḍārabah*

In an absolute *muḍārabah,* the *muḍārib* possesses the following powers implied in the contract.[59]

1. He possesses the authority to buy and sell, because this is the means through which the *muḍārabah* achieves its primary purpose of earning a profit. Trading is not possible without this authority. According to Abū Ḥanīfah, this authority does not permit him to trade with his wife, children or his parents. His two disciples disagree and maintain that he has such authority by virtue of the contract.

   If he buys at exorbitant rates as compared to those prevailing in the market, his purchase is deemed to be for his own account

---

[56]Ibn Rushd, *Bidāyat al-Mujtahid,* vol. 2, p. 248.

[57]Al-Kāsānī, *Badā'i' al-Ṣanā'i',* vol. 8, p. 3606.

[58]Ibn Rushd, *Bidāyat al-Mujtahid,* vol. 2, p. 239.

[59]See §1414 of the *Majallat al-Aḥkām* for the details.

and not for the *muḍārabah.*[60] He may buy and sell on credit up to the extent of the capital employed, but he cannot exceed the limit imposed by the capital for such a purchase. If he does exceed this limit the purchase is for his own account. This is the Ḥanafī opinion, and the opinion of the Ḥanbalīs appears to be quite similar.[61] As for the Shāfi'īs, they do not permit sale and purchase on credit, except by express permission, and the contract of *muḍārabah* is rendered void if this condition is violated.[62] The Mālikī jurists permit sale on credit without express permission, but not purchase.[63] The *muḍārib* possesses the right to negotiate a rescission (*iqālah*).[64]

The *Majallah* explaining the credit and cash sales by the *muḍārib* implies that prices cannot be varied by giving trade discounts, but it is permissible to sell on credit for reasonable periods, that is, periods that conform with the usual commercial practice.[65] The opinions of the jurists on trade discounts are not very clear. There appears to be no logical reason, according to the rules of *ribā,* why a trade discount cannot be given.[66]

2. The *muḍārib* possesses the authority to appoint agents for the trade. All that a *muḍārib* can do himself may be delegated to another person by virtue of the contract of *muḍārabah* as this is the commercial practice, "because *muḍārabah* is more general than agency, and he can utilize the authority that is lesser in status (inherent in it)."[67]

3. He can hire services and may also let them out on hire. Al-Kāsānī says:

---

[60] Loc. cit.

[61] Ibn Qudāmah, *al-Mughnī,* vol. 5, pp. 23, 40, 48.

[62] Al-Ramlī, *Nihāyat al-Muḥtāj,* vol. 5, p. 229.

[63] Al-Khirashī, *Sharḥ al-Mukhtaṣar,* vol. 6, 216.

[64] Ibn Qudāmah, *al-Mughnī,* vol. 5, p. 44.

[65] *Majallat al-Aḥkām al-'Adlīyah,* §1414. See also al-Kāsānī, *Badā'i' al-Ṣanā'i',* vol. 8, pp. 3607–08.

[66] For a discussion of this issue, see this author's *The Concept of Ribā and Islamic Banking,* pp. 74–75.

[67] Al-Kāsānī, *Badā'i' al-Ṣanā'i',* vol. 8, p. 3607. This means that *muḍārabah* is a higher level contract as compared to agency. In fact, agency is part of it, therefore, he has the authority to employ this lower level contract that is included within it.

> He has the authority to hire workers who labor with the wealth as this is the commercial practice. A human being cannot carry out all tasks by himself and is in need of hired services. Further, the *muḍārib* has the authority to rent houses for storing goods, because he cannot preserve these assets without them. He may also hire boats and beasts of burden, because the transportation of goods from one place to the other is a way of earning profit, and he cannot do this all by himself."[68]

4. The *muḍārib* is authorized to travel with the wealth of the *muḍārabah*. Al-Kāsānī says:

> As the contract has been concluded independent of a particular location it will be observed in an unrestricted manner, and also because the meaning of the word *muḍārabah* is a supporting evidence. *Muḍārabah* is derived from *ḍarb fī al-arḍ* and that means traveling.... This is the opinion of Abū Ḥanīfah and Muḥammad, and is also one opinion of Abū Yūsuf as narrated by Muḥammad. In a narration of the authors of *Imlā'* the *muḍārib* does not have this right. It is also narrated from him that he made a distinction on the basis of whether the person does business in a settled manner and also whether he has the right to claim transportation costs."[69]

5. The right to deposit the goods as well as bailment also belongs to the *muḍārib,* because this too is the usual commercial practice. Some jurists impose a condition of necessity for this, but that is obvious.

6. The *muḍārib* has the right to give the goods of the *muḍārabah* to another by way of *biḍā'ah.* In its literal meaning *biḍā'ah* is the giving of one's goods to another for trading when the person accepting them is not going to share the profits derived. Some types of bailment would be covered in this. This too is justified on the basis of commercial practice, because the

[68]Ibid. p. 3707.

[69]Ibid. p. 3708.

muḍārib has the right to hire such services so giving them for the same purpose free of charge is considered better.[70] The Ḥanbalīs uphold an opinion, which is the preferred view, that the *muḍārib* does not have the right to give the goods of the *muḍārabah* on *biḍā'ah*.[71] This appears to be the opinion of the Mālikīs as well.

7. Assignments and endorsements. The *muḍārib* has the right to assign claims and debts on the basis of *ḥawālah* as it is an essential part of trade.[72]

8. The *muḍārib* has the right to pledge property in lieu of the debts of the *muḍārabah*. He may also accept such pledges or mortgages for the debts owed to the *muḍārabah*. The reason is that these are methods for the satisfaction of claims.[73] It should not be concluded from this, however, that the *muḍārib* or a partner in any other partnership may mortgage the property of the partnership for raising cash loans. The reason is that the raising of cash business loans is not permitted. Al-Sarakhsī declared this *bāṭil* in what has preceded as doing so would be in clear violation of the principles of *ribā* as spelled out in the contract of *ṣarf*.[74] The type of mortgage permitted to the *muḍārib* is for credit purchases made by him. This is permitted due to a precedent laid down in a tradition.

Powers that may be granted through express stipulations

The *muḍārib* does not have the authority to do the following, unless these acts are expressly permitted.

1. He does not have the authority to sell or purchase on credit beyond the limits imposed by the capital. In other words, he does not have *wilāyat al-istidānah*. If the *muḍārib* makes such a purchase on credit, it is not permitted and the excess will be considered a personal debt of the *muḍārib*. *Istidānah* is a

---

[70] Ibid. pp. 3606–07.

[71] Ibn Qudāmah, *al-Mughnī*, vol. 5, p. 71.

[72] *Majallat al-Aḥkām al-'Adlīyah*, §1414.

[73] Al-Kāsānī, *Badā'i' al-Ṣanā'i'*, vol. 8, p. 3707.

[74] For the details see Imran Ahsan Nyazee, *The Concept of Ribā and Islamic Banking* (Islamabad, 1995).

way of increasing the capital of the business and this can be permitted by the *rabb al-māl* alone.[75]

Just as he does not have the right to increase the capital through *istidānah,* he does not have the right to repair, improve or manage the existing assets of the *muḍārabah* through this method. For example, if the *muḍārib* purchases cloth with the entire wealth of the partnership and then wishes the delivery of this cloth, by asking the suppliers to bear the cost of transportation, it is not permitted, because he would be incurring a debt beyond the capital of the *muḍārabah.* This would become a personal debt if he does so.[76]

2. He does not have the right to make gifts and donations, unless he takes specific permission from the *rabb al-māl.* He does not even possess the right to give something away as a gift or charity as each is a donation.

3. Likewise, he cannot give a loan to another or assign claims to another where they are not offset by other claims, because each is a kind of charitable donation. He can do so, however, if instructed by the investor. Al-Kāsānī says: "If the investor has authorized him to operate according to his considered opinion, it pertains to sale and purchase... and donation is not a permitted act in *muḍārabah* nor is *istidānah.*"[77] We can safely conclude from this that he cannot make contributions to political campaigns either.

4. Even the emancipation of a slave is not implemented, although it is under other circumstances.

Powers that do not require express permission, but may be included in a general provision

The *muḍārib* may be granted a broad authority to act according to his considered opinion in all matters, however, the authorities mentioned in the previous section are not covered by this. This statement by the investor allows the *muḍārib* to undertake those acts that may not be implied by the unrestricted contract.[78] Al-Kāsānı says:

---

[75]Al-Kāsānī, *Badā'i' al-Ṣanā'i',* vol. 8, p. 3616.

[76]Ibid. p. 3615.

[77]Ibid. p. 3617.

[78]Ibid. 3625.

> The category of acts that the *muḍārib* may undertake if he is authorized to act according to his considered opinion, even when these have not been stipulated are: *muḍārabah, sharikah* and *khalṭ*. Thus, he has the right to employ the assets of the *muḍārabah* for another *muḍārabah* with someone else or to enter into a partnership with someone else by way of *sharikat al-'inān*. He also has the right to mingle the wealth of the *muḍārabah* with his own wealth when the *rabb al-māl* tells him to act on his considered opinion. He does not have the right to do any of the above things if he has not made this statement.[79]

Al-Kāsānī has provided detailed reasons as to why these acts are allowed.

17.3.5 The Restricted *Muḍārabah*

The restricted *muḍārabah* is one in which some limitations have been placed upon the acts of the *muḍārib*. It is obvious that these restrictions will have to be made by stipulating them in the contract. In all the other details, the *ḥukm* of the restricted *muḍārabah* is the same as the absolute *muḍārabah*.

17.4 Liability of the Partners for the Debts of the *Muḍārabah*

The liability of the *rabb al-māl* and the *muḍārib* for the debts of the *muḍārabah* is a very important topic for modern applications. It is well known that the liability for loss is that of the investor or the *rabb al-māl*, but there may be cases where the *muḍārib* is exceeding his lawful authority. In such cases of the exercise of unlawful authority by the *muḍārib*, he may also be held liable for all or part of the debts of the partnership. Some of these details have already been studied in the first part of the study. In this section, the topic is summarized under the following subsections:

1. Liability prior to *wilāyat al-istidānah*.

   (a) Liability prior to the commencement of transactions.

---

[79] Loc. cit.

(b) Liability after commencement of transactions.

2. Liability after *istidānah*.

The general rule is that a *muḍārib* may buy on credit up to the extent of the capital of the *muḍārabah*. He has to stop doing this when the accounts payable are equal to the capital employed. If he wishes to make further purchases on credit, he has to take special permission from the *rabb al-māl*. This authority is called *wilāyat al-istidānah* or the authority for raising debts beyond the limit of the capital. The details of the operation of this authority will be elaborated below.

17.4.1 Liability of the investor and the worker for the debts of the *muḍārabah* before *istidānah* and before commencement of transactions

Al-Sarakhsī says: "If the investor gives him a thousand *dirhams* by way of *muḍārabah*, concluded on half profits, and this capital is lost before he could buy anything with it, the *muḍārabah* becomes void, because of the loss of its subject-matter."[80] Thus, there would be no liability for the *muḍārib* (worker) and whatever is lost is a loss for the investor. The *muḍārabah* becomes void, because its subject-matter was lost before the commencement of operations. The position is the same if the money was lost while in possession of the *muḍārib* or his agent. If, however, the money had been delivered to the agent and was destroyed in his hands, but the *muḍārib* took some counter-value from the agent, the *muḍārabah* is still valid. The taking of such compensation is like the taking of the price/value of the wealth.[81] It should be obvious here that the value received must not violate the provisions of the contract of *ṣarf*, that is, cash compensation cannot be received for the *dirhams*.

17.4.2 Liability after purchase, but before *wilāyat al-istidānah*

We have stated in what has preceded that the *muḍārib* has the right to purchase on credit to the extent of the capital that is in his possession or has been employed in the business. The liability for debts of the *muḍārabah* when credit purchases are being made to the extent of the capital has two cases:

---

[80] Al-Sarakhsī, *al-Mabsūt*, vol. 22, 169.

[81] Al-Kāsānī, *Badā'i' al-Ṣanā'i'*, vol. 8, p. 3664.

Liability after purchase, but before the realization of any profit.

Al-Sarakhsī explains this as follows:

> If a person gives to another a thousand *dirhams* by way of *muḍārabah* on half profits, and he (the worker) buys something with it, and the thousand are then destroyed before he could pay the seller, then, the *muḍārib* will go back to the *rabb al-māl* for a similar amount. The reason is that the capital was a trust (*amānah*) in his hands after the purchase, as it was before it, and is therefore a loss of the capital. The purchase, however, was not void due to the loss of a thousand. The *muḍārib* is a worker for the *rabb al-māl* in this purchase and he has recourse to him for what has become due by virtue of the agreement. For this reason he recovers another thousand from the *rabb al-māl* and delivers it to the seller.
>
> If he takes the (second) thousand from the *rabb al-māl* and does not pay it till such time that this too is lost, he has the right to recover yet another thousand. Likewise, all amounts that are lost out of those that he took into his possession until he makes the payment. Each of these amounts that he takes from the investor are held in trust in his possession.... The capital is a trust in his hands and he, therefore, has the right of recourse time and again until the payment reaches the seller, as against possession by the agent.[82]

We understand from this that:

1. The liability of the *rabb al-māl* in this case is unlimited, that is, it is not limited to the extent of the capital contributed by him the first time. His liability is unlimited and stays so irrespective of the fact that the capital is lost once or a number of times. The *muḍārib* will have the right to claim further amounts till the payment is finally made.

2. Whatever the *muḍārib* receives this way is added to the capital. Thus, if the *muḍārib* takes another thousand to pay the seller,

[82] Al-Sarakhsī, *al-Mabsūt*, vol. 22, p. 169. See also al-Kāsānī, *Badā'i' al-Ṣanā'i'*, vol. 8, p. 3665.

the capital increases to 2000 and so on. If the *muḍārib* sells the thing purchased for 1500, there is no profit, even though it was bought for 1000. The net profit and loss will be taken into account here.

3. It appears from this case that there is a difference between *muḍārabah* and *wakālah* (agency) in this respect. Al-Kāsānī has the following to say:

> The distinction between an agent and a *muḍārib* is that if the money is destroyed in the hands of the agent, and he recovers it once from the *rabb al-māl,* he cannot recover it a second time if he loses it. The *muḍārib,* on the other hand, can recover it each time it is lost. The reason for the distinction is that the agency is terminated with the conclusion of the purchase by the agent, because the purpose of the agency is the acquisition of ownership and not the seeking of profit. Thus, when he makes the purchase the purpose is achieved and the agency is terminated with it. The agent is liable for the price owed to the seller. If it was lost in his possession before he could pay the seller, the principal became liable to the agent for what the agent is liable for to the seller. If he, therefore, takes possession of it once more, his claim is settled and he cannot claim it again.[83]

According to this reasoning, the *muḍārabah* is a continuing affair, while agency was granted for a specific purpose. As soon as this purpose was achieved, the relationship was terminated and there was no further legal justification for holding the principal liable. The reason why the agent is permitted a one time recourse to the principal is that the first amount was being held in trust and the title to the property had not passed to the principal. The loss of the first amount, therefore, had nothing to do with the purchase. The agent could recover the amount once, because title had now passed to the principal and he was still liable even though the agency had expired. He was, therefore, liable for the loss of this amount just once.

[83] Al-Kāsānī, *Badā'i' al-Ṣanī',* vol. 8, p. 3665

There is no reason, however, why an agency cannot be a continuing affair, especially if it is a general agency and is concluded as a continuing affair for a general purpose, or even for a series of specific purposes.

Liability after purchase and after the realization of profits

Al-Sarakhsī says:

> He gives to a person one thousand *dirhams* as *muḍārabah* for half profits, and this worker buys a slave with them whose value is two thousand (*dirhams*). He then takes possession and sells him for two thousand. With the two thousand he purchases a slave girl, but has not paid the amount of two thousand when it is lost. The *muḍārib* has recourse to the *rabb al-māl* for one thousand five hundred and compensates from his personal wealth the remaining five hundred. The reason is that the *muḍārib* is acting for himself in the purchase of one-fourth of the slave girl in consideration of his share of the profits. He, therefore, has no recourse to the *rabb al-māl* for the part of the agreement that pertains to him with respect to this fourth. For the remaining three-fourths he is still working for the *rabb al-māl* according to the agreement.[84]

Al-Sarakhsī goes further to illustrate how profits will be calculated and shared after this transaction and in further transactions. He continues:

> If he pays this two thousand to the seller and takes possession of the slave girl, and then sells her off for five thousand, he is entitled to one-fourth of this price. This is due to the portion that he purchased for himself and paid the price out of his personal assets. Three-fourths of the price belongs to the *muḍārabah*. The *rabb al-māl* first takes his two thousand five hundred from this, because he paid this in two parts, and we have explained that whatever the *rabb al-māl* pays is added to the capital. The profit, however, is not realized except after the capital reaches the *rabb al-māl*. When he takes all his capital,

[84] Al-Sarakhsī, *al-Mabsūṭ*, vol. 22, p. 169.

the remaining amount is profit to be shared as stipulated (for the *muḍārabah*).[85]

We conclude from the above that:

- The liability of the *rabb al-māl* is not limited to the extent of his capital that he contributed the first time rather it is unlimited till such time that the claims are fully met. **Once the profits have arisen and have been re-employed in the business,** the liability of the *muḍārib* is also unlimited to the extent of his share, which is now represented by his re-employed share in the profits. The *muḍārabah,* therefore, stands converted to a kind of *sharikah* in which profits are shared in a unique way as in the following point.

- All amounts paid by the *rabb al-māl* are added to the capital irrespective of its actual existence. The part of the loss borne by the *muḍārib* as well as his earned profits become his capital in the business, and these are to be excluded from the business of the *muḍārabah* at the time of the accounting period. If this amount is re-employed in the business, it will be considered as *khalṭ* of his own wealth with the wealth of the *muḍārabah.* The sharing of profits in such a business will follow the following sequence: future profits will first be allocated on the basis of the ratios of *khalṭ;* the *muḍārib* will take the profits that have arisen from this capital; from the remaining assets, the capital of the *rabb al-māl* will then be set aside; whatever remains is the profit of the *muḍārabah* and will be shared between the *rabb al-māl* and the *muḍārib* in accordance with the agreed upon ratio for the *muḍārabah.* This is what has been explained by al-Sarakhsī in the passage above.[86]

What we do not understand from the text of the jurists is:

- That if the capital of the *muḍārabah* is increased in the books of the partnership when the *rabb al-māl* replaces the lost capital, what will be the limit of the capital for purposes of *istidānah?* In other words, will the authority of *istidānah* be needed once the limit of the original capital is reached or will it be based on the new limit created by the replacement of lost capital.

---

[85]Loc. cit.

[86]See also al-Kāsānī, *Badā'i' al-Ṣanā'i'*, vol. 8, p. 3666.

- Whether the capital added to the *muḍārabah* either by the re-employment of profits or by direct *khalṭ* by the *muḍārib,* when he mixes his own capital with that of the *muḍārabah,* will cause the same problems with respect to *istidānah?*

- What will happen to the liability of the *muḍārib* with respect to these problems?

17.4.3 When the *muḍārib* purchases on credit beyond the capital limit without lawful authority

This has already been explained in the first part under fundamental concepts. It is stated briefly here that any purchases made in excess of the capital limit, when the *muḍārib* does not possess *wilāyat al-istidānah,* is for his personal account; he is liable for it and he takes its profit and the *rabb al-māl* has nothing to do with this excess. Accordingly, we may conclude that the *rabb al-māl* has no liability for this, but the worker has unlimited liability in this case and he cannot have recourse to the *rabb al-māl* for such excess.

This does not mean that the *rabb al-māl* has now acquired limited liability, that is, limited to the extent of his share. The liability for debts arising out of all the transactions lawfully undertaken by the *muḍārib* is still unlimited for the *rabb al-māl.*

17.4.4 Liability of the *rabb al-māl* and the *muḍārib* for debts after lawful *istidānah*

When the *rabb al-māl* permits the *muḍārib* to purchase on credit beyond the capital amount, he grants him *wilāyat al-istidānah.* This gives rise to a *sharikat al-wujūh* between them, which has separate rules of its own. This is similar to the relationship that arises when profits are re-employed in the business. The *muḍārabah* in such a case becomes a cluster of separate yet related contracts. The credit partnership created through *istidānah* requires that profits arising from such a partnership be shared equally between the investor and the *muḍārib.* Al-Kāsānī says: "Likewise, *istidānah,* which creates after authorization a *sharikat al-wujūh,* and is a contract over and above the *muḍārabah.*[87] About such purchases, and the sharing of profits in them, al-Sarakhsī says: "The rest is shared by them in equal ratios, because the authority of *istidānah* is absolute, and the commodity

[87]Ibid., vol. 8, p. 3617.

purchased on credit is owned (jointly and) equally by them. This equality between them, with respect to the purchased item, does not permit an inequality of profit."[88]

We understand from all this that:

- After the authority of *istidānah* a *sharikat al-wujūh* is formed between the *rabb al-māl* and the *muḍārib*. This new *sharikah* is one layer above the underlying *muḍārabah* and is dependent upon it.
- This contract will make the liability of the worker unlimited as well.
- The profit arising from transactions undertaken through this partnership will be shared equally. This is the case when the ratio of ownership in the property purchased on credit is not specified, because *wilāyat al-istidānah* is absolute. If such a ratio is specified, profit will also be shared in the same ratio.

What we do not understand from the text of the jurists is:

- That the creation of a *sharikat al-wujūh* will bring in new rules. The basic rule is that both the worker and the investor will become principals and agents for each other. The *sharikat al-wujūh* will authorize the *rabb al-māl* to buy and sell on credit, that is, participate in the management of the *muḍārabah* to the extent of credit purchases beyond the limit imposed by the original capital.

17.4.5 No liability for the *rabb al-māl* in *qarḍ*

The word *qarḍ* (loan) may be understood in two meanings in Islamic law. The first is in the meaning of an interest free loan for which the period of repayment is fixed. The obvious purpose of such a loan would be its employment in business. The second meaning is that of *qarḍ ḥasan,* which is also an interest free loan, but it has no fixed period of repayment. It may be recalled the next day or it may be delayed till the time of financial ease of the debtor.

Islamic law down not acknowledge the first type of *qarḍ,* because it falls within the prohibitions of the contract of *ṣarf,* that is, of

[88] Al-Sarakhsī, *al-Mabsūṭ,* vol. 22, pp. 178–79.

ribā.[89] The only type of *qarḍ* acknowledged by Islamic law is *qarḍ ḥasan,* and this loan is usually of a personal nature, however, one may also utilize it in one's business. This is the loan that al-Sarakhsī recognizes in the following passage:

> (Suppose) he orders him to raise debts through *istidānah* against the wealth (of the *muḍārabah*) or against the credit of the *rabb al-māl,* and he does so purchasing a slave girl for the *muḍārabah.* Thereafter, he raises a loan (*qarḍ*) of a thousand *dirhams* against the *muḍārabah* and purchases a(nother) slave girl with it. This second purchase is deemed to be for his personal account, and he is personally liable for the *qarḍ.* Among the jurists are those who say that *istidānah* pertains to purchase on credit, and raising of loans (*qarḍ*) is something different. It (raising of cash loans), therefore, is not included in an unqualified authority of *istidānah.* **The correct view is to say that granting the authority to raise loans is *bāṭil* (void).**
>
> Do you not see that if he had ordered a person to raise a loan of one thousand for him from a certain person, and the person did so the one thousand would be for the person raising the loan and not for the one who ordered him. The reason is that *qarḍ* is compensated with a similar (*mithl*) fungible and is a liability of the borrower. If the counter-value is his liability, the borrower becomes the owner of the *qarḍ,* and he is in no need of the command of another for doing this. Giving an order for raising a loan is identical to giving an order for begging, which is *bāṭil.* Whatever is obtained through begging belongs to the beggar and not to another. Once this is established, we may say that whatever the *muḍārib* raises as a loan goes into his personal ownership."[90]

This passage explains to us that there is no concept of a business loan in Islamic law. All that is acknowledged is a charitable loan, which is identical to begging. Even when a charitable loan is raised

---

[89]For the details see Imran Ahsan Khan Nyazee, *The Concept of Ribā and Islamic Banking* (Islamabad: Niazi Publishing House, 1995).

[90]Al-Sarakhsī, *al-Mabsūṭ,* vol. 22, p. 180.

it does not belong to the business; it is owned personally by the borrower, and he alone is liable for it personally. Even if we were to acknowledge that a business firm, as a juristic person, may raise an interest free loan for itself, the problem would be that no period of repayment can be fixed for it, and the corporation may be asked to pay it back the next day. Business cannot function this way.

This concept of Islamic law has devastating consequences for many of the schemes of banking and finance designed by modern institutions on the recommendations of modern scholars. Islamic business has to be a loan free business; it has to be based on the principles of true participation.

17.5 Termination of the *Muḍārabah*

Muḍārabah, like any other partnership, is a terminable (*ghayr lāzim*) contract. It is terminated by all acts that terminate *wakālah* (agency). Thus, it is terminated by:

1. Rescission and proscriptions pertaining to transactions.
2. The termination of the period, if it was for a limited period.
3. Extinction of the capital of *muḍārabah* after its possession and before commencement of transactions.
4. Insanity of either party.
5. Death of the *muḍārib* or *rabb al-māl*.
6. The order of the court, if one of the parties joins the *dār al-ḥarb*. In this case, it would be categorized as an enemy partnership.

Al-Kāsānī says:

> As for an explanation of acts that annul the contract of *muḍārabah*, the contract is annulled by rescission and proscriptions restricting transactions, however, in the case of rescission and proscriptions the conditions of making these known to the other party must be fulfilled. Further, the (entire) capital must be in the shape of *'ayn* (liquid assets) at this time. If it is in the shape of goods that are not acceptable, then, should be converted to *dirhams* and *dīnārs* so that they become cash assets.[91]

[91] Al-Kāsānī, *Badā'i' al-Ṣanā'i'*, vol. 8, p. 3662.

This implies that the dissolution of the *muḍārabah* will take effect once the following conditions have been met:

1. Notice of dissolution should be given to the other party.

2. The assets of the partnership should be converted to fungibles or cash assets.

The second condition alone is required in cases like those of the enemy partnership, insanity, and death, that is, the assets should be converted to cash to give effect to the dissolution. Al-Kāsānī says: "It does not matter whether the *muḍārib* has knowledge of the death of the *rabb al-māl,* because it is dissolution by operation of the law (*ḥukmī*) and does not depend upon notice to the other party, as in *wakālah.* If the assets are in the shape of goods, then, the *muḍārib* should sell them to convert them into cash."[92] The same applies to apostasy.

17.6 Shortcomings of the *Muḍārabah* Contract

The contract of *muḍārabah* is being considered an ideal contract in terms of modern corporate finance. Unfortunately, the contract suffers from some shortcomings, and if it is applied in its strictly traditional form it will lose its importance. Some of these shortcomings have been noted in the preceding discussion. The following, however, can prove fatal to the form or life of this contract:

1. The first shortcoming appears to be that it is not considered a partnership, and is in reality a combination of agency and *ijārah.* There is no harm in this, but if that is its nature, a better contract can be designed today that will serve the same purpose.

2. The contract is considered important today, because there is no liability for the worker in this contract. This is, in fact, a mere illusion. As soon as profits emerge and are re-employed in the business, the worker acquires liability as a partner to the extent of his share of the profits re-employed in the business. Let us take a simple transaction as an example. Let us assume that a *muḍārabah* is formed that provides for the equal

[92] Loc. cit.

sharing of profits between the worker and the investor. Let us also assume that the capital given was $1000 and the worker purchases wheat with this amount. After one week prices rise and he sells the wheat for $2000. In this amount the profit is $1000 out of which $500 belongs to the worker. If the entire amount is employed in the business, the worker becomes a partner to the extent of his $500. In other words, he will become liable for the debts of the partnership in proportion to his 25% share. For the remaining he will continue to be a *muḍārib.* This was only the first transaction. If the transactions continue for a longer period, say a year, the share of the *muḍārib* may increase manifold and he will acquire unlimited liability along with the investor according to *al-kharāju bi'ḍ-ḍamān.* We have provided several quotations from al-Sarakhsī to show how this takes place. This reduces the utility of this contract, at least for modern banks.

3. The *muḍārib,* according to Ḥanafī law, is permitted to buy on credit within the limitations of the capital employed. In other words, if the capital invested is $1000, the *muḍārib* is allowed to purchase on credit to the extent of $1000 and no more. Supposing he eyes a very good business opportunity and is need of buying on credit up to $3000, he cannot do so, unless he acquires authority authority from the investor, and authority that is called *wilāyat al-istidānah.* Let us assume that the investor does grant him such authority. As soon as the authority is granted, a new relationship is created between the investor and the worker for the additional credit purchase of $2000. This is a *sharikat al-wujūh,* which means that the worker and the investor are now regular partners and are equally liable for the debts with respect to the additional credit purchase of $2000. The advantage of the *mudārabah* vanishes again, as soon as this happens.

4. Finally, and this shortcoming is not because of *muḍārabah,* but due to the rules for the prohibition of *ribā.* The issue is about raising loans other than credit purchases. This has been discussed at length above and elsewhere. Islamic businesses cannot raise cash loans. Al-Sarakhsī quoted above says: **"The correct view is to say that granting the authority to raise loans is *bāṭil* (void)."**

Chapter 18

Muzāra'ah and *Musāqāh*

Muzāra'ah and *musāqāh* are not considered partnerships in modern times and even the earlier jurists were inclined to consider them forms of *ijārah* (hire). Nevertheless, both are forms of enterprise organization that should be given due importance for determining the nature of modern enterprises engaged in farming and agriculture. These forms are being discussed here, because a discussion of the second category of partnerships will not be complete without an examination of these two forms. In this chapter the general features of these two forms will be described to see how the earlier jurists have applied the rules of Islamic enterprise organization.

18.1 *Muzāra'ah* (Share-cropping)

In this section we will discuss the meaning of *muzāra'ah,* its legal justification, elements and types, conditions and termination.

18.1.1 The meaning of *muzāra'ah*

The jurists begin with an analysis of the term *muzāra'ah* and discuss whether its grammatical form implies work by both partners, when in practice only one person does the work.[1] Al-Kāsānī verifying the use of the term as proper quotes a number of other terms that have similar grammatical forms, but involve work from one side. One such term is *mu'ālajah* (treatment), where it is the physician alone who is doing the work.[2] The jurists also compare the term *muzāra'ah*

[1] Al-Kāsānī, *Badā'i' al-Ṣanā'i',* vol. 8, p. 3807; al-Marghinānī, *al-Hidāyah,* vol. 4, p. 53; al-Zayla'ī, *Tabyīn al-Ḥaqā'iq,* vol. 5, p. 278.

[2] Al-Kāsānī, *Badā'i' al-Ṣanā'i',* vol. 8, p. 3808.

with the term *mukhābarah* with some considering them similar, while others making a distinction on the basis of who supplies the seed needed for sowing. Some jurists maintain that *mukhābarah* was the name of the arrangement undertaken with the people of Khaybar.[3]

Technically, it means a contract for cultivation of land in return for part of the produce in accordance with the conditions stipulated by law.[4] The *Majallah*, in section 1413, defines it as follows: "*Muzāra'ah* is a type of partnership with land contributed by one party and work by another—that is, the land is cultivated and yield is shared by them."[5] A later Mālikī jurist 'Ulaysh describes it as follows: "*Muzāra'ah* is a partnership for cultivation and its contract is *ghayr lāzim* (terminable) prior to sowing and either party to this partnership for cultivation may revoke it."[6] It is, however, to be noted that the Mālikīs do not assign the same meaning to *muzāra'ah* as is done by the Ḥanafīs and Ḥanbalīs.

18.1.2 Legal justification of *muzāra'ah*

We will begin with the position taken by the Ḥanafīs along with the dissenting view of the founder of the school, Abū Ḥanīfah. The views of the other schools will then follow.

The Ḥanafī view

The Ḥanafī jurists disagreed about the contract of *muzāra'ah* with Abū Ḥanīfah maintaining that it is not legally justifiable. Abū Yūsuf and Muḥammad al-Shaybānī held that it is legally maintainable. These two companions of Abū Ḥanīfah argue as follows:

1. That the Prophet (peace be upon him) made the contract with the people of Khaybar for half of the produce, and this provides a precedent.[7]

---

[3]Ibn Qudāmah, *al-Mughnī,* vol. 5, p. 417.

[4]Al-Zayla'ī, *Tabyīn al-Ḥaqā'iq,* vol. 5, p. 278; Al-Kāsānī, *Badā'i' al-Ṣanā'i',* vol. 8, p. 3807; al-Marghinānī, *al-Hidāyah,* vol. 4, p. 53; Ibn Qudāmah, *al-Mughnī,* vol. 5, p. 412.

[5]*Majallat al-Aḥkām al-'Adlīyah,* §1431.

[6]Muḥammad 'Ulaysh, *Taqrīrāt 'alā al-Sharḥ al-Kabīr* on the margin of al-Dasūqī, *Ḥāshiyah,* vol. 3, p. 372.

[7]Ibn 'Umar is reported to have said that the Prophet (peace be upon him) made a *mu'āmalah* (agreement) with the people of Khaybar for a part of the

2. It is a contract of partnership with wealth from one party and labor by the other, which is the same thing as *muḍārabah* on the basis of analogy (*qiyās*).

3. It is based on necessity. The owner of the land may not be in a position to cultivate the land himself, while one who is able to work may not have land. Necessity, therefore, requires that they come to such an arrangement and conclude the contract. This is different from giving animals or birds to another on the basis of *muzāra'ah,* because the labour of the worker is not effective in generating the yield.

4. The practice of the Companions and their followers till this day has left precedents on which we may rely.

Abū Ḥanīfah, on the other hand, gives the following arguments:

1. The tradition in which the Prophet (peace be upon him) proscribed the contract of *mukhābarah.*[8]

2. Permitting *muzāra'ah* amounts to getting a rent for what is produced by the (personal) labour of the worker, and is similar to asking the miller to share the profit generated through milling, that is, purely his labour. Further, the wages for such hiring of services are unknown or non-existent. All this makes it void. This amounts to strict analogy from the general principle that no compensation for personal labour can be shared, as in begging; there can be no partnership in begging. It also opposes the principle that wages for labour must be known.

3. The transaction of the Prophet (peace be upon him) with the people of Khaybar was a type of *kharāj* imposed on them due to their submission and not a type of *muzāra'ah. Kharāj* is of two types. The first is one in which the *imām* imposes a fixed levy in accordance with what the land is able to bear. The second type is the taking of a part of the produce as *kharāj.* Both types are valid. It appears that the people of Khaybar were being subjected to the second type. The evidence for this argument is that the Prophet (peace be upon him) did not

---

yield of fruit and crops." This tradition is reported in the *Ṣaḥīḥ* compilations. See al-Shawkānī, *Nayl al-Awṭār,* vol. 6, p. 7.

[8]Ibid., vol. 6, pp. 15–16.

stipulate a fixed period for them. Had it been *muzāra'ah,* he would have done so. The reason is that *muzāra'ah,* according to those who permit it, is not valid without stipulation of a period. There are further details in this argument pertaining to the arrangement with the people of Khaybar.[9]

The *fatwā,* however, was given on the basis of the opinions of Abū Yūsuf and al-Shaybānī. The main reason advanced was necessity and the practice of the people. Analogy advanced by Abū Ḥanīfah was given up on the basis of practice and *ḍarūrah.*[10] A breach of analogy on the basis of a stronger principle would amount to *istiḥsān* according to the principles of *uṣūl al-fiqh.*

Land, labour and capital

It appears that the real distinction between the two views within the Ḥanafī school is somehow concealed within the details given by later jurists. To understand this distinction, we have to step back and look at the fundamental concepts discussed in the first part of the study. We said there that entitlement to profit is based on a corresponding liability to bear the loss. The second point we raised is that the bases of entitlement to profit is either capital (*māl*), labour (*'amal*), and *ḍamān* or the surety that you will pay for the loss when you are not contributing anything. The two principles when combined tell us that **in business you are allowed to gain on what you can lose.** When you give money, you also accept the accompanying risk of loss. It should be noted here that we are not talking about potential loss or the loss due to the capital staying idle. We are talking about loss in the original principal sum. The same goes for labour, as the entire labor can be lost. *Ḍamān* amounts to the same thing as capital, with the difference that nothing is being paid in advance. We now raise the question: Is land a basis for entitlement to profit? The reply would be that if a loss can occur in land, it should also be entitled to profit. Abū Ḥanīfah appears to be saying that no loss can occur in land and it cannot be a basis for entitlement to profit. As *muzāra'ah* is the sharing of profit, the owner of land cannot be allowed the

[9] The arguments from both sides can be seen in al-Zayla'ī, *Tabyīn al-Ḥaqā'iq,* vol. 5, p. 278; al-Marghinānī, *al-Hidāyah,* vol. 4, p. 53–54; al-Kāsānī, *Badā'i' al-Ṣanā'i',* vol. 8, pp. 3808.

[10] Al-Zayla'ī, *Tabyīn al-Ḥaqā'iq,* vol. 5, p. 279; al-Marghinānī, *al-Hidāyah,* vol. 4, p. 54.

profit or yield because land is not subject to loss. Abū Yūsuf and al-Shaybānī, on the other hand, appear to be saying that the seed contributed by the landowner should be considered his capital and his land should be assigned the status of real estate, because of which additional profits have been permitted in regular partnerships based upon labour (*sharikat al-'amal*), whether *'inān* or *mufāwaḍah.*

According to Abū Ḥanīfah, then, *muzāra'ah* is not valid, because land is not a basis for entitlement to profit. It is obvious that such a land can be rented out or leased by the owner, unless he wishes to manage it or cultivate it himself. We will see that Mālik appears to say something similar, and so does al-Shāfi'ī in his own way.

Views of the Mālikī school

Ibn Rushd says that the Mālikī opinion permits the renting of land for everything except food.[11] For this opinion he relies upon the same tradition about *mukhābarah* that is relied upon by Abū Ḥanīfah. The tradition proscribes the renting of land with its yield.[12] The Mālikī jurists go into the details of the different types of *kirā'* (renting, leasing) of land.[13] Most of these are partnerships in tools, implements and land. The *muzāra'ah* proper that is permitted by the Ḥanafī school is not allowed by the Mālikīs.

Views of the Shāfi'ī school

The Shāfi'īs maintain that *mukhābarah* is not permitted. This, in their view, is a contract in which the seed is provided by the worker. They maintain that all the four schools consider it void.[14] In such an arrangement, the landowner would be participating on the basis of land alone, which is not a basis for entitlement to revenue or profit. The Shāfi'īs permit *muzāra'ah* only when it is subservient to *musāqāh.* In this case, there must be some fruit bearing trees on the land or the land should be between two groves that are part of the contract of *musāqāh.* They justify this on the basis of the arrangement with the people of Khaybar.[15]

---

[11] Ibn Rushd, *Bidāyat al-Mujtahid,* vol. 2, p. 221.

[12] Ibid. p. 222.

[13] Al-Dasūqī, *Ḥāshiyah,* vol. 3, p. 372; Saḥnūn, *al-Mudawwanah al-Kubrā,* vol. 5, p. 52.

[14] Al-Ramlī, *Nihāyat al-Muḥtāj,* vol. 5, pp. 245–46.

[15] Loc. cit.

Views of the Ḥanbalī school

The views of the Ḥanbalī school are similar to those of Abū Yūsuf and al-Shaybānī. They give identical arguments and even reproduce the arguments of necessity.[16] It is not clear what principles are being invoked by the Ḥanbalīs. In fact, their reliance on necessity creates a methodological problem. The Ḥanafīs could invoke *ḍarūrah* on the basis of the principle of *istiḥsān,* but the Ḥanbalīs do not believe in this principle. How then are they invoking necessity and *ḍarūrah?*

THE CONCLUSION WE DRAW FROM THIS DISCUSSION is that *muzāra'ah* proper is permitted by Abū Yūsuf and Muḥammad al-Shaybānī on the basis of necessity anchored in *istiḥsān.* The Ḥanbalī school follows these views without explaining the basis of their reliance. Abū Ḥanīfah, Mālik and al-Shāfi'ī consider *muzāra'ah* to be unlawful. Is the necessity mentioned by those who permit it sufficient? Is there some other necessity today.

In our view, necessity requires the opposite today. We believe that tenancy on the basis of sharing of profits should be declared unlawful. The landowners should rely on some other arrangement for deriving a yield from their land. The large landowners should form corporations having hired labour to cultivate their lands. The rent on land may be permitted as an expense for such corporations. The profits of these corporations should be taxed like other corporations. The small landowners should either join cooperative societies for the management of their land or should cultivate it themselves. Partnerships are also possible. All such enterprises should be taxed. The only exemption from tax should be given to the person cultivating the land himself. Those who cannot do all this may rent out their land (*kirā'*). This should solve the "tax on agriculture" problem being faced in Pakistan today and also lead to a consolidation of holdings through firms.

If such a measure is adopted, it is likely to put an end to the possible confrontation between the feudals and the industrialists as well, because both will depend on hired labour for promoting their industry. This is not a novel idea; agriculture is being practised all over the world on the basis of hired labour. Besides solving practical problems, the abolition of tenancy would be more in line with the view of the majority of the Muslim jurists.

---

[16] Ibn Qudāmah, *al-Mughnī,* vol. 5, 418, 421.

18.1.3 *Rukn* and Types

According to the Ḥanafīs, *muzāra'ah* has a single *rukn* and that is that *ṣīghah* (offer and acceptance). The landowner says to the tenant, "I give you this land by way of *muzāra'ah* on the condition that your share out of its produce is so much." The tenant responds with, "I accept" or "I agree" or any other statement that indicates his willingness. The offer may also be made by the tenant.[17]

The types of *muzāra'ah* are as follows:

1. Land, implements, seed, and animals are provided by the landowner and work is undertaken by the tenant. This is permitted (by those who permit it as a whole).
2. Land is provided by the landowner and the rest of the things mentioned are provided by the tenant. This too is permitted by some.
3. Land and seed from the owner and the rest by the tenant. This too is permitted.
4. There are a number of other types in which the inputs are varied. Some of these are permitted by Abū Yūsuf and some by Muḥammad al-Shaybānī.[18]

18.1.4 Conditions of *Muzāra'ah*

Al-Kāsānī says that "conditions are essentially of two types: those that are conditions for the validity of the contract, according to those who permit *muzāra'ah* and the conditions that vitiate the *muzāra'ah*."[19]

Conditions validating the contract

The conditions validating the contract are either related to *muzāra'ah* itself, or to the seed, or to the profit, to implements, to yield, the

---

[17]Al-Kāsānī, *Badā'i' al-Ṣanā'i'*, vol. 8, p. 3808; *Majallat al-Aḥkām al-'Adlīyah*, §1432.

[18]For the details of all these types see al-Kāsānī, *Badā'i' al-Ṣanā'i'*, vol. 8, pp. 3816–18; al-Zayla'ī, *Tabyīn al-Ḥaqā'iq*, vol. 5, p. 278.

[19]Al-Kāsānī, *Badā'i' al-Ṣanā'i'*, vol. 8, p. 3809.

land, and others to the duration of the contract. Some of these are summarized below.[20]

The conditions for the *muzāri'*. These are two: First, that he should be sane. It is to be noted that majority is not a condition for the validity of this contract and a discriminating minor may enter into this contract. Freedom too is not a condition. Second, that he should not be an apostate. This view is derived on the principles laid down by Abū Ḥanīfah, though he does not consider *muzāra'ah* to be valid in any case. His two leading disciples permit such a *muzāra'ah.*

The conditions for the *zar'*. It should be clearly stated what is to be sown, that is, the seed, unless the landlord tells him to sow whatever type he likes.

The conditions for the *mazrū'*. The product sown should be something useful and amenable to cultivation.

The conditions for the produce (*khārij*). The produce should be mentioned in the contract, and it should be stated that it belongs to them together, otherwise it will negate the very idea of a partnership. The share should be specified clearly whether it is half, one-third or whatever. The share should not be specified in terms of some specified items of the produce.

The conditions for the land (*mazrū' fīh*). The land should be cultivable. It should be clearly delineated. It should be handed over the the *muzāri'*, that is, the owner should enable the worker to till the land and work on it.

The conditions for the provision of the seed. If the seed is provided by the tenant, he is the one who is hiring the land for the contract. If it is provided by the landlord, then, he is hiring the services of the tenant. These arrangements also indicate the types of *muzāra'ah* that are permitted. Animals and implements are considered subservient to the main contract.[21]

---

[20] These conditions have been reproduced from al-Kāsānī's text. Ibid., vol. 8, pp. 3812–3822.

[21] Ibid., vol. 8, p. 3816.

The duration of the contract. It is necessary to stipulate the duration for which the contract is made, otherwise it leads to *jahālah* and disputes as to the sharing of the produce. This is according to strict analogy (*qiyās*), but the Ḥanafīs permit an undetermined period as well on the basis of *istiḥsān,* but the validity in this case extends to the first produce alone.

Conditions vitiating the contract

Some of these are those that are contrary to the conditions validating the contract as mentioned above. There are others that pertain to the storage and preservation of the produce after the season. This work is not part of the *muzāra'ah* and may be done by the landlord.

18.1.5 The *aḥkām* (legal effects) of *muzāra'ah*

The legal effects are of three types: effects of a valid *muzāra'ah;* effects of a *fāsid* (unenforceable) *muzāra'ah;* and effects of a rescinded *muzāra'ah.*[22]

The effects of a valid *muzāra'ah*

The valid *muzāra'ah* is a terminable contract (*'aqd ghayr lāzim*) for the tenant, but is binding upon the owner of the land. If the tenant says to the landlord after the conclusion of the contract that he does not want to continue, he has the right to do so.

The work that is essential for the *muzāra'ah* like cultivation and sowing is for the tenant to perform, while work that is not essential to it like transportation and harvesting is a joint liability.

The produce is to be shared by both in accordance with the stipulated shares. If the land does not produce anything, then, there is nothing for either, and the tenant is not entitled to wages for his work nor is the landlord entitled rent for his land irrespective of who provided the seed.

The effects of a vitiated *muzāra'ah*

The tenant has no obligation to perform any work in such a contract. The produce is entirely for the owner of the seed, whether this was the tenant's or the landlord's. The other person will be provided

[22]Ibid., vol. 8, pp. 3822–3830.

reasonable wages or rent as the case may be. Reasonable rent or wages are only due when there has been some utilization of the land, that is, if the land has been tilled and there is no produce, the wages and rent are still due.[23]

The effects of a rescinded *muzāra'ah*

Rescission may take place before the commencement of cultivation or after it. If it is rescinded prior to cultivation, there is nothing for the worker. If it is rescinded after cultivation and the land produces something and has been harvested, the produce is to be shared by them as stipulated. If it has not been harvested, it is still to be shared by them along with the work that is left, and the tenant will be paid reasonable wages for this remaining work.[24]

18.1.6 Rescission of the *muzāra'ah*

The *muzāra'ah* comes to an end either expressly or impliedly. Express termination is by *faskh* or *iqālah* (negotiated rescission). It is implied when the tenant is prevented from working on the land or when the period of the *muzāra'ah* is over.

The *muzāra'ah* is also terminated with the death of the tenant and the rights will pass to the heirs.[25] If the landlord dies the tenant will continue till the produce is harvested and the new landlord cannot evict him.[26]

18.2 *Musāqāh* or *Mu'āmalah*

In this section we will discuss the meaning of *musāqāh*, its legal justification, elements and types, conditions and termination.

18.2.1 The meaning of *musāqāh*

Technically, "it is a contract of work for part of the produce along with the conditions of validity,"[27] or "it is a contract (*mu'āmalah*)

---

[23] Ibid. p. 3825.
[24] Ibid. p. 3829.
[25] Ibid. p. 3828.
[26] *Majallah*, §1440.
[27] Al-Kāsānī, *Badā'i' al-Ṣanā'i'*, vol. 8, p. 3831.

for the caring of trees for part of their fruit."[28] The author of *al-Mughnī* says: "*Musāqāh* is the giving of trees to another so that he undertakes to water them and performs all other associated work for a known part of their produce."[29] Al-Dasūqī says: "It is a contract for serving trees and whatever is associated with it for part of the produce or for the whole lot of it."[30]

The *Majallah* calls it "a type of *sharikah* so that the trees are contributed by one party and their care is undertaken by the other, with their fruit being divided between them."[31]

18.2.2 Legal justification of *musāqāh*

The Ḥanafīs disagreed about its validity on the same lines as in *muzāra'ah* with the same evidences and arguments. Abū Ḥanīfah did not consider it valid, while his two disciples did.[32] Likewise, the Ḥanbalīs permitted it in agreement with Abū Yūsuf and al-Shaybānī. As for the Shāfi'īs, al-Ramlī says that "the source for it is the *mu'āmalah* of the Messenger of Allah (peace be upon him) with the Jews of Khaybar with respect to their date palms and their land for what would be produced by them."[33] According to the Mālikīs, *musāqāh* is permitted as an exemption from the following rules:[34]

1. *Ijārah* with unknown wages;
2. Renting of land with what it produces;
3. Sale of fruit prior to the process of ripening, in fact, prior to its existence; and
4. *Gharar,* because the worker does not know what the quantity will be.

---

[28] Al-Ramlī, *Nihāyat al-Muḥtāj,* vol. 5, p. 242.

[29] Ibn Qudāmah, *al-Mughnī,* vol. 5, p. 391.

[30] Al-Dasūqī, *Ḥāshiyah,* vol. 3, p. 539.

[31] *Majallah,* §1441.

[32] Al-Kāsānī, *Badā'i' al-Ṣanā'i',* vol. 8, p. 3831.

[33] Al-Ramlī, *Nihāyat al-Muḥtāj,* vol. 5, p. 242.

[34] Ibn Rushd, *Bidāyat al-Mujtahid,* vol. 2, p. 244; al-Dasūqī, *Ḥāshiyah,* vol. 3, p. 539; al-Khirashī, *Sharḥ al-Mukhtaṣar,* vol. 6, p. 227.

Al-Khirashī says that the basis for this is the transaction by the Prophet (peace be upon him) with the Jews of Khaybar, and the cause is the need for it.[35]

18.2.3 The *rukn* (element) of *musāqāh*

The *rukn* (element) of *musāqāh* is offer and acceptance. Thus, if the owner of the trees says to the worker: "I have delivered my trees to you by way of *musāqāh* so that you may take such and such share from its fruit," and the worker accepts, then, the *musāqāh* is formed.[36] *Musāqāh* has a single element according to the Ḥanafīs. As for the majority, Ibn Rushd says: "It has four elements: the subject-matter specific to it; the portion for which it has been concluded; the description of the work required by the contract; and the period for which it has been concluded and is permitted."[37] This distinction is found throughout the law of contract and is well known.

18.2.4 The conditions of *musāqāh*

Al-Zayla'ī says that the conditions of *musāqāh* differ from those of *muzāra'ah* is four respects. He says:

> The conditions of *musāqāh,* in their view, are the same as those of *muzāra'ah,* except in four matters: First, if either one of them refuses to perform the contract, he is to be forced to perform it as there is injury involved in it. This is different from the case of the owner of seed, who cannot be forced. Second, if the period is over, access to the trees is to be given without rent and work is to be done without wages, and we will explain this in *muzāra'ah* with wages.... Third, if a third party is entitled to the trees, the worker will be entitled to reasonable wages from such a party, while in *muzāra'ah* the value of the crop is to be paid. Fourth, if the period needs to be determined, it will be presumed by way of *istiḥsān* as the season of the crop is well known.[38]

---

[35] Al-Khirashī, *Sharḥ al-Mukhtaṣar,* vol. 6, p. 228. For a full discussion of this text and the views of the jurists, see Ibn Rushd, *Bidāyat al-Mujtahid,* vol. 2, p. 245.

[36] Al-Kāsānī, *Badā'i' al-Ṣanā'i',* vol. 8, p. 3831; *Majallah,* §1442.

[37] Ibn Rushd, *Bidāyat al-Mujtahid,* vol. 2, p. 245.

[38] Al-Zayla'ī, *Tabyīn al-Ḥaqā'iq,* vol. 5, p. 284.

Conditions specific to the parties

The parties to the contract must be sane. *Bulūgh* (majority), however, is not a condition, and nor is freedom. It is stipulated that the parties should not be male apostates. As for a female apostate, her contract is valid.[39]

Conditions specific to the subject-matter

Ibn Rushd says that "they disagreed about the subject-matter of *musāqāh*. Dāwūd said that it is not permitted except in date-palms, while al-Shāfiʻī said that it is permitted in date palms and grapevines. Mālik said that it is permitted in all basic fruits. . . ."[40] The Ḥanbalīs also named certain fruit trees like date palms and vineyards. Ibn Qudāmah, after naming the fruit trees, says: "The conclusion is that *musāqāh* is permitted in all fruit bearing trees, and this is the opinion of the Khulafā'. . . ."[41]

Al-Kāsānī says: "Among the conditions is that the subject-matter delivered should be fruit bearing trees whose yield improves with labour."[42] Here we find a distinction between the method of the majority schools and the method of the Ḥanafīs. The majority merely count cases, while the Ḥanafīs make a broad rule that will cover most cases.

Conditions specific to the stipulated shares

According to al-Kāsānī the condition is that a share be stipulated for each one of the parties. If the entire yield is to be given to one party the *musāqāh* is void.[43] The Mālikīs have a different view. Ibn Rushd states that a share can be stipulated for each party or the entire yield may be given to the worker. He admits, however, that in this case it will amount to a gift and will not be *musāqāh*. Mālik made the same stipulation for *qirāḍ*, but then he had to call it *qarḍ*.[44] This conforms with the definition of *musāqāh* given by the Mālikīs

[39] Al-Kāsānī, *Badā'iʻ al-Ṣanā'iʻ*, vol. 8, p. 3831.

[40] Ibn Rushd, *Bidāyat al-Mujtahid*, vol. 2, p. 245.

[41] Ibn Qudāmah, *al-Mughnī*, vol. 5, pp. 392–93.

[42] Al-Kāsānī, *Badā'iʻ al-Ṣanā'iʻ*, vol. 8, p. 3832.

[43] Loc. cit.

[44] Ibn Rushd, *Bidāyat al-Mujtahid*, vol. 2, p. 248.

and recorded earlier in this section. An obvious condition is that the specified share should be a percentage of the undivided whole.[45]

Conditions specific to work

The primary work in this contract is the watering of the trees, whether this is through wells or other means.[46] As the entire work is to be done by the worker, it is imperative that he be given complete access to the land and the trees.[47] To this the Ḥanabalīs add a host of details like the tilling of the land under the trees and taking care of the animals and so on.[48]

Conditions specific to the duration of the contract and the time for the conclusion of the contract

Some jurists specify that the contract should be concluded before the fruit has begun to ripen, but others disagree.[49] The reason is that the labour of the worker has no role to play once the fruit has ripened.

As for the duration of the contract, the jurists maintain that it should not be uncertain.[50] The Ḥanafīs maintain that this is not necessary for the validity of the contract and would be construed to include the first fruit that is harvested. They base this on *istihsān*.[51]

Conditions that render the contract void

The major stipulations that render the contract void are the giving of the entire yield to one party, or the stipulation of the share in known quantities, the stipulation of work for the owner of the trees, or the stipulation of transportation and storage after the division for the worker.[52]

---

[45]Ibn Qudāmah, *al-Mughnī*, vol. 5, p. 395; al-Kāsānī, *Badā'i' al-Ṣanā'i'*, vol. 8, p. 3832.

[46]Ibn Rushd, *Bidāyat al-Mujtahid*, vol. 2, p. 247.

[47]Al-Kāsānī, *Badā'i' al-Ṣanā'i'*, vol. 8, p. 3832.

[48]Ibn Qudāmah, *al-Mughnī*, vol. 5, pp. 401–402.

[49]Ibn Rushd, *Bidāyat al-Mujtahid*, vol. 2, p. 249.

[50]Loc. cit.

[51]Al-Kāsānī, *Badā'i' al-Ṣanā'i'*, vol. 8, pp. 3832–33.

[52]Loc. cit.

18.2.5 The *aḥkām* (legal effects) of the contract

Musāqāh is a binding (*lāzim*) contract, and according to Mālik it may be inherited.[53] Whatever work is required on the trees is the liability of the worker, and whatever expenditure is required is to be borne by the trees and thus to be shared by the parties in proportion to their shares.[54] If the trees do not produce anything then none of the parties is entitled to anything in the shape of lost wages or rent. The worker does not have the right to sub-let his tanancy to another, unless the owner permits him.[55]

In the case of a vitiated (*fāsid*) contract, the worker is not to be forced to perform the contract with work. The entire yield will belong to the owner and the worker will be entitled to reasonable wages. The wages will be given even if the trees produce nothing, unlike a valid contract.[56]

18.2.6 Rescission of the contract

The rules are the same as those for *muzāra'ah,* and the reason for this could be that the worker is a thief and so on.[57] The contract is rescinded due to the death of either party as in the case of *muzāra'ah.*

---

[53]Ibn Rushd, *Bidāyat al-Mujtahid,* vol. 2, p. 250; al-Kāsānī, *Badā'i' al-Ṣanā'i',* vol. 8, p. 3835.

[54]Al-Kāsānī, *Badā'i' al-Ṣanā'i',* vol. 8, p. 3834.

[55]Ibid. p. 3835.

[56]Ibid. 3836.

[57]Ibid. p. 3837.

Part V

Islamic Form of Partnerships for the Modern World

In the previous parts of this study, we have attempted to understand the general principles of enterprise organization in Islamic law and then examined how these principles are applied by the jurists to develop the two categories of partnerships. In this part we shall embark upon a more creative task; namely, to apply the same principles to institutions and situations of the modern age, and to see how the existing forms can be amended or new forms can be devised to meet the demands of the present age.

We will begin this part with a brief discussion on what are the major issues facing the Muslim world in the field of business organization. Some of these matters were considered in the introduction to this study, but there is a need to be more specific so that we may be able to identify what can be discussed at present and what issues need to be dealt with in other more focused studies.

The first chapter in this part will, therefore, be devoted to major issues in the field of corporate law and finance.

The second chapter will deal with partnership forms that do not need legal personality. This is the area covered by the existing partnership law. The partnership law applied in Pakistan, for example, is old; it needs to be revamped in any case. In the second chapter, in this part, we will examine the partnership law applied in Pakistan and analyze some of the provisions of this law in the light of our study in the previous three parts. This should reveal to us the provisions that would clash with the general principles of Islamic law. Proposals will be made where necessary.

An extension of the same idea will be found in the third chapter. Partnership law in the modern world has changed shape somewhat to meet the demands of the present times. The law in Pakistan should be improved to suit modern conditions. In this last chapter it will be shown how Islamic law may employed for the design of new forms that are likely to be useful in the context of Islamic banking and finance. Some other issues relating to this shall, God willing, be taken up in a separate study.

Chapter 19

Basic Issues in Corporate Law and Finance for Islamic Law

The most important issue facing the Muslims today is that of Islamic banking. Islamic banks are being established with increasing speed, but the biggest problem they face may be phrased as follows: How to invest the money that is entrusted to them by sincere Muslims in Islamically permitted securities and to provide a lawful return to their investors that is free of *ribā?* Most of the securities on which the modern system is constructed are built upon the paper issued by the corporations, the financial assets, whether these corporations are engaged in the banking business or in manufacturing or trading or something else. Ultimately, each security or financial instrument, whatever its nature, is linked to the creation of wealth, and this wealth in the modern world is created mostly within the corporation. Unless the corporation is Islamized, there is very little chance of success in Islamizing its securities and all the derivatives arising from the them. The future of Islamic banking depends on the success we have in Islamizing the corporation. The main task facing the Muslim scholars, in our view, is the Islamization of the modern business corporation. Each issue related to such Islamization is, therefore, important.

This does not mean that partnerships are confined to the field of small business. Certain forms of partnership, especially the limited liability partnership has been employed quite successfully as a means of financing by financial institutions. This form is not accepted by the Pakistani law of partnership. A new section—section 6A—has been introduced into the law that attempts, possibly, to achieve the same result. It is felt, however, that the matter should be approached directly and anlyzed in the light of Islamic law. A limited liability partnership may become one of the most important forms of financing of small and medium sized businesses in the Muslim world.

In this chapter, we shall list some of the issues that appear important to us. All of these cannot be taken up in this study, but identifying the issues will help identify the fields of study that need to be developed if Islamization of banking and commercial law are to be undertaken seriously. Some of the fields of study envisaged pertain to law, while others involve finance as well as management. Whatever the field, it will always need nourishment from Islamic law. It is, therefore, felt that these fields be developed in accordance with some coherent plan.

The fields to which this coherent plan should ultimately reach out are: Islamic corporate law including corporate governance and control; Islamic corporate finance and financial engineering; primary and secondary markets and securities regulation including issues like insider trading; and finally Islamic management techniques. Work on most of these fields cannot be undertaken unless certain basic issues are settled first. For example, how can we talk about corporate governance and control when we do not even understand how the basic relationships between the shareholders, the corporation, the board of directors, and the management are viewed by Islamic law. What precisely are the contracts with which such relationships are regulated?

It is for this reason that a simple approach was adopted in this study. The fundamental principles of Islamic law were first identified. The application of these principles to the traditional law of business by the earlier jurists was studied. The knowledge gained has now placed us in a position to examine modern applications in the light of the same principles. Before we begin applying the principles of Islamic law to individual applications, there is a need to look at the total picture and to undertstand the nature of the whole project. It is only after some kind of consensus is developed on the issues that one can move further. The list that follows extends beyond some of the basic issues. The issues are listed under the following three headings: 1) those that are specific to corporations; 2) those that are specific to partnerships; and 3) issues that are common to both. Out of these issues, those to be taken up in this study will then be identified.

19.1 Corporation Specific Issues

There are three major issues that need to be tackled under this heading. The first deals with the concept of the corporation. The second concerns the new model of the Islamic corporation. The third is the area of corporate governance and control.

19.1.1 The Concept of the Modern Corporation

The concept of the corporation, as stated above, has two aspects. The first deals with legal personality and whether it can be accomodated within Islamic law. The second aspect concerns the modern business corporation that has been constructed out of legal personality. Even if the concept of legal personality is acceptable, as many modern Muslim scholars are insisting, it does not mean that it gives a blanket approval to the modern business corporation. Does the manner in which the modern corporation is implemented violate certain basic principles of Islamic commercial law? Can the modern corporation function even after accepting the prohibition of *ribā?* Is the structure of the legal relationships between the shareholders, and between the shareholders and the corporation, acceptable to Islamic law? Are the securities issued by the corporation, beginning with the ordinary shares, legal? These and other related questions are very important. All these have been considered in another study tentatively entitled "Corporations and Islamic Law" that is being completed simultaneously with the present study.

19.1.2 The Model of the Islamic Corporation

In the study on corporations, after having identified how the concept of a fictitious personality can be accomodated into Islamic law and also what is wrong with the modern business corporation, a new model of the Islamic corporation has been constructed. This model attempts to satisfy all or most of the objections raised against the existing model. In other words, it tries to satisfy, all or most of the principles of Islamic law. Further, the new model is intended to be as efficient as the existing system if not better, and if implemented should enable us to move over to it with the minimum effort.

19.1.3 Corporate Governance and Control

Corporate governance according to Islamic principles is a very important area. It should be made to conform to Islamic principles. This cannot be done under the present model of the corporation. The attempt to extrapolate the rules of Islamic business organization from *fiqh* and to apply them to problems of corporate governance and control under the existing system is not only difficult, it is also futile. It is like transplanting organs from one being to a completely different being. The only way this can be done is by the creation of a new model of the business corporation that conforms with Islamic law. This new model has already been proposed, as stated above. Once the new model is implemented and the underlying relationships established in terms of Islamic law, this area should be dealt with exhaustively and comprehensively.

19.2 Partnership Specific Issues

The law of partnership studied in the preceding parts of this study shows that it is considerably developed and can serve modern needs. Nevertheless, there are two issues that need to be dealt with urgently, if Islamic law of partnerships is to function smoothly in the modern world. The first concerns legal personality for a partnership, so that it may become a going concern and avoid excessive transaction costs. The other issue deals with the limited partnership in which one or more partners may have limited liability, while sharing the profits of the partnership. These two issues are important, because these forms, if implemented, will facilitate financing of small businesses by banks. The acceptance of the concept of fictitious personality by Islamic law should apparently mean that there is no obstacle in assigning such personality to partnerships as well. Likewise, if limited liability can be managed for the shareholders of a corporation, then, why not for some of the partners too. We shall examine both issues in some detail in the last chapter and make proposals.

19.3 Common Issues

There are certain basic issues that concern corporations as well as partnerships. These are listed below:

1. **Limited Liability for Shareholders and Partners.** The major problem here is the creation of limited liability in the light of the principles of Islamic law.

2. **Ribā-free Financing of Corporations and Partnerships.** This is the most important issue for Islamic banking. It is a complex issue and represents a real challenge for Islamic corporate finance. The present study is an attempt to clear the way for the development of this field. Hopefully, this area will be taken up for consideration in the near future.

3. **Ribā-free Capital Investments for Corporations and Partnerships.** This is to be included in the study on corporate finance in the light of the principles of Islamic law. The emphasis will be on using the funds obtained through financing in lawful investments.

4. **New Securities and Securities Regulation.** This issue can only be taken up once progress has been made in the area of corporate finance.

5. **Derivatives, hedging, speculation and *gharar*.** These problems will also be taken up in the study on corporate finance.

19.4 Issues Dealt With in This Study

It should be clear to the reader by now what this study is mainly concerned with. However, the issues to taken up are listed below:

1. The analysis of the existing partnership law in the light of the principles of Islamic law.

2. The creation of partnerships with legal personality so as to cut down transaction costs involved in the partnership form.

3. The designing of the Islamic limited liability partnership.

In addition to these issues, the modern applications of *muḍārabah* should have been analyzed in this study. This analysis, however, is being avoided due to space constraints. A separate monograph will hopefully be devoted to the Pakistani modaraba law in he light of our findings in the present study.

Chapter 20

Partnerships Without Legal Personality: Existing Law

The Federal Shariat Court of Pakistan examined the law of contract as applicable in Pakistan in 1982 and within this law the partnership law was also considered. This judgement was not published, but a copy obtained from the Court shows that no changes were suggested in the law of partnership. The present chapter is a renewed effort to examine this law in the light of Islamic principles identified in this study.

There are two basic principles of business law in Islam. The first is the principle of prohibition of *ribā* and the second is the principle of liability, which is stated in a tradition as *al-kharāju bi al-ḍamān.* The other principles, like *gharar* and other sub-principles, are but corollaries of these two principles. We have seen the application of these two main principles and their corollaries in the previous chapters of this study. The principles have also been applied to the concept of the modern corporation in another study.[1]

These two principles and the sub-principles derived in the previous chapters are being applied in the present chapter to examine the law of partnership as applied in Pakistan. The comments and proposals will appear after the words *Comment:* and *Proposal:* in what follows. Part of the text of the Partnership Act, 1932 has been reproduced without the footnotes.

It may be mentioned here that the Islamic partnerships that are more or less identical to the existing law are the Ḥanafī *'inān* based on *kafālah* and a similar partnership in the Ḥanbalī school

[1]See Imran Ahsan Khan Nyazee, *Islamic Law of Business Organization: Corporations* (to be published).

that they call *mufāwaḍah.* Unfortunately, the Ḥanafī jurists just acknowledged this important form without going into its details. The analysis presented by the Ḥanbalī jurists is also not adequate. The major difference between the Ḥanafī *'inān* with *kafālah* and modern law pertains to the concept of agency employed. The Ḥanafī school makes a distinction between the *ḥukm* and *ḥuqūq* of the contract, and then covers up the shortcomings through the contract of surety included in the partnership. Modern law achieves the same thing with the wider concept of agency. The Ḥanafī approach is more precise as far as legal analysis is concerned, however, it is not possible to change the existing law so as to make it conform completely with the Ḥanafī concepts as this will entail unnecessary hardship. It is, therefore, proposed to make a few suggestions for changes in the light of the general principles of Islamic business organization. The provisions to be amended would relate generally to the following points:

1. The issues of *ḍamān,* that is, liability for debts, especially in situations where profits are being earned without a corresponding liability for loss, like the minor admitted to the benefits of the partnership and the transferee to whom a partner has assigned his interest.

2. The issues of interest as in the case of a creditor entitled to share in the profits or other charges on which interest is due.

3. The issues pertaining to *wilāyat al-istidānah.* The concept of agency that governs this law is different from that applied by the Muslim jurists and would provide the same rules that are provided by the contract of surety (*kafālah*) under Islamic law, yet the issue or buying on credit and of raising debts should be clarified within the law and should not be implied. It will serve no useful purpose to suggest that the distinction between the *ḥukm* of the contract and its *ḥuqūq* be inserted into the existing law. In fact, it may prove to be detrimental as the law in countries like Pakistan has now been practiced for a long time on the basis of the Western concept of agency. Further, if the purpose is being achieved by this law and there is no clash with the major provisions of Islamic law, it would be better to leave it undisturbed. The Ḥanafite distinction between the *ḥukm* and *ḥuqūq* of a contract will be employed only where new forms are suggested and that too if it is essential, and there is no other way of getting the desired results.

In what follows, only the relevant provisions of the Pakistani law have been reproduced.

4. *Definition of "partnership", "partner", "firm", and "firm name".*— "Partnership" is the relation between persons who have agreed to share the profits of a business carried on by all or any of them acting for all.

Persons who have entered into partnership with one another are called individually "partners" and collectively "a firm", and the name under which their business is carried on is called the "firm name".

Comment: The definition of a partnership is correct according to Islamic law. As pointed out in this study, the emphasis in Islamic law is also on the relationship established between the partners. This relationship is judged through the contracts of *'inān* and *mufāwaḍah,* which in turn regulate the relationship through the contracts of agency (*wakālah*) and the contract of surety (*kafālah*). The contract of *kafālah* does not come into play in a modern partnership, because the concept of agency is much wider and achieves the same result.

The concept of the firm, as explained in the first part of this study, is acceptable in Islamic law. The acceptance, however, is based on the contract of *kafālah* underlying an Islamic partnership. Due to the wider concept of agency employed here the contract of *kafālah* is not needed. Further, there appears to be no reason to disturb the existing law and introduce the Ḥanafī concept of agency with an accompanying distinction between the *ḥukm* of a contract and its *ḥuqūq*.

The concept of the firm has been mistaken for legal personality by some.[2] This does not seem to be correct. The concept of the firm in Islamic law is identical to the concept of the firm in this Act.

In addition to the above, this definition does not give separate treatment to partnership based upon wealth, labour or creditworthiness. In other words, the formation of such specialized partnerships is left to the agreement of the parties. They may agree to become partners in any arrangement they like. In fact, the contract of *muḍārabah* may also be said to be included in this definition, although the position of the *muḍārib* will be that of the employee as contemplated in §6 Explanation 2(b). The *muḍārib* will be treated as a worker and not as a partner, and will, therefore, have no liability for the debts of the firm. If, however, the profits earned by the

[2]See the opinions of Abraham L. Udovitch and S.M. Hasanuzzaman in the chapter on the Fundamental Concepts I at page 55.

worker are re-employed in the partnership, he may be admitted to the partnership on the basis of such a contribution; Islamic law does the same.

5. *Partnership not created by status.*—The relation of partnership arises from contract and not from status;

and in particular, the members of a Hindu undivided family carrying on a family business as such, or a Burmese Buddhist husband and wife carrying on business as such are not partners in such business.

Comment: The *Majallah* states in §1398 that where some partners are dependent upon other partners, like a son being dependent upon his father, the partnership is not acknowledged by Islamic law, even when there is a contract between the partners. Perhaps, the relationship between a father and a son can be justified on the basis of the tradition: "You and your wealth are for your father." A husband and wife, however, are treated as independent persons in Islamic law. A partnership between them should be acceptable, when there is a contract, and even tax considerations should not be able to set aside such a relationship.

6. *Mode of determining existence of partnership.*—In determining whether a group of persons is or is not a firm, or whether a person is or is not a partner in a firm, regard shall be had to the real relation between the parties, as shown by all relevant facts taken together.

Explanation 1.—The sharing of profits or of gross returns arising from property by persons holding a joint or common interest in that property does not of itself make such persons partners.

Comment: The term *sharikah* can be used for such an arrangement, but it will be called *sharikat al-milk* co-ownership that may be giving rise to profits. The term *sharikat al-'aqd* or contractual partnership cannot be used here. For a partnership to exist under Islamic law it has to be the result of a contract.

Explanation 2.—The receipt by a person of a share of the profits of a business, or of a payment contingent upon the earning of profits or varying with the profits earned by a business, does not of itself make him a partner with the persons carrying on the business;

and, in particular, the receipt of such share of payment—

(*a*) by a lender of money to persons engaged or about to engage in any business,

Proposal: There is no doubt that such an arrangement cannot be called a *sharikah* in Islamic law. The problem in such an arrangement is that the relationship is unlawful according to Islamic law. It violates the principle of prohibition of *ribā,* because it amounts to an exchange of currency for currency with an excess.[3]

It is believed that the relationship conceived in this provision has many similarities with, and could be a prototype for, the ordinary share of the corporation. The reader is expected to reflect upon this point.[4]

Proposal: It is proposed that the arrangement of a lender of money sharing the profits of a parntership be declared unlawful.

(*b*) by a servant or agent as remuneration,

(*c*) by the widow or child of a deceased partner, as annuity, or

(*d*) by a previous owner or part owner of the business, as consideration for the sale of the goodwill or share thereof,

does not of itself make the receiver a partner with the persons carrying on the business.

Comment: The definition of *māl* in Islamic law may be said to include goodwill as well as intellectual property rights. The Islamic Fiqh Academy (OIC) has issued a ruling to this effect and the Federal Shariat Court of Pakistan too has acknowledged such rights.

6-A. *Act not to apply to certain relationships.*—Nothing contained in this Act shall apply to a relationship created by any agreement between a banking company and a person or a group of persons providing for sharing of profit and losses arising from or relating to the provision by the banking company or finance to such person or group of persons.

Explanation.—For purposes of this section, "banking company" and "finance" shall have the same meaning as in the Banking Tribunals Ordinance, 1984.]

Proposal: This section has been introduced recently to provide protection to banks and financial institutions, apparently against the provisions of unlimited liability for debts that may be invoked when financing is undertaken on the basis of profit sharing. The section, besides distorting the existing law of partnership, is also vague and is against the principles of good legislation.

It is proposed that this section be repealed and be replaced with clearly spelt out forms that will provide limited liability to banks

[3]For further details see the author's book *The Concept of Ribā and Islamic Banking* as well as the study on Islamic Law of Business Organization: Corporations.

[4]For further details see *Corporations and Islamic Law* by the author.

and financial institutions. Some such forms, based on Islamic law, are being proposed in the next chapter. The main idea in such proposals is to permit the creation of limited partnerships as well as partnerships that have legal personality. The Companies Ordinance, 1984 envisages such an arrangement, but for companies alone.[5]

7. *Partnership at will.*—Where no provision is made by contract between partners for the duration of their partnership, or for the determination of their partnership, the partnership is "partnership at will"

Comment: This conforms with the provision of Islamic law that the contract of partnership is *ghayr lāzim.*

8. *Particular partnership.*—A person may become a partner with another person in particular adventures or undertakings.

Comment: This type of partnership is called *sharikah khāṣṣah* in Islamic law, as against the *sharikah ʿāmmah* or general partnership, which is formed to deal in all kinds of goods and trade. This classification is also linked to general and special agency.

9. *General duties of partners.*—Partners are bound to carry on the business of the firm to the greatest common advantage, to be just and faithful to each other, and to render true accounts and full information of all things affecting the firm to any partner or his legal representative.

Comment: The contract of *amānah* underlying all Islamic partnerships governs the fiduciary relationship between the partners.

10. *Duty to indemnify for loss caused by fraud.*—Every partner shall indemnify the firm of any loss caused to it by his fraud in the conduct of the business of the firm.

Comment: The provisions of *taʿaddī*, negligence, and *ghaṣb* may govern this provision.

11. *Determination of rights and duties of partners by contract between partners.*—(1) Subject to the provisions of this Act, the mutual rights and duties of the partners of a firm may be determined by contract between partners, and such contract may be express or may be implied by a course of dealing.

Such contract may be varied by consent of all the partners, and such consent may be express or may be implied by a course of dealing.

Comment: The contract may be varied and the duties and powers of partners may be changed by granting general or specal agency

[5]See sections 111 and 112 of the Companies Ordinance, 1984. These sections have been reproduced in the next chapter.

in Islamic law. The Shāfi'ī and Ḥanbalī jurists provide for the termination of agency of one partner so as to prevent him for acting on behalf of the partnership. This arrangement permits him to act to the extent of his own share. This provision of Islamic law is rejected, and rightly so, by the Ḥanafīs as it leads to the dissolution of the partnership.

Authority to buy on credit: It should be clearly stated under this section that each partner conducting business on behalf of the partnership has the right to buy on credit to the extent of the capital of the firm, and any credit purchase beyond that needs special authority from all the partners (*wilāyat al-istidānah*). This problem will be removed if the contract of surety (*kafālah*) is specifically introduced into the partnership, although the Western concept of agency that governs this partnership law achieves the same result. The issue, however, should be clarified in the law. The authority of *istidānah* may either be deemed to be implied by the partnership contract and may be restricted specifically by the partners or it may not be included in the implied contract and be spelled out specifically. Islamic law prefers the latter.

(2) *Agreements in restraint of trade.*—Notwithstanding anything contained in section 27 of the Contract Act, 1872, such contracts may provide that a partner shall not carry on any business other than that of the firm while he is a partner.

Comment: This provision is supported by the principles underlying the Ḥanafī partnership concluded as *mufāwaḍah.* For the details refer to the chapter on *mufāwaḍah,* according to the Ḥanafīs, in this study.

12. *The conduct of the business.*—Subject to contract between the partners—

(*a*) every partner has a right to take part in the conduct of the business;

Comment: This also implies that a partner may be designated as a "sleeping partner." Islamic law does not permit the existence of a sleeping partner. It must be stipulated that every partner will take part in the conduct of the business. A partner may, if he chooses, abstain from taking part in the business of the partnership, if the other partners agree, but the contract itself cannot stipulate this.

(*b*) every partner is bound to attend diligently to his duties in the conduct of the business;

(*c*) any difference arising as to ordinary matters connected with the business may be decided by a majority of partners, and every partner shall have the right to express his opinion before the matter is decided, but no change may be made in the nature of the business without the consent of all the partners; and

(*d*) every partner has a right to have access to and to inspect and copy any of the books of the firm.

13. *Mutual rights and liabilities.*—Subject to contract between the partners—

(*a*) a partner is not entitled to receive remuneration for taking part in the conduct of the business;

Comment: This may be changed by agreement and additional profits provided for work or remuneration paid.

(*b*) the partners are entitled to share equally in the profits earned, and shall contribute equally to the losses sustained by the firm;

Comment: This provision states the presumption that profits are divisible and losses apportioned in equal shares. It may be changed by express agreement. Contribution to losses, however, is linked to the ratio of profits: if profits are being shared equally losses will be borne equally. It is also possible under the law to excuse a partner from bearing any loss.

Proposal: It is proposed that to give effect to the Islamic principle of liability (*ḍamān*) in the context of this Act, it should be stated that each partner will be liable for contributing to losses and entitlement to profit will be based on such liability for loss, irrespective of the contribution made to the capital of the firm. Actually, the liability to bear loss should be the basic criterion for determining whether a person is a partner in a firm.

(*c*) where a partner is entitled to interest on capital subscribed by him, such interest shall be payable only out of profits;

Proposal: This provision is unlawful according to Islamic law and should be repealed. It is null and void according to the principles of the prohibition of *ribā*.

(*d*) a partner making, for the purposes of the business, any payment or advance beyond the amount of capital he has agreed to subscribe is entitled to interest thereon at the rate of six per cent. per annum.

Proposal: Should be repealed on the same grounds as above. If a partner makes a payment on behalf of the partnership such a payment may be included in the capital of the partnership in return for sharing profits.

(e) the firm shall indemnify a partner in respect of payments made and liabilities incurred by him—

(i) in the ordinary and proper conduct of the business, and

(ii) in doing such act, in an emergency, for the purpose of protecting the firm from loss, as would be done by a person of ordinary prudence, in his own case, under similar circumstances; and

(f) a partner shall indemnify the firm for any loss caused to it by his wilful neglect in the conduct of the business of the firm.

14. *The property of the firm.*—Subject to contract between the partners, the property of the firm includes all property and rights and interests in property originally brought into the stock of the firm, or acquired, by purchase or otherwise, by or for the firm or for the purposes and in the course of the business of the firm, and includes also the goodwill of the business.

Unless the contrary intention appears, property and rights and interests in property acquired with money belonging to the firm are deemed to have been acquired for the firm.

Comment: This provision may clash with the provisions of Islamic law about *ikhṭilāṭ*. Modern transactions have become quite complex and the rules of *ikhṭilāṭ* cannot be followed. *Ikhṭilāṭ* should be assumed to have taken place throught the contract itself. The major purpose of *ikhṭilāṭ* is to create co-ownership and then determine the extent of liability for losses or debts. This is achieved by an express statement about liability for loss as indicated above. With the exclusion of *ikhṭilāṭ*, this section may be said to be in accordance with the provisions of Islamic law

According to Islamic law, the property of the firm is held in co-ownership among the partners and that is what determines the issues of *ḍamān*.

15. *Application of the property of the firm.*—Subject to contract between the partners, the property of the firm shall be held and used by the partners exclusively for the purposes of the business.

Comment: Same as above.

16. *Personal profits earned by partners.*—Subject to contract between the partners,—

(*a*) if a partner derives any profit for himself from the any transaction of the firm, or from the use of the property or business connection of the firm or the firm name, he shall account for that profit and pay it to the firm;

Comment: This is supported by the principles underlying the Ḥanafī *mufāwaḍah.* See the chapter on *mufāwaḍah* for the details.

(*b*) if a partner carries on any business of the same nature as and competing with that of the firm, he shall account for and pay to the firm all profits made by him in that business.

Comment: This too is required by the contract of *mufāwaḍah* and has been explained under that contract.

18. *Partner to be agent of the firm.*—Subject to the provisions of this Act, a partner is the agent of the firm for the purposes of the business of the firm.

Comment: This is the same as the Islamic forms of partnership. Islamic law also provides for the insertion of the contract of surety into the partnership, but this is mainly due to the narrower concept of agency in Ḥanafī law as well as the distinction made between the *ḥukm* of the contract and its *ḥuqūq*. As indicated in the earlier chapters, Islamic law is much more precise on this issue than modern law, but the modern concept of agency may be permitted to continue as the people are used to it. It is only in some new forms that the Ḥanafī provisions may have to be introduced.

25. *Liability of a partner for acts of the firm.*—Every partner is liable, jointly with all other partners and also severally, for all acts of the firm done while he is a partner.

Comment: Islamic law provides for unlimited liability in both forms, that is, joint and several. Pakistani law differs from British and American law on this point where liability is joint and not several. The main idea in these systems is that the collective assets of the firm must first be exhausted before partners are involved individually. Islamic law creates joint liability through the contract of *kafālah* and not agency, unlike the existing law. Liability through *wakālah* is several and that too for the managing partner or the partner undertaking the transactions.

26. *Liability of the firm for wrongful acts of a partner.*—Where, by the wrongful act or omission of a partner acting in the ordinary course of the business of a firm, or with the authority of his partners, loss or injury is caused to any third party, or any penalty is incurred, the firm is liable therefor to the same extent as the partner.

Comment: This too is supported in Islamic law through the contract of surety rather than agency.

27. *Liability of firm for misapplication by partners.*—Where—

(*a*) a partner acting within his apparent authority receives money or property from third party and misapplies it, or

(*b*) a firm in the course of its business receives money or property from a third party and the money or property is misapplied by any of the partners while it is in the custody of the firm,

the firm is liable to make good the loss.

Comment: This too is supported in Islamic law through the contract of surety rather than agency.

29. *Rights of transferee of a partner's interest.*—(1) A transfer by a partner of his interest in the firm, either absolute or by mortgage, or by the creation by him of a charge on such interest, does not entitle the transferee, during the continuance of the firm, to interfere in the conduct of the business, or to require accounts, or to inspect the books of the firm, but entitles the transferee only to receive the share of profits of the transferring partner, and the transferee shall accept the account of profits agreed to by the partners.

(2) If the firm is dissolved or if the transferring partner ceases to be a partner, the transferee is entitled as against the remaining partners to receive the share of the assets of the firm to which the transferring partner is entitled, and, for the purpose of ascertaining that share, to an account as from the date of the dissolution.

Comment: This provision should be examined in the light of the provisions for *ḍamān*, that is, whether the transferee is entitled to the profits of the firm without offering any kind of *ḍamān*. As the transferring partner does not cease to be a partner and he is offering *ḍamān*. This arrangement should be a private one between the partner transferring his interest and the transferee, and the firm should have nothing to do with the transferee.

30. *Minors admitted to the benefits of the partnership.*—(1) A person who is a minor according to the law to which he is subject may not be a partner in a firm, but, with the consent of all the partners for the time being, he may be admitted to the benefits of partnership.

(2) Such minor has a right to such share of the property and of the profits of the firm as may be agreed upon, and he may have access to and inspect and copy any of the accounts of the firm.

(3) Such minor's share is liable for the acts of the firm, but the minor is not personally liable for any such act.

Proposal: This provision is unlawful according to Islamic law, because it violates the principle of *al-kharāju bi al-ḍamān*. The minor is enjoying the profits of the firm while he is not fully liable for its debts. The provision should be repealed and replaced with Islamic provisions that permit the authorized minor to enter into a partnership with the consent of the *walī*, and become liable as a full partner. For the details see §10.9 in this study.

36. *Rights of outgoing partner to carry on competing business.*—(1) An outgoing partner may carry on a business competing with that of the firm and he may advertise such business, but, subject to contract to the contrary, he may not—

(*a*) use the firm name,

(*b*) represent himself as carrying on the business of the firm, or

(*c*) solicit the custom of persons who were dealing with the firm before he ceased to be a partner.

(2) *Agreements in restraint of trade.*—A partner may make an agreement with his partners that on ceasing to be a partner he will not carry on any business similar to that of the firm within a specified period or within specified local limits; and, notwithstanding anything contained in section 27 of the Contract Act, 1872, such agreement shall be valid if the restrictions imposed are reasonable.

Comment: This provision is unlawful according to Islamic law as it attempts to restrict the legal capacity of a person, however, further research is needed on the issue.

54. *Agreements in restraint of trade.*—Partners may, upon or in anticipation of the dissolution of the firm, make an agreement that some or all of them will not carry on a business similar to that of the firm within a specified period or within specified local limits: and notwithstanding anything contained in Section 27 of the Contract Act, 1872, such agreement shall be valid if the restrictions imposed are reasonable.

Comment: See comments under section 36(2).

Chapter 21

Partnerships With Legal Personality: New Proposals

The existing law of partnership in Pakistan, as seen in the previous chapter, does not acknowledge the entity concept for partnerships. In other words, a partnership is not assigned legal personality. Although a partnership may sue and be sued in its own name after the registeration formalities, it is not a legal person. Partnerships have been assigned legal personality by some legal systems. In the United States, after a long debate stretching over a century, the Uniform Partnership Act has now acknowledged the entity concept for partnerships and it is expected that many states will adopt its recommendations. In Britain, and hence in Pakistan, the thinking appears to be that there is no need to assign personality to partnerships when private companies can be formed under company laws. There are, however, some advantages in assigning legal personality to partnerships, besides making this legal form inexpensive for the small businessman. As there appears to be no reason why legal personality cannot be assigned to partnerships, while retaining unlimited liability for the partners, the modern trend is to grant legal personality to the partnership by its mere formation.

Another feature in which the Pakistani law lags behind even the British law is in acknowledging the limited partnership. There was some reluctance in Britain in the early days about this form of partnership, but it was later accepted. In Pakistan, the law of partnership retained the shape it was given in the 19th century, and has not taken advantage of some of the forms available in the rest of the world.

In the present chapter, we would like to propose that if the concept of a fictitious person is acceptable in Islam, legal personality should not only be retained for companies and corporations, but should also be assigned to partnerships. In addition to this, the limited partnership should be acknowledged by the Partnership Act or a new law should be framed for this. A combination of legal personality and the limited partnership, it is believed, will go a long way in promoting the Islamic forms of financing for small as well as large businesses by Islamic banks and financial institutions.

We will briefly examine the issue of corporate personality as it is viewed in Islamic law and then describe the nature of the limited partnership. A proposal will then be made about the form in which a limited partnership may be accepted in Islamic law.

21.1 Corporate Personality and Islamic Law

There has been a prolonged debtate about the existence of the concept of a fictitious person (*shakhṣīyah i'itbārīyah*) in Islamic law. Most modern scholars insist that this concept was known to Islamic law, while some are doubtful whether Islamic law was aware of this concept. The truth is that the earlier Muslim jurists were fully aware of the concept, but they rejected it for the system they were dealing with. This does not mean that the concept cannot be accepted in Islamic law. We have analyzed the issue at great length in our study on *Corporations and Islamic Law* and shown how, and with what conditions, this concept may be accepted.

Accepting corporate personality within the fold of Islamic law does not mean that all institutions based on this concept automatically become legal. The implementation of the concept in different forms needs separate analysis. A model of the business corporation has been presented in the above mentioned study where the manner in which the business corporation should be implemented has been discussed at length. Such an implementation needs some minor changes to the existing structure of the business corporation, but these changes will enable the corporation to issue securities that are free from *ribā,* and it will also meet most of the requirements of the general principles of the Islamic law of business organization. A similar model will be implemented in this chapter for the limited partnership.

The following conclusion was drawn, after a detailed analysis, in the study on corporations about the acceptance of the corporate personlality:

In the light of the above, it appears that the ruler may assign a restricted or limited *dhimmah* to a non-human on the following conditions:

1. That no religious duties will be expected of a fictitious person. In other words, the fictitious person will not be subject to the *khiṭāb* of *'ibādāt,* and will not be liable for any religious duty or obligation that may flow from it. Thus, it will have no liability for *zakāt,* for *ṣadaqah* or for any other religious task.[1] These duties pertain to the *'aḥd* of the *'abd* with the Creator.
2. That some form of *'aql* must be associated with the fictitious person. This *'aql* may be that of one individual or group of individuals like the board of directors. The *ahliyat al-adā'* will always be associated with this source of *'aql,* and so will the liability for such acts.
3. That a concept of dual title of ownership must be associated with a fictitious person. Any property held by the fictitious person in its own name must be assumed to be held on behalf of the members of this fictitious person as a result of *khalṭ* or mingling of capitals. The fictitious person, if permitted by its members, may have the full right of disposal and transaction in this property. The reason and rationale of this stipulation of dual ownership will be explained later. For the present moment it may be said that it will avoid many complications and facilitate the smooth operation of the Islamic law of business organization through corporate personality.

The last point in the above conclusion pertains to dual ownership, and this has been proposed to meet some of the objections raised on the basis of the principles of *ribā* and liability. It should not be too difficult to implement in practice and to justify on the basis of the general principles of Islamic law.

---

[1] In the system to be proposed in the next part of this study, *zakāt* will be levied on the wealth of the shareholders rather than on the corporation.

The main idea is that corporate personality, around which the modern world is organized, may be accepted as Islamic with certain conditions and then utilized to implement different models of business enterprise. The Islamic model of the corporation has already been discussed elsewhere and the model of the limited partnership is discussed in this chapter.

21.2 The Nature of the Limited Partnership

The limited partnership may be considered to be the exact opposite of the Islamic contract of *muḍārabah.* In *muḍārabah,* it is the investor who has unlimited liability and bears the risk of business, but in the limited partnership the investor's risk is limited to the extent of his share. In other respects, the position of the investor may be similar. For example, in both forms the investor does not interfere in the management of the firm.

The limited partnership was called commenda, or the partnership *en commandite* in France.[2] "A limited partnership is a form of business organization, having any variety of activities and business objectives, which is made up of a general partner who organizes and manages the partnership and its operations, and limited partners who contribute capital, having limited liability, and assume no active role in day-to-day business affairs."[3] The limited partnership is, therefore, a combination of:

1. one or more partners whose liability for the debts and obligations of the firm is unlimited, and
2. one or more partners whose liability for such debts and obligations is limited in amount, and
3. the right to take part in the management of the affairs of the firm is confined to the partner or partners with unlimited liability.[4]

This form of partnership was first regulated in France in 1673, while in England it was introduced with the Limited Partnership Act, 1907. In the United States, the limited partnership exists in

---

[2]Lindley, *The Law of Partnership,* p. 799.

[3]*Finance and Investment Handbook* (New York: Barrons, 1995) p. 39.

[4]Lindley, *The Law of Partnership,* p. 799.

almost every jurisdiction, having been introduced by France in the state of Louisiana when it was under French control.

In the United States today, limited partnerships or LPs as they are called, may be both public and private. Some are even listed on the stock exchange. From the investors point of view, the biggest drawback of the limited partnership has been the lack of liquidity. After the 1980s, inspired by the tax reform, some sponsors began marketing programs featuring depository receipts, which represent unit interests and can be traded in the open marketplace. Liquidity provided this way is a feature of *master limited partnerships,* which was a mid-1980s innovation.[5] The main advantage of limited partnerships has been that financial and tax events flow directly to the investor. Starting in 1998, however, these partnerships will be taxable as corporations and this appears to have slowed down the interest in these forms.

We are not concerned, for the present, with the financial and tax advantages that may be given to these partnerships, but with the legal form they will adopt when viewed through the eyes of Islamic law.

21.3 Designing the Islamic Limited Partnership

In the chapter on *muḍārabah,* we have indicated some of the problems that arise in the traditional form. In the next chapter, we will take up the analysis of its modern form. The conclusion is that the contract of *muḍārabah* may not be the ideal form for modern times due to its inherent problems and its somewhat temporary nature. As compared to this, the limited partnership adapted to suit the requirements of Islamic law may be a better alternative.

It may be stated at the outset that the limited partnership or what it seeks to achieve in form may be possible under the company laws as well. This can be achieved by permitting a combination of limited as well as unlimited liability within the same company. This form, if designed, would face the same objections that have been raised against the structure of the modern corporation.[6] It is for this reason that a separate form is being proposed here—one in which the tax and financial benefits may flow directly to the investor. The

---

[5] *Finance and Investment Handbook* (New York: Barrons, 1995) p 38.

[6] See the author's study on *Corporations and Islamic Law (to be published shortly).*

form of the limited partnership proposed here may be considered as something that falls midway between the traditional partnership and the modern corporation. The basic structure proposed here follows a pattern similar to the model of the Islamic corporation proposed in another study.

21.3.1 The guiding principles for the new Islamic limited partership

The structure of the limited parternship proposed will attempt to meet the following goals:

- It will attempt to maintain the principle of *al-kharāju bi al-ḍamān* and all its requirements.
- It will attempt to uphold the principle of prohibition of *ribā* and ensure that no transaction undertaken by the limited partnership can be suspected of bearing *ribā* in any form.
- The new form will attempt to preserve the corollaries of these two principles in terms of ownership of the assets of the business by the partners with unlimited liability along with the creation of *ḍamān* (liability) through ownership and other means.
- It will attempt to affirm each relationship of a partner with the partnership in terms of some basic contract like *wakālah, kafālah, ijārah* and *amānah* so that the principles of Islamic law can be applied in a clean and obvious manner.

The same or similar rules were adopted for the new Islamic model of the corporation with limited liability for its members.

21.3.2 The foundations on which the limited partnership is erected

The following assumptions are made:

1. **Legal personality.**—The limited partnership will be a legal person created by the agreement of the partners.
2. **Wakālah and kafālah not sharikah to be the basis for the participation of the working or general partners.**—The relationship of the working partners, having unlimited liability, with the partnership will be based either on the Ḥanafī

concept of *wakālah* along with *kafālah* or simply on the modern concept of agency. In other words, the partnership will be an agent of the partners with unlimited liability. The concept of sharing of profits will be avoided here as the entire residual profits will be passed on to the working partners in proportion to their shares.

3. **The limited partners will enter into a simple *sharikat al-'inān* with the partnership and this will be based on the Ḥanafite form of wakālah.**— The contract of *wakalah* applied will be based on the Ḥanafite view so that a distinction between the *ḥukm* or a contract and its *ḥuqūq* is maintained.[7] The *sharikah* will be formed between the partnership and the limited partner and the partnership will be acting as the agent of the general partners in this *sharikah.*

4. **Dual Ownership of Capital and Assets.**—The capital and assets of the partnership will belong to the general and limited partners and will be held in the form of a co-ownership. The partnership as a legal person will hold these assets on behalf of all the partners with full right of disposal. This will create a kind of dual ownership, and may require *ijtihād* for approval.

5. **Sale of shares by the partners.**—The general partners will not be permitted to sell their shares without the permission of the other general partners. As compared to this, the limited partners may divide their investment into smaller units and dispose of their shares to any outsider. In other words, securitization of the investment of the limited partners will be permitted.

6. **Istidānah and liability of shareholders.**—The general partners may grant the authority of raising credit beyond the limits of the invested capital (*wilyat al-istidānah*) to the partnership. As a result of this, they will have unlimited liability. The unlimited liability will arise through the modern concept of agency, or through the contract of *kafālah,* if the Ḥanafite concept of agency is adopted even for these partners. The limited partners, on the other hand, will deny such authority to the parntnership on the assumption that the limited partners

[7] This form of *wakālah*, it has been suggested elsewhere, may be restricted to the law of business organization alone and not extended to all contracts.

will always have limited liability even if the partnership does exercise such authority. In practice, however, the need to raise credit beyond the limits of the invested capital may never arise, because of the structure proposed here. The determination of the limit for *istidānah* will be tied to the net assets of the partnership at any one time and not to the capital contributed.

7. **Entitlement to profit.**—The limited partners will share the profit with the partnership according to the terms of the *'inān* partnership concluded. After settling the accounts of the limited partners, the general partners will share the entire profit earned by the partnership in proportion to their shares.

8. **Creditors and third parties will be able to sue the general partners.**—As the general partners will be the principlals of the partnership on the basis of the modern concept of agency, third parties will be able to sue them for the debts of the partnership either jointly or severally along with the partnership. Third parties will not be able to sue the limited partners, becuase the *ḥuqūq* of each contract will revert to the agent, on the basis of the Ḥanafī form of *wakālah,* and this is the concept of agency on which their relationship will be based.

9. **Banks and financial institutions will be limited partners.**—The partnership will rasise money from the financial institutions by making them limited partners. As indicated above, this relationship will be based on the simple Ḥanafī *'inān,* with a distincition made between the *ḥuqūq* and the *hukm* of contracts. This arrangement through the concept of dual ownership will make the financial institutions owners of the assets of the partnership and thus avoid the cost of mortgages and trust deeds, but this may be possible if desired.

10. **Priority of claims for limited partners at the time of dissolution.**—In their claims against the partnership, the *'inān* investors will have top priority after those who have given trade credit to the corporation. The limited partners will have priority over the general partners, because the partnership will primarily be the agent of the shareholders and will be doing business for them.

In the design of the new model of the Islamic limited partnership, it would be appropriate to take into account the different ways in which the limited partnership has been implemented. Of particular relevance would be the Uniform Partnership Act that has proposed the new forms of partnership based on the entity concept.

21.4 An Identical Provision in the Company Law

The Companies Ordinance, 1984 provides for a form that is almost identical to a limited partnership proposed above. Sections 111 and 112 of the Ordinance provide as follows:

> 111. *Limited company may have directors with unlimited liability.*—(1) In a limited company, the liability of the directors or of any director may, if so provided by the memorandum, be unlimited.
>
> (2) In a limited company in which the liability of any director is unlimited the directors of the company, if any, and the member who proposes a person for election or appointment to the office of director, shall add to that proposal a statement that the liability of the person holding that office will be unlimited and the promoters and officers of the company, or one of them, shall, before that person accepts the office or acts therein, give him notice in writing that his liability will be unlimited.
>
> (3) If any director or proposer makes default in adding such a statement, or if any promoter or officer of the company makes default in giving such a notice, he shall be liable to a fine which may extent to two thousand rupees and shall also be liable for any damage which the person so elected or appointed may sustain from the default,, but the liability of the person elected or appointed shall not be affected by the default.
>
> 112. *Special resolution of limited company making the liability of directors unlimited.*—(1) A limited company, if so authorised by its articles, may, by special resolution, alter its memorandum so as to render unlimited the liability of its directors or of any director.
>
> (2) Upon the passing of any such special resolution, the provisions thereof shall be as valid as if they had been originally contained in the memorandum:

> Provided that an alteration of the memorandum making the liability of any of the directors unlimited shall not apply, without his consent, to a director who was holding the office from before the date of the alteration, until the expiry of the term for which he was holding office on that date.

Apparently, this provision achieves what has been proposed above, especially with the granting of personality to limited partnerships. Yet, there are some differences. These are as follows:

1. There are some objections to the form of companies found in the existing law. These have been discussed in a separate study on *Corporations and Islamic Law*. The form of the limited partnership proposed here takes into account those objections and conforms with the provisions of Islamic law.

2. In the form of a limited company with unlimited liability for some directors, there will be some directors who have limited liability and yet they are participating in the management of the company. In the limited partnership, on the other hand, all members or investors with limited liability will not be participating in the management of the business.

3. The formation of a company is cumbersome and entails expenses that may not be suitable for small business.

4. A higher standard of documentation is required of a company that may not be expected of a limited partnership, depending on the law that may be made.

5. A company will be subjected to more taxes as compared to a partnership for which the income may be divided among the partners before it is taxed.

Having said this, it must be acknowledged that both forms combined may be able to provide great flexibility for the entrpreneur as well as the financial institutions financing the business. The form of the companies, of course, needs to be reexamined and amended in the light of Islamic law, and this has already been proposed in the independent study mentioned earlier.

Select Bibliography

Abū Dāwūd Sulaymān ibn al-Ashāth al-Sijistānī (817 or 18-889). *Sunan Abū Dawūd.* Trans. Ahmad Hasan. 3 vols. Lahore, 1984.

Aḥmad 'Alī 'Abd Allāh. *al-Shakhṣīyah al-I'tibārīyah fī al-Fiqh al-Islāmī.* Khartoum, n.d.

'Alī al-Khafīf. *al-Sharikāt fī al-Fiqh al-Islāmī.* Cairo, n.d.

Anson, Sir William R. *Principles of the English Law of Contract.* 12th ed. London: ELBS & Oxford University Press, 1967.

Bahr al-'Ulūm, Muḥammad 'Abd al-'Alī ibn Niẓām al-Dīn Muḥammad al-Anṣārī al-Lakhnawī (d. 1180/1766). *Fawātiḥ al-Raḥamūt Sharḥ Musallam al-Thubūt* on the margin of Al-Ghazālī. *Al-Mustaṣfā min 'Ilm al-Uṣūl.* 2 vols. Cairo, 1324.

Al-Bahūtī, Manṣūr ibn Yūnus ibn Ṣalāḥ al-Dīn. *Kashshāf al-Qinā' 'an Matn al-Iqnā'.* Cairo, 1968.

Barrons. *Finance and Investment Handbook.* New York: Barrons, 1995.

Buchanan, N. S. *The Economics of Corporate Enterprise.* 1940.

Commission of Ottoman Jurists (1867–77). *Majallat al-Aḥkām al-'Adlīyah.* Constantinople, 1305 AH.

Commission of Sulṭān Muḥīy al-Dīn Awrangzeb 'Ālamgīr (1659–1707). *al-Fatāwā al-'Ālamgīrīyah.* 6 vols. Būlāq, 1310 A.H.

Al-Dabūsī, Abū Zayd 'Ubayd Allāh ibn 'Umar 'Īsā (d. 430/1039). *Ta'sīs al-Naẓar.* Cairo, n.d. 1-78. Followed by al-Karkhī. *Risālah fī Uṣūl.* 80–87 with comments by al-Nasafī.

Al-Dasūqī, Muḥammad ibn Aḥmad ibn 'Arafah. *Ḥāshiyat 'alā al-Sharḥ al-Kabīr li-Abī al-Barakāt Sīdī Aḥmad al-Dardīr 'alā Mukhtaṣar al-Khalīl.* Cairo: 'Īsā al-Bābī al-Ḥalabī wa-Shurakāh, 1931–34.

Dias, R. W. M. *Jurisprudence.* London: Butterworths, 1985.

Drucker, Peter F. *The Concept of the Corporation.* New York: The New American Library, 1964.

Farrar, J. H. *Company Law.* London: Butterworths & Co., 1985.

Financial Accounting Standards Board. *Objectives and Concepts of Financial Accounting, Presentation and General Disclosure Standard and Information about the Organization.* Jeddah, 1994.

Hasanuzzaman, S. M. "Limited Liability of Shareholders: An Islamic Perspective." *Islamic Studies.* 28:4. Islamabad: IRI, 1989.

Ḥassān, Ḥusayn Ḥamid. *al-Madkhal li Dirāsat al-Fiqh al-Islāmī.* Cairo, 1979.

Ibn 'Ābidīn, Muḥammad Amīn ibn 'Uthmān ibn 'Abd al-'Azīz. *Radd al-Muḥtār 'alā al-Durr al-Mukhtār Sharḥ Tanwīr al-Abṣār.* Cairo: Muṣṭafā al-Bābī al-Ḥalabī, 1966.

Ibn al-Humām al-Siwāsī al-Iskanadarī, Kamāl al-Dīn Muḥammad. *Fatḥ al-Qadīr 'alā al-Hidāyah Sharḥ Bidāyat al-Mubtadī.* Cairo: Muṣṭafā al-Bābī al-Ḥalabī, 1389/1970.

Ibn Nujaym, Zayn al-'Ābidīn ibn Ibrāhīm (d. 970/1563). *Al-Ashbāh wa al-Naẓā'ir.* Cairo, 1387/1968.

————. *al-Baḥr al-Rā'iq Sharḥ Kanz al-Daqā'iq.* Cairo, 1893.

Ibn Qudāmah, Muwaffaq al-Dīn Abū Muḥammad 'Abd Allāh ibn Aḥmad ibn Muḥammad. *al-Mughnī fī Fiqh Imām al-Sunnah Aḥmad ibn Ḥanbal al-Shaybānī.* Cairo: al-Maṭba'ah al-Salafīyah wa-Maktūbātuhā, 1962.

Ibn Rushd, Abū al-Walīd Muḥammad ibn Aḥamad ibn Muḥammad (al-Ḥafīd) (d. 594/1198). *Bidāyat al-Mujtahid wa Nihāyat al-Muqtaṣid.* 2 vols. Cairo, n.d.

'Īsā 'Abduh. *al-'Uqūd al-Shar'īyah al-Ḥākimah.* Cairo: Dār al-I'tiṣām, 1977.

Islamic Fiqh Academy. *Majallat Majma' al-Fiqh al-Islāmī.* vol. 7:1. Jeddah: 1992.

Al-Jaṣṣāṣ al-Rāzī, Abū Bakr Aḥmad ibn 'Alī (d. 370/981). *Aḥkām al-Qur'ān.* 2 vols. Istānbūl, 1355/1916.

Al-Karkhī, 'Abd Allāh ibn al-Ḥusayn (d. 340/935). *Risālah fī al-Uṣūl.* On pp. 78–87 following al-Dabūsī (430/1039). *Ta'sīs al-Naẓar.* Cairo, n.d.

Al-Kāsānī, Abū Bakr ibn Mas'ūd (d. 587/1191). *Badā'i' al-Ṣanā'i' fī Tartīb al-Sharā'i'*. 10 vols. Cairo, 1968.

Kelsen, Hans. *General Theory of Law and State.* Trans. Wedberg. 1945.

———————. *Pure Theory of Law.* Trans. Knight. 1967.

al-Khayyāṭ, 'Abd al-'Azīz. *al-Sharikāt.* 2 vols. Amman: Wizārat al-Awqāf, 1971.

Al-Khirashī, Abū 'Abd Allāh Muḥammad. *Sharḥ al-Mukhtaṣar.* Cairo, 1318.

Al-Marghinānī al-Rushdānī Burhān al-Dīn, 'Alī ibn Abū Bakr ibn 'Abd al-Jalīl al-Farghānī. *Kitāb al-Hidāyah Sharḥ Bidāyat al-Mubtadī.* Cairo, 1368/1948.

Modaraba (Floatation and Control) Ordinance, 1982.

Al-Muzanī, Abū Ibrāhīm Ismā'īl ibn Yaḥyā (d. 264/878). *Mukhtaṣar.* On the margin of Al-Shāfi'ī (204/802). *al-Umm.* 7 vols. in 4. Cairo, 1388/1968.

Al-Nawawī, *Matn al-Minhāj* on the margin of al-Ramlī, Shams al-Dīn Muḥammad ibn Abū al-'Abbās Shihāb al-Dīn Aḥmad ibn Aḥmad ibn Ḥamzah. *Nihāyat al-Muḥtāj li-Sharḥ al-Minhāj.* Cairo, 1967.

Nyazee, Imran Ahsan. *The Concept of Ribā and Islamic Banking.* Islamabad: Niazi Publishing House, 1995.

———————. *Theories of Islamic Law.* Islamabad: International Institute of Islamic Thought & Islamic Research Institute, 1994.

Posner, Richard A. *Economic Analysis of Law.* Boston: Little, Brown and Company, 1972.

Posner, R. A and Scott, K. E. *Economics of Corporation Law and Securities Regulation.* 1980.

Al-Qudūrī al-Baghdādī, Abū al-Ḥusayn Aḥmad ibn Muḥammad. *Kitāb al-Mukhtaṣar.* Cairo, n.d.

Al-Ramlī, Shams al-Dīn Muḥammad ibn Abū al-'Abbās Shihāb al-Dīn Aḥmad ibn Aḥmad ibn Ḥamzah. *Nihāyat al-Muḥtāj li-Sharḥ al-Minhāj.* Cairo, 1967.

Report of the Panel of Bankers and Experts submitted to the Council of Islamic Ideology. Islamabad, 1982.

Ṣadr al-Sharīʻah al-Thānī al-Maḥbūbī, ʻUbayd Allāh ibn Masʻūd (d. 747/1346). *Sharḥ Wiqāyat al-Riwāyah fī Masā'il al-Hidāyah* on the margin of ʻAbd al-Ḥakīm al-Afghānī. *Kashf al-Ḥaqā'iq: Sharḥ Kanz al-Daqā'iq*. 2 vols. in 1. Cairo, 1318.

Saḥnūn, ʻAbd al-Salām ibn Saʻīd ibn Ḥabīb al-Tanūkhī. *al-Mudawwanah al-Kubrā*. Cairo: Maṭbaʻat al-Saʻādah, 1905.

Sanhūrī, ʻAbd al-Razzāq. *Maṣādir al-Ḥaqq fī al-Fiqh al-Islāmī*. Beirut: Dār Iḥyā' al-Turāth al-ʻArabī, n.d.

Al-Sarakhsī, Abū Bakr Muḥammad ibn Abī Sahl Aḥmad (d. 490/1097). *Uṣūl al-Sarakhsī*. Ed. Abū al-Wafā' al-Afghānī. 2 vols. Cairo, 1372.

———————— *Kitāb al-Mabsūṭ*. 30 vols. Cairo, 1324–31/1906-13.

Schamell, Earnest H. *Lindley on the Law of Partnership*. 12th ed. London: Sweet and Maxwell, 1962.

Al-Shāfiʻī, Muḥammad ibn Idrīs (d. 204/820). *Kitāb al-Risālah fī Uṣūl al-Fiqh*. Ed. Aḥmad Muḥammad Shākir. Cairo, 1358.

————————. *al-Umm*. 7 vols. in 4. Cairo, 1388/1968.

Al-Shaybānī , Muḥammad ibn al-Ḥasan (d. 189/805). *Kitāb al-Aṣl*. Ed. Abū al-Wafā' al-Afghānī. 3 vols. Cairo, 1954.

————————. *Kitāb al-Buyūʻ wa al-Salam*. (Part of *Kitāb al-Aṣl*) Ed. Chafik Chehata. Cairo, 1954.

————————. *Kitāb al-Makhārij fī al-Ḥiyal*. Ed. J. Schacht. Leipzig, 1930.

Al-Shīrāzī, Abū Isḥāq Ibrāhīm ibn ʻAlī (d. 482/1083). *al-Muhadhdhab fī Fiqh Madhhab al-Imām al-Shāfiʻī*. 2 vols. Cairo, n.d.

Al-Ṭaḥāwī, Abū Jaʻfar Aḥmad ibn Muḥammad ibn Salamah al-Ḥajrī (d. 321/933). *Al-Mukhtaṣar fī al-Fiqh*. Cairo, 1370.

————————. *Kitāb al-Shurūṭ al-Kabīr*. Baghdad, 1966.

————————. *Kitāb al-Shurūṭ al-Kabīr*. Baghdād, 197-?.

Udovitch, Abraham L. *Profit and Partnership in Medieval Islam*. Princeton, 1976.

ʻUlaysh, Muḥammad. *Taqrīrāt ʻalā al-Sharḥ al-Kabīr*, on the margin of al-Dasūqī, Muḥammad ibn Aḥmad ibn ʻArafah. *Ḥāshiyat ʻalā al-Sharḥ al-Kabīr li-Abī al-Barakāt Sīdī Aḥmad al-Dardīr ʻalā*

Mukhtaṣar al-Khalīl. Cairo: ʿĪsā al-Bābī al-Ḥalabī wa-Shurakāh, 1931–34.

Uniform Partnership Act, 1994 (USA).

Usmani, Muhammad Taqi. "The Principle of Limited Liability From the Shariah Viewpoint." *New Horizon.* Aug.–Sept., 1992.

Wakin, Jeannette. *Function of Documents in Islamic Law.* Albany, 1972.

Glossary

'abd: slave; servant; *'abd ma'dhūn* is a slave who has been authorised by his master to handle business on his behalf.

abdān: see *sharikat al-'abdān.*

'aḥd: covenant; here it is used in the context of *dhimmah* (personality), which is considered by the jurists a covenant with the Creator.

aḥkām: Plural of *ḥukm* (rule); the *aḥkām* of a contract (legal effects) as distinguished from its *ḥuqūq* (rights of performance of the contract)—the Ḥanafīs make a distinction between the two.

ahliyah: Legal capacity.

ahliyat al-adā': Legal capacity for execution.

ahliyat al-wujūb: Legal capacity for the acquisition of rights and obligations.

ajānib: plural of *ajnabī* (stranger); those who are not co-owners in a property.

ajal: period; duration for which delivery is delayed.

ajnabī: stranger; see *ajānib.*

ajr al-mithl: reasonable wages; wages to which a person would be entitled under normal circumstances; wages paid to a *muḍārib* in a *fāsid muḍārabah.*

a'māl: plural of *amal* (work) that is required in a partnership or on the basis of which a partnership is formed.

amānah: trust; the contract of *amānah* gives rise to fiuciary relationships and duties.

'amal: work; conduct.

amīn: trustee; see *amānah.*

amwāl: plural of *māl* (wealth); wealth that is contributed as capital in a partnership.

'aqd: agreement; contract.

'aqd ghayr lāzim: a contract that is terminable at the will of the parties, like partnership.

'aql: reason; fourth interest secured by the *sharī'ah* and recognized as a purpose of the law; the existence of *'aql* is an essential condition for *ahliyat al-adā'*.

'arḍ: land; according to most jurists land is not eligible for entitlement to profit as compared to other things that are: wealth, labour, credit-worthiness (*ḍamān al-thaman*).

arkān: The elements or essential ingredients of an act, without which the act is not legally valid.

arsh: compensation for injury caused.

aṣl: origin; root; foundation; source of law; established case that forms the basis of the extension of the *ḥukm* in *qiyās* (analogy); a principle of law; principal amount in a debt; see *ra's al-māl*.

athmān muṭlaqah: absolute currencies; the term is usually applied to *dīnārs* and *dirhams*.

'ayn: The corpus or substance of a thing. A thing present as distinguished from one that is absent at the time of the contract. In Ḥanafī terminology, it is a thing that is to be determined through weight or measure during a transaction of sale.

a'yān: Plural of *'ayn*.

badal: substitute; substitute compensation.

bāligh: person who has attained puberty, the outward sign of majority and discretion, in the absence of which jurists determine different ages for the presumption of puberty.

bāṭil: Nullity; void.

bay': comprehensive term that applies to sale as well as many other transactions that are not strictly referred to as sales in positive law; bilateral contract; exchange.

biḍā'ah: goods given to another for trading without giving wages or sharing profits (like a shopkeeper leaving his shop with another shopkeeper during his absence).

bulūgh: the attainment of puberty; see *bāligh*.

buṭlān: see *bāṭil*.

ḍamān: compensation; liability.

ḍamān al-'amal: liability underlying a partnership formed on the basis of labour, where the partner is liable for performing the contract or completing the work accepted by either partner.

ḍamān al-māl: liability for the debts of the partnership; the usual form of liability underlying all partnerships, especially one formed on the basis of wealth.

ḍamān al-talaf: liability for damaging or destroying property accepted by the partnership for value-added work.

ḍamān al-thaman: liability underlying a partnership formed on the basis of credit-worthiness where each partner is liable, jointly and severally, for paying the prince of goods bought on credit.

dār al-ḥarb: enemy territory not under the jurisdiction of a Muslim state.

dār al-Islām: area under the juridiction of the Muslim state.

ḍarūrah: Necessity. A principle used for permitting forbidden things in case of duress or extreme hardship.

ḍarb fī al-arḍ: journeying through the earth seeking the bounty of Allāh; justifying basis for *muḍārabah.*

dayn: receivables; the term does not apply to cash loans for which the word *qarḍ* is used; see *qarḍ.*

dayn bi al-dayn: the exchange of a debt for a debt (prohibited on the basis of a tradition and unanimously by the jurists on the basis of *ijmā'*).

dhimam: see *sharikat al-dhimam.*

Dhimmī: non-Muslims subject of the state.

dhimmah: equivalent of legal personality in positive law; receptacle for the capacity for acquisition; see *ahd.*

faḍl: excess; used for *ribā*, which is excess in the exchange of twc counter-values, whether determined through weight or measure or realized through delay in the delivery of one of the counter-values.

fāsid: vitiated; irregular; unenforceable; used in the sense of voidable in the positive law, but a contract is voidable at the option of the parties, while the *fāsid* contract can become valid only if the offending condition is removed.

fāsid ijārah: the *ḥukm* (rule) for a vitiated *muḍārabah, muzāra'ah* or *musāqāh.*

fasād: see *fāsid.*

faskh: rescission.

fulūs: plural of *fals* (copper coin).

gharar: uncertainty; hazard that is likely to lead to a dispute in a contract; does not mean speculation in goods or currencies or the acquisition of huge profits.

ghaṣb: usurpation; abduction.

ghayr lāzim: contract terminable at the will of either party.

ḥīlah: legal device.

ḥajar: interdiction, usually for *safah* (prodigality).

ḥamīl: surety; the term is used by Ḥanbalī jurists for *kafīl.*

ḥawālah: indorsement; assignment; aval.

hibah: gift.

ḥiyal: plural of *ḥīlah* (legal device).

ḥujjah: legal proof or authority.

ḥukm: rule; command; precription; the *ḥukm* of a contract is a term for the legal effects of the contract.

ḥukman: legally, though not actually.

ḥuqūq: rights; the rights of performance of a contract that belong to the agent according to the Ḥanafīs.

i'ārah: lending utensils and non-fungibles.

ibāḥah: permissibility.

iḥyā' al-mawāt: reviving barren lands.

ījāb: obligation as distinguished from *wujūb* (duty).

ijārah: hire; renting.

ijmā': consesus of opinion of jurists on a rule of law.

ijmā' ṣukūtī: consensus where some jurists give tacit approval to the rule pronounced by others.

ijtihād: effort of the jurist to derive the law on an issue by expending all the available means of interpretation at his disposal and by taking into account all the legal proofs related to the issue.

ikhṭilāṭ: mixing of shares so that they can no longer be separated.

'ilm al-shurūṭ: conveyancing; drafting of legal documents.

'inān: rein of an animal; type of partnership; see *sharikat al-'inān.*

'inān khāṣṣ: the *'inān* partnership that is formed for a particular project or for trading in a particular commodity or in which the agency granted to the partners is restricted.

inqilāb: coversion; conversion of *mufāwaḍah* into *'inān.*

intihā': end; termination; termination or dissolution of a partnership.

iqālah: negotiated rescission.

irtihān: pledging; mortgaging.

ishtirāk: equivocality; participation; partnership.

isnād: The chain of transmission of a tradition.

isqāṭ: The extinction of a right.

istidānah: raising or building up credit through credit purchases; does not apply to the raising of cash loans; see *istiqrāḍ.*

istiḥqāq al-ribḥ: entitlement to profit; basis for entitlement to profit.

istiḥsān: principle according to which the law is based upon a general principle of the law in preference to a strict analogy pertaining to the issue, the principle is used by the Ḥanafīs as well as the Mālikīs.

istiqrāḍ: the raising of cash loans for business purposes, declared *bāṭil* by al-Sarakhsī as it is against the principle of prohibition of *ribā.*

'iwaḍ: compensation; counter-value.

jā'iz: permissible; permissible contract.

jahālah: uncertainty; uncertainty in a contract that may lead to a later dispute; see *gharar.*

juz' shā'i': a share that is undivided and completely mixed up with the shares of the other partners, that is, it is to be found in each particle of the property.

kātib: scribe.

kafālah: contract of surety; guarantee; bail; posting a bond.

kafālah bi al-thaman: surety for paying the price or sum if unpaid by the person originally liable.

kafālah bi-al-nafs: bail; surety for producing the body of the person wanted.

kafīl: surety; person providing the surety; guarantor.

al-kharāj bi al-ḍamān: a principle based upon a tradition; it is, perhaps, the most influential principle in Islamic law, applies to contracts, damages and even crimes.

khārij: produce.

khalṭ: mixing of shares; see *ikhṭilāṭ.*

khamr: wine from grape juice.

kharāj: revenue from land.

khiyārāt: plural of *khiyār* (option).

kirā': rent for land, permitted by Mālik ibn Anas.

lāzim: binding; binding contract.

māl: wealth.

majhūl: unknown; uncertain.

makrūh: abominable; reprehensible; disapproved.

manāfi': plural of *manfa'ah* (benefits; usufruct; profits; utility).

manfa'ah: see *manāfi'.*

mazrū': the crop to be cultivated.

mazrū' fīh: land given out by way of *muzāra'ah.*

milk: ownership; property.

milk mushtarak: co-ownership; joint ownership.

milkīyah: ownership.

mithl: fungible; things sold by weight or measure, and for which one quantity or measure is a substitute for another.

mu'āmalah: transaction; agreement; term used for the agreement concluded by the Prophet (peace be upon him) with the people of Khaybar.

mu'ayyan: ascertained; determined; commodity ascertained through weight or measure for purposes of sale.

mubāḥ: permissible.

mubāshir: person who commits an act personally and of his own volition rather than through another person.

muḍārabah: contract of partnership and sharing of profits in which the investor provides all the capital and is liable for the loss.

muḍārib: the worker in a contract of *muḍārabah.*

mudabbar: a slave whom his master has declared to be free upon the master's death.

mufāwaḍah: a basic contract of partnership based on *wakālah* and *kafālah* that requires full commitment from the partners and to achieve this purpose tries to maintain equality in the capital, labour, liability and legal capacity and also declares each partner to be a surety for the other—it is converted into the *'inān* partnership if such equality is disturbed.

mukātab: a slave with whom his master has concluded the contract of *kitābah* by virtue of which the slave buys his freedom and agrees to pay for it in instalments.

mukhābarah: another name for the contract of *musāqah* derived from the transaction with the Jews of Khaybar.

muqāraḍah: another name for *muḍārabah* used by the Mālikīs; see also *qirāḍ.*

muqtaḍā 'aqd al-'inān: implied contract of *'inān;* conditions implied by the mere use of the word *'inān* in the contract of partnership.

murābaḥah: sale at stated cost price and mark-up.

musāqāh: contract for the watering of trees between the owner of land and a worker on the condition of sharing the produce.

mushā': the undivided share of a person in every particle of joint property.

mushārakah: see *sharikah.*

musharika: term used in Pakistan for *mushārakah.*

muṭālabah: demand; demand by a creditor for the satisfaction of debts from the dealing partner or from the other partners.

muzāra'ah: contract for the cultivation of land between the owner of the land and the worker with the condition of sharing the produce.

muzāri': tenant.

nabīdh: beverage made from dates; mead of dates.

nasī'atan: by way of *nasī'ah,* that is, with a delay in the delivery of one or both counter-values in a contract of exchange (*bay'*).

naṣṣ: text; word or text with a single meaning; text from the work of a jurist.

niẓām: institution; term used in Saudi law for the corporation, in place of the usual term *sharikah,* in Arab law.

qabūl: acceptance.

qarḍ: loan, especially an interest-free loan in which the period of repayment is not fixed; a loan in which the period is fixed is permitted by Islamic law, even if it is without interest, because it is hit by the stipulations of the contract of *ṣarf.*

qarḍ ḥasan: gracious loan without interest in which the benefit to be derived is gifted by the owner to the beneficiary—without this charitable act, the use of the money for a period would be considered an unjustified excess transferred to the beneficiary also called *ribā al-nasī'ah.*

qirāḍ: another name given by the Mālikīs to the contract of *muḍārabah,* from the word *qarḍ.*

qiyās: analogy; syllogism.

ra's al-māl: capital; principal amount invested.

rabb al-arḍ: owner of land.

rabb al-māl: investor; owner of capital.

radd bi-al-'ayb: return of goods after a sale due to defects in the goods.

rahn: pledge; mortgage.

ribā: interest; unlawful excess in the exchange of two counter-values where the excess is measurable through weight or measure (called *ribā al-faḍl*) or is measurable through time (called *ribā al-nasī'ah.*

rukn: element; part of an act without which the act is not complete or valid; essential ingredient or element of a contract.

ṣīghah: form of the contract.

ṣabī: minor.

ṣadaqah: charity; also used for *zakāt.*

salam: contract in which an advance payment is made for a delayed delivery of goods.

ṣarf: contract for the exchange of gold, silver, and currencies whether the currency or commodity exchanged is the same from both sides or is different, that is, whether dinārs are exchanged with dīnārs or dīnārs are exchanged with dirhams.

shakhṣīyah i'itbārīyah: juristic person; artificial personality; corporate personality.

sharīk: partner.

sharikah: partnership; in Egyptian law the term is used for joint-stock companies and corporations as well, but is qulified with an adjective to indicate its nature: thus, *sharikah musāhamah* for a public limited company or a corporation whose capital has been subscribed to by the general public.

sharikah 'āmmah: general partnership; a partnership in which each partner is a general attorney for the other partners; a partnership that permits trading in all types of goods.

sharikah khāṣṣah: special partnership; partnership for a single venture or for trading in a particular item; partnership in which each partner is a special attorney of the other partners.

sharikah musāhamah: in Egyptian law it is the name for a corporation or for a public limited company.

sharikat a'māl: partnership in which participation by the partners is based on labour or skill, but the partnership has to be of the type *'inān* or *mufāwaḍah.*

sharikat al-'amal: see *sharikat al-a'māl.*

sharikat al-'aqd: a partnership created through contract as opposed to co-ownership that may be the result of a joint purchase or agreement or it may result from inheritance or from some other legal situation.

sharikat al-'inān: a basic contract of partnership based on agency in which participation may either be on the basis of wealth or labour or credit-worthiness, and in which equality of contribution or legal capacity is not necessary.

sharikat al-abdān: another name for *sharikat al-a'māl.*

sharikat al-amwāl: a partnership in which participation is based on the contribution of wealth by all partners, but the partnership has to be of the type *'inān* or *mufāwaḍah.*

al-sharikah dhāt al-mas'ūlīyah al-maḥdūdah: the name for a private limited company in Egyptian law.

sharikat al-dhimam: a term used by the Mālikīs to indicate a situation where two or more persons are buying goods on credit—it is different from the Ḥanafī *sharikat al-wujūh* insofar as it requires the physical presence of all the partners at the time of purchase.

sharikat al-ibāḥah: a common right of individuals to gather, possess and own free commodities.

sharikat al-jabr: mandatory co-ownership created by an act of law, like inheritance.

sharikat al-māl: see *sharikat al-amwāl.*

sharikat al-mafālīs: a partnership between persons whose assets have been reduced to copper coins and who have to buy on the basis of credit-worthiness; see *sharikat al-wujūh.*

sharikat al-milk: co-ownership.

sharikat al-muḍārabah: see *muḍārabah.*

sharikat al-mufāwaḍah: see *mufāwaḍah.*

sharikat al-ṣanā'i': partnership between artisans; a form of *sharikat al-a'māl.*

sharikat al-taqabbul: partnership for the acceptance of work, which is the same thing as a partnership based on labour or skill.

sharikat al-wujūh: partnership based on credit-worthiness of the partners in which the ratio of profit and loss is based on the liability borne, but the partnership has to be of the type *'inān* or *mufāwaḍah.*

shirā' bi al-nasī'ah: credit-purchase.

shirkah: another form of the term *sharikah.*

shuf'ah: preemption.

shurūṭ: conditions; the name given to the art of conveyancing in Islamic law.

ta'addī: transgression; delict; wrong; tort.

ta'yīn: ascertainment of the goods sold through weight or measure.

tabarru': act of charity.

tafwīḍ: delegation.

takhrīj: derivation; a methodology practised by the *faqīh,* and that is based upon reasoning from principles.

takhṣīṣ: restriction; restriction of the meaning of a text.

tamlīk: transferring ownership.

tamyīz: discretion; sense of discriminating between right and wrong evident in the behaviour of a minor.

taqabbul al-'amal: acceptance of work by either partner in a partnership based on labour.

tarjīḥ: preference of one legal evidence over another in the derivation of the rules of law.

taṣarruf: act; right to transact; right of disposal of property.

tawliyah: sale at a discount.

tawqīt: limiting duration of contract or another legal act.

dirāhim tijārīyah: currecny accepted by the traders as valid for commercial transactions amongst them although it did not meet the conditions laid down for currency.

tijārah: trade; business.

'urbūn: earnest money.

'urf: usage; custom.

'urūḍ: property that includes goods, slaves and even real estate.

wadī'ah: contract of deposit; bailment.

wakālah: agency.

wakālah 'āmmah: general agency.

wakālah khāṣṣah: special agency.

wakālah qāṣirah: restricted agency.

wakīl: agent.

walī: guardian.

waqf: charitable trust; testamentary trust.

waṣīyah: bequest.

wilāyah: guardianship.

wilāyat al-istidānah: authority granted by one partner to another to buy on credit beyond the limit of the capital of the partnership.

yaḍribūna fi al-arḍ: journeying through the earth seeking the bounty of Allah.

zakāt: obligatory religious dues on wealth.

zar': seed; crop to be sown.

Index